Jesus Among Her Children

HARVARD THEOLOGICAL STUDIES
55

CAMBRIDGE, MASSACHUSETTS

Jesus Among Her Children

Q, Eschatology, and the Construction of Christian Origins

Melanie Johnson-DeBaufre

DISTRIBUTED BY

HARVARD UNIVERSITY PRESS

FOR

HARVARD THEOLOGICAL STUDIES

HARVARD DIVINITY SCHOOL

Jesus Among Her Children:
Q, Eschatology, and the Construction of Christian Origins

Harvard Theological Studies 55

Series Editors:
François Bovon
Francis Schüssler Fiorenza
Peter B. Machinist

Cover design: Eric Edstam
Cover art: Eucharistic banquet. Crypt of the Sacraments. Early Christian fresco, 1st half 3rd century C.E. Catacomb of S. Callisto, Rome, Italy. Reproduced with permission from Art Resources

Johnson-DeBaufre, Melanie.
    Jesus among her children : Q, eschatology, and the construction of Christian origins / Melanie Johnson-DeBaufre.
        p. cm. -- (Harvard theological studies ; 55)
    Includes bibliographical references (p.   ) and indexes.
    ISBN 0-674-01899-0 (pbk. : alk. paper)
    1. Q hypothesis (Synoptic criticism). 2. Jesus Christ--Historicity.
3. Eschatology. 4. Bible. N.T. Gospels--Feminist criticism. I. Title.
II. Harvard theological studies ; no. 55
    BS2555.52.J64   2005
    226'.06--dc22
                                                                      2005031520

This book is printed on acid-free paper.

For My Parents,

Don and Jean Johnson

Whose welcoming table

gave me my first glimpse

of the Basileia *of God*

Contents

Acknowledgements   xi
Abbreviations   xiii
Short Titles   xv

Introduction
IT'S THE END OF THE WORLD AS WE KNOW IT   1
  Debates About Jesus, Q, and Eschatology   3
  Entering the Debate   8
  Ethics of Interpretation   11
    Practices of Critical Reflexivity   12
    Practices of Textual Re-Reading   14
    Practices of Public Debate   16
  Interpreting the Sayings Source Q   17
  Interpreting the *Basileia* of God   20
  A Note About the Book's Organization   24

Part I: The Children of *Sophia*: De-Centering Q's Jesus

Chapter One
ESCHATOLOGY AND IDENTITY: Q'S JESUS AND CHRISTIAN DIVERSITY   27
  Christian Origins and Christian Identity in a Diverse World   29
  Equating Jesus' Identity with Christian Identity   33
  Fixing Jesus' Identity with Scholarly Taxonomy   35
  Theological Taxonomies and Christian Identity   38
  Conclusion   41

Chapter Two
ESCHATOLOGY AND COMMUNITY: TRADITIONS OF SOLIDARITY IN Q 7:18–35   43
  Sophia is Vindicated by All Her Children: Q 7:31–35   45
  Should We Expect Another? Q 7:18–23   62
  The Least in the *Basileia* are Greater: Q 7:24–28   68
  Rethinking "This Generation"   78

Chapter Three
**ESCHATOLOGY AND THEOLOGY: THE JUDGMENTAL JESUS AND
JOHN'S OPENING SPEECH IN Q 3:7–9, 16–17**   81
   John at the Beginning of Q   82
   The Judgment and the Interpretation of Q 3:7–9, 16–17   85
      A Judgmental Jesus and the Redaction of Q   87
      John's Doctrine of the Future   91
   Invoking Q's Symbolic World: Q 3:7–9, 16–17   95
   Bear Fruit Worthy of Repentance: Q 3:7–9   99
   Bearing Good Fruit Throughout Q   102
      Redacting the Judgment   104
      Judging the Children of Abraham   106
   Introducing Jesus as the Coming One: Q 3:16–17   108
   Conclusion   112

Part II: Jesus Among the Children of *Sophia*: Re-Focusing Q's Jesus

Chapter Four
**ESCHATOLOGY AND CHRISTOLOGY: THE PROBLEM OF THE
UNIQUENESS OF JESUS**   115
   Apologetics and Christian Origins   116
   Eschatology Renders Jesus and Q Incomparably Unique   118
   Christology and the Uniqueness of Jesus   122
   Dispensing with Apologetics?   124
   Conclusion   128

Chapter Five
**ESCHATOLOGY AND THE *BASILEIA*: THE UNIQUENESS OF
JESUS IN Q 11:14–26**   131
   Establishing the Text   132
   Q 11:20 and the Interpretation of Q 11:14–26   137
   Claiming the Common Ground   139
      Against the Disasters of Divisiveness: Q 11:15–18   140
      The Sons of the Accusers and the Basileia *of God: Q 11:19–20*   144
         1. THE REDACTIONAL SOLUTION TO THE PERCEIVED INCOMPATIBILITY   146
         2. THE HERMENEUTICAL SOLUTION TO THE PERCEIVED INCOMPATIBILITY   147
         3. DISSOLVING THE INCOMPATIBILITY   152
      Common Ground and Exclusion: Q 11:21–26   154
   Conclusion   165

Chapter Six
**ESCHATOLOGY AND APOCALYPTIC: THE SON OF HUMANITY
IN Q 11:16, 29–32**   169
   Establishing the Text   170
   Q 11:30 and the Interpretation of Q 11:16, 29–32   174
   Others Request a Sign   178
   This Evil or Sorry Generation   181
   Seeking a Verifiable Sign   186
   There's Something about the "Son of Humanity"   190

CONCLUSION   195

BIBLIOGRAPHY   203
INDEX OF ANCIENT SOURCES   219
INDEX OF SUBJECTS   229

Acknowledgments

This study places the communal vision of the *basileia* of God at the center of an interpretation of Q. It is appropriate, therefore, to recognize the community of teachers, colleagues, friends, and family who have shaped my thinking and values and who have supported me throughout its completion. My greatest thanks go to my doctoral advisors Elisabeth Schüssler Fiorenza and Helmut Koester. Throughout my master's and doctoral programs they shared with me their keen interest in the history of early Christianity, their love of the texts and materials of the ancient world, and their critical insights into the hermeneutical process. Professor Schüssler Fiorenza's path-breaking work on feminist hermeneutics and the ethics of interpretation has empowered me to find my own voice and a place from which to do engaged scholarship. Throughout the project she generously shared her time with me and provided vital insights at crucial junctures. Professor Koester's meticulous and creative exegetical work has significantly shaped my approach to early Christian texts. I am grateful for his unflagging support of me and my desire to find my own way in the forest of Q scholarship and exegesis. It has been my great pleasure to work with these two scholar-teachers. Our common ground has always been a commitment to creating community and to envisioning a just world.

Over the years, many teachers and colleagues have shared their insights and energies with me. Special thanks goes to Professor Larry Wills of Episcopal Divinity School, who provided detailed feedback and kind support throughout the entire project. I am grateful to Professor Bernadette Brooten of Brandeis University whose Introduction to the New Testament class at Harvard first fostered my love of antiquity and early Christianity. She gave me my first job as a researcher and has been a dedicated colleague and friend over the years. Professor Richard Horsley at the University of Massachusetts has always encouraged me in my work and models well the life of scholarship as an ongoing collegial conversation.

The staff of Harvard Theological Studies has been very helpful in seeing this revised dissertation into print: series editors François Bovon, Francis Schüssler Fiorenza, and Peter Machinist; typesetters - Cory Crawford, Richard Jude Thompson and Randall Short; proofreaders - Randall Short and Richard Jude Thompson. Special thanks go to managing editor Dr. Margaret Studier for her care and encouragement and copy editor Glenn Snyder for his professionalism and consistency.

During my years at Harvard Divinity School, I benefited greatly from the collegial atmosphere of the New Testament department and particularly the Doctoral Dissertation Seminar. Professors François Bovon, Karen King, Allen Callahan, and Ellen Aitken each in their own way provided me with important perspectives and encouragement. The friendship and insights of my fellow graduate students have been invaluable to me. I particularly thank Shelly Matthews, Cynthia Kittredge, Valerie Cooper, Anne Marie Luijendijk, Susan Abraham, Greg Schmidt Goering, Jalane Schmidt, Yuko Taniguchi, Laura Beth Bugg, and Nicole Kelley.

Both Harvard Divinity School and Luther College have been generous with institutional support throughout my graduate work. I especially thank Dean Bill Craft and Professor Terry Sparkes for making it possible for me to continue to work on this project after beginning my teaching at Luther. My colleagues Kristin Swanson, Gereon Kopf, and Guy Nave provided support and encouragement at important points in the process. The enthusiasm of the students at Luther College reminded me often of why I love teaching and learning about the Bible and Christian history.

My sister Melissa Widitor and my dear friends Denise Buell, Lori Pearson, and Laura Nasrallah have stood by me at all times. Their insights, humor, and love have enriched my life in more ways than I can say. I am even more speechless when it comes to my parents, Donald and Jean Johnson. Their tireless support of my interests and commitments have made much that I have done possible. My lovely daughter Grace Johnson-DeBaufre was born in the first semester of my doctoral program. Although her growing height reminded me of the ticking clock, her delightful sense of humor and loving spirit kept me going. My partner and best friend Eric Johnson-DeBaufre has been beside me from the beginning. He has made this ending possible with his remarkable intellect, his deep sensitivity, and his lovely, cathartic humor. He knows the depth of my thanks.

Abbreviations

AAR	American Academy of Religion
ABD	*Anchor Bible Dictionary.* Edited by D. N. Freedman. 6 vols. New York, 1992
ANF	*Anti-Nicene Fathers*
BAG	Bauer, W., W. F. Arnt, and F. W. Gingrich. *Greek-English Lexicon of the New Testament and Other Early Christian Literature,* Chicago, 1957
BETL	Bibliotheca ephemeridium theologicarum lovaniensium
Bib	*Biblica*
BibS	Biblische Studien
BTB	*Biblical Theology Bulletin*
BZ	*Biblische Zeitschrift*
CBQ	*Catholic Biblical Quarterly*
Cr St	*Cristianesimo nella Storia*
Did.	*Didache*
Ep.	*Epistula.* Edited by Abraham J. Malherbe, *The Cynic Epistles. Missoula, Mont.: Scholars, 1977.*
ExpTim	*Expository Times*
FB	Forschung zur Bibel
HTR	*Harvard Theological Review*
HTS	Harvard Theological Studies
IDBSup	*Interpreter's Dictionary of the Bible: Supplementary Volume.* Edited by K. Crim. Nashville, 1976
IQP	International Q Project
JAAR	*Journal of the American Academy of Religion*
JBL	*Journal of Biblical Literature*
JFSR	*Journal of Feminist Studies in Religion*
JSNT	*Journal for the Study of the New Testament*
JSNTSup	Supplement to the Journal for the Study of the New Testament
JSOT	*Journal for the Study of the Old Testament*
JTS	*Journal of Theological Studies*

LSJ	H. G. Liddell and R. Scott, *Greek-English Lexicon with a Revised Supplement*. Rev. by Sir Henry Stuart Jones. Oxford: Clarendon, 1996.
NovTSup	Novum Testamentum Supplements
NPNF[1]	*Nicene and Post-Nicene Fathers*, Series 1
NRSV	New Revised Standard Version
NTS	*New Testament Studies*
NovT	*Novum Testamentum*
P. Oxy,	*Oxyrhynchus Papyri*
Pss. Sol.	*Psalms of Solomon*
RSV	Revised Standard Version
SBLSP	*Society of Biblical Literature Seminar Papers*
TB	Theologische Bücherei: Neudrucke und Berichte aus dem 20. Jahrhundert
TDNT	*Theological Dictionary of the New Testament.* Edited by G. Kittel and G. Friedrich. Translated by G. W. Bromiley. 10 vols. Grand Rapids, 1964–1976
TZ	*Theologische Zeitschrift*
WMANT	Wissenschaftliche Monographien zum Alten und Neuen Testament
WUNT	Wissenschaftliche Untersuchungen zum Neuen Testament
ZNW	*Zeitschrift für die neutestamentliche Wissenschaft und die Kunde der älteren Kirche*
ZWT	*Zeitschrift für wissenschaftliche Theologie*

Short Titles

Allison, *Jesus Tradition*
    Allison, Dale C., Jr. *The Jesus Tradition in Q*. Harrisburg, Pa.: Trinity, 1997.

Bultmann, *History*
    Bultmann, Rudolf. *The History of the Synoptic Tradition*. Translated by John Marsh. New York and Evanston: Harper & Row, 1963. Translation of *Die Geschichte der Synoptischen Tradition*. Göttingen: Vandenhoeck & Ruprecht, 1921.

Hoffmann, *Studien*
    Hoffmann, Paul. *Studien zur Theologie der Logienquelle*. Münster: Aschendorff, 1972.

Horsley and Draper, *Whoever Hears*
    Horsley, Richard A., and Jonathan A. Draper. *Whoever Hears You Hears Me*. Harrisburg, Pa.: Trinity, 1999.

Jacobson, *First Gospel*
    Jacobson, Arland D. *The First Gospel: An Introduction to Q*. Sonoma, Calif.: Polebridge, 1992.

Kirk, *Composition*
    Kirk, Alan. *The Composition of the Sayings Source: Genre, Synchrony, and Wisdom Redaction in Q*. NovTSup 91. Leiden: Brill, 1998.

Kloppenborg Verbin, *Excavating Q*
    Kloppenborg Verbin, John S. *Excavating Q: The History and Setting of the Sayings Gospel*. Minneapolis: Fortress, 2000.

Kloppenborg, *Formation*
    Kloppenborg, John S. *The Formation of Q: Trajectories in Ancient Wisdom Collections*. Philadelphia: Fortress, 1987.

Kloppenborg, *Q Parallels*
    Kloppenborg, John S. *Q Parallels*. Sonoma, Calif.: Polebridge, 1988.

Lührmann, *Redaktion*
Lührmann, Dieter. *Die Redaktion der Logienquelle*. Neukirchen-Vluyn: Neukirchener Verlag, 1969.

Mack, *Lost Gospel*
Mack, Burton L. *The Lost Gospel: The Book of Q and Christian Origins*. San Francisco: HarperSanFrancisco, 1993.

Piper, *Wisdom*
Piper, Ronald A. *Wisdom in the Q-Tradition*. Cambridge: Cambridge University Press, 1989.

Robinson, *Critical Edition*
Robinson, James M., Paul Hoffmann, and John S. Kloppenborg. *The Critical Edition of Q*. Hermeneia. Minneapolis: Fortress, 2000.

Schulz, *Q*
Schulz, Siegfried. *Q: Die Spruchquelle der Evangelisten*. Zürich: Theologischer Verlag, 1972.

Schüssler Fiorenza, *Politics*
Schüssler Fiorenza, Elisabeth. *Jesus and the Politics of Interpretation*. London and New York: Continuum, 2000.

Tuckett, *Q*
Tuckett, Christopher M. *Q and the History of Early Christianity*. Edinburgh: T&T Clark, 1996.

Vaage, *Galilean Upstarts*
Vaage, Leif E. *Galilean Upstarts: Jesus' First Followers According to Q*. Valley Forge, Pa.: Trinity, 1994.

It's the End of the World As We Know It

The image on the front cover of this book tells a story familiar to biblical scholars. We have precious little material from early Christians, and it is often enigmatic. Who are the seated figures? Are they men or women? Why do they lift their hands? Are they early Christians or does this frieze depict a scene from the time of Jesus and his followers? Our material is quite fragmentary. It must be pieced together and, like the frieze, patched up in order to fill the gaps and hold together something resembling a whole. Not surprisingly, interpreters draw on their own knowledge, expectations, and experiences to solve the puzzles and fill in the holes. This book is both an attempt to interpret portions of an elusive and fragmentary "text"—the sayings source "Q"[1]—and an exploration of the ways in which our interpretation of it is shaped by our expectations and interests.

The particular set of interests that shape this book are signaled by its title, *Jesus Among Her Children*, which alludes to the saying in Q 7:35: "But *Sophia* is vindicated by all her children." This familial image of the children of *Sophia*-God[2] stands in Q alongside the more familiar corporate

---

[1] "Q" is short for the German *Quelle* or "source"; it refers to the hypothetical sayings collection used by Matthew and Luke in the composition of their gospels. Many scholars have argued for the existence of such a text as part of the Two-Source hypothesis, which seeks to explain the literary relationship among the Synoptic Gospels. For a history of Q scholarship and a reconstruction of the text of Q using Matthew and Luke, see Robinson, *Critical Edition*. For an extensive explication of the Q hypothesis, see Kloppenborg Verbin, *Excavating Q*.

[2] I have not translated the Greek term σοφία ("wisdom") so that the gender of the word is apparent. The feminine σοφία more clearly brings to mind the personification of God in the Hebrew Scriptures and Apocrypha (Prov 8:1–36, 9:1–6, and *Wis* 7:22–8:1) than the neutral and abstract notion of God's wisdom. I have capitalized *Sophia* because God's Wisdom is personified in Q as a parent who has children (Q 7:35) and as one who sends out prophets and sages (Q 11:49).

theo-political vision in the Jesus tradition: the *basileia* of God.[3] What happens when we interpret Q as primarily concerned with articulating these communal self-understandings and promoting a certain set of values for those who see themselves in this way? What happens when we assume that Q presents Jesus as one among many of *Sophia*'s children rather than as a unique and singularly significant one? These questions point to the hermeneutical key of this book: that we see things differently when we look from a different perspective, or if we ask a different set of questions. I have found that interpreters of Q often place the person of Jesus at the center of their questions. Who was the historical Jesus? How did others understand him and respond to him? These questions have a way of ensuring that the texts we are reading can and will answer them. These questions also produce and re-produce a view of Christianity as originally and always about how one understands and responds to Jesus, which has implications for how Christians understand both interreligious difference and the diversity within Christianity. Where is the basis for solidarity and common ground to be found? Is it with those who hold the same views of Jesus or with those who hold the same values of the *basileia* of God? This question resonates with a common historical question: did the audience of Q understand itself as similar to or different from other first-century Jews. If so, based on what—its views of Jesus, its self-understanding, its values and commitments? These are the questions that inspired and infuse this book. Rather than reading Q as being *about* Jesus and his eschatological uniqueness, we will examine Q as using Jesus to *think about* the communal vision of the *basileia* of God and the collective identity of the people as children of *Sophia*.

In order to lay the groundwork for the hermeneutical reflections and exegetical experiments that follow, it is helpful to situate this project in three contexts: (1) the scholarly debates about the historical Jesus, Q, and eschatology; (2) the changes in the field in the last several decades; and (3) an area of research that is expressly interested in developing an ethics of interpretation, that is, attending to both the way that interpretation is done and the effects of our interpretations. We begin below by outlining these three discursive locations. Following this discussion, we take up some of the basic issues that must be addressed in a book about Q, particularly one that works with the "*basileia* of God" but does not set out to discover its meaning. The chapter concludes with a note about the organization of the book.

---

[3]For a discussion of the use and translation of "*basileia* of God," see pp. 20–24 below.

Debates about Jesus, Q, and Eschatology

In the past two decades there has been a lot of attention paid to the historical Jesus, both among scholars and in the public arena. Q has figured prominently in these discussions and has been popularized and scrutinized in such places as the public work of the Jesus Seminar and the widely-read books of John Dominic Crossan. Within the academy, a wide range of New Testament scholars have renewed the debate over the eschatological outlook of Jesus and his first followers, drawing upon Q as evidence. In *The Birth of Christianity*, Crossan devotes thirty-two pages to defining the term "eschatology" and differentiating among the eschatologies of the synoptic sayings source (Q), the *Gospel of Thomas*, and the sayings common to both texts.[4] He does so because there is "considerable terminological confusion"[5] in historical Jesus research over the meaning and historical appropriateness of categories such as "eschatology," "eschatological," and "apocalyptic." While Crossan attempts to clarify the meaning and usefulness of these expressions, others ask whether historical-critical scholars should stop using a modern doctrinal category[6] to describe early Christian perspectives on the future.[7] This book asks what is at stake in this debate about "eschatology." What do we accomplish by arguing that Jesus and Christian beginnings were "eschatological" or "apocalyptic" or "non-eschatological"? What can we learn from our debates about eschatology, Jesus, and Q? One of the things we learn is that biblical scholarship participates in

[4]John Dominic Crossan, *The Birth of Christianity* (San Francisco: HarperSanFrancisco, 1998) 257–89.

[5]Crossan borrows this assessment from Marcus Borg, *Jesus in Contemporary Scholarship* (Valley Forge, Pa.: Trinity, 1994) 9.

[6]The *Oxford English Dictionary* defines eschatology as "the department of theological science concerned with 'the four last things: death, judgment, heaven, and hell.'" It cites the first use of "eschatology" in English in 1844. Gerhard Sauter credits the Lutheran theologian Abraham Calov with coining the term in his *Systema locorum Theologicorum* (1677) as a title of the last section, which deals with the "last things" (*de novissimis*), such as "death and the state after death, the resurrection of the dead, the last Judgment, the consummation of the world, hell and everlasting death, and, finally, life everlasting" ("The Concept and Task of Eschatology—Theological and Philosophical Reflections," *Scottish Journal of Theology* 41 [1988] 499). The category came into prominence in European historical-Jesus scholarship with the work of Albert Schweitzer.

[7]See, for example, Ron Cameron, "The Anatomy of a Discourse: On 'Eschatology' as a Category for Explaining Christian Origins," *Method and Theory in the Study of Religion* 8 (1996) 231–45.

larger contemporary discussions of the essence of Christianity. By present-ing historical reconstructions of Christian origins that confirm or challenge particular understandings of the central message of Christianity, biblical interpreters take sides in the ongoing struggle to define Christianity and to shape Christian identity in a changing world.

Biblical scholars have been debating the eschatology of Jesus for some time. At the end of the nineteenth century, Johannes Weiss's *Jesus' Proclamation of the Kingdom of God*[8] posited an eschatological mind-set for Jesus. This book "came as a shock to the theological world,"[9] because Weiss countered the familiar Jesus of contemporary theology with a historical Jesus who was very different. The prevailing German Protestant theology, represented most clearly by Weiss's father-in-law, Albrecht Ritschl, saw Jesus as proclaiming the "kingdom of God" as a moral program for individual religious experience and for the evolution of an ideal society. Weiss protested this interpreta-tion of Jesus' preaching by arguing that the historical Jesus—in his Jewish apocalyptic context—proclaimed the "kingdom of God" as a wholly future event, entirely determined by the actions of God, not humanity. In the face of theology and historical Jesus research in which Jesus was made to look like "us" and thus to authorize "us," Weiss argued for a completely foreign Jesus—a figure wholly defined by the mythic world of Jewish apocalyptic expectation.

Weiss so significantly changed the terms of the debate about Jesus that Albert Schweitzer credited him with adding a third

> great alternative which the study of the life of Jesus had to meet. The first was laid down by [David Friedrich] Strauss: *either* purely historical *or* purely supernatural. The second had been worked out by the Tübingen school and [Hans Julius] Holtzmann: *either* Syn-optic *or* Johannine. Now came the third: *either* eschatological *or* non-eschatological![10]

---

[8]Johannes Weiss, *Jesus' Proclamation of the Kingdom of God* (ed., trans., and intro. Richard Hyde Hiers and David Larrimore Holland; foreword by Rudolf Bultmann; Philadelphia: Fortress, 1971); trans. of *Die Predigt Jesu vom Reiche Gottes* (Göttingen: Vandenhoeck & Ruprecht, 1892).

[9]Rudolf Bultmann, foreword to *Proclamation*, by Weiss, xi. Bultmann's assessment of Weiss's work was first published in *Theologische Blätter* (18 [1939] 242–46) and was republished as a foreword to the third edition of Weiss's *Predigt* in 1964.

[10]Albert Schweitzer, *The Quest of the Historical Jesus* (New York: Macmillan, 1968) 238 (Schweitzer's emphasis); repr. of *The Quest of the Historical Jesus* (trans. W. Montgomery; New York: Macmillan, 1910); trans. of *Von Reimarus zu Wrede* (Tübingen: J. C. B. Mohr [Paul Siebeck], 1906).

Schweitzer's *The Quest of the Historical Jesus*, a monumental critique of the results of nineteenth-century research on the life of Jesus, sides with Weiss and presents a Jesus that challenged contemporary theological appropriations of Jesus. For Schweitzer, the eschatological Jesus was immune to being made "sympathetic and universally intelligible to the multitude" by "a popular historical treatment." "The historical Jesus," he says, "will be to our time a stranger and an enigma."[11] For both Weiss and Schweitzer, the historical Jesus is a stranger and a foreigner to the contemporary world because of his eschatology, in this case, his Jewish apocalyptic worldview.

Although Q studies was at its infancy in the early twentieth century, already a scholar of the liberal German theological tradition found in Q an historical "other" different from the "other" of Weiss and Schweitzer's eschatological Jesus. Published in 1907, a year after Schweitzer's *Quest*, Adolf von Harnack's *The Sayings of Jesus*[12] presents Q's view of Jesus as historically preferable to the recently hailed priority of Mark:

> The portrait of Jesus as given in the sayings of Q has remained in the foreground. The attempts which have been made to replace it by that of St. Mark have met with no success. . . . The collection of sayings [Q] and St. Mark must remain in power, but the former takes precedence. Above all, the tendency to exaggerate the apocalyptic and eschatological element in our Lord's message, and to subordinate to this the purely religious and ethical elements, will ever find its refutation in Q.[13]

For Harnack, the eschatological and apocalyptic elaborations of Mark are absent from the unbiased Q. Although Weiss and Schweitzer's view of Jesus prevailed in German scholarship, Harnack's assessment of Q suggests that all three scholars were actively engaged in the theological debates of their time.

These debates continue today. In the academy, much recent discussion of eschatology and Christian origins focuses on three scholarly contributions: (1) John Kloppenborg's proposal for the redactional strata of Q;

---

[11] Ibid., 399.

[12] Adolf von Harnack, *The Sayings of Jesus: The Second Source of St. Matthew and St. Luke* (trans. J. R. Wilkinson; New York: Putnam, 1908); trans. of *Sprüche und Reden Jesu. Die Zweite Quelle des Matthäus und Lukas* (Leipzig: J. C. Hinrichs, 1907).

[13] Ibid., 250–51.

(2) the hypothesis that the historical Jesus was a Cynic-like wisdom teacher; and (3) the work of the Jesus Seminar.[14] All three in one way or another differentiate wisdom (or, sapiential) traditions from apocalyptic ones in Q. While Kloppenborg does not equate "sapiential" with "non-eschatological," Burton Mack does by suggesting that if a sapiential setting was the "generative matrix" of earliest Christianity, then Jesus (or the Q people) should not be read in an eschatological context.[15] Mack's position is analogous to the Jesus Seminar's "fifth pillar" of contemporary scholarship, that is, "the liberation of the non-eschatological Jesus of the aphorisms and parables from Schweitzer's eschatological Jesus."[16] The combined rhetorical force of these contributions and others like them led James Robinson to declare in 1991 that this change from a pervasive eschatological interpretation of Jesus' preaching to a consensus against such an interpretation marks a "paradigm shift" and a "Copernican revolution" in the field of Jesus research.[17]

However, the extent of the debate over the eschatology of Jesus or Q suggests not a new consensus but an ongoing struggle over interpretations of Jesus and Q.[18] Both Christopher Tuckett's *Q and the History of Early Christianity* and Dale Allison's *The Jesus Tradition in Q* present alternative approaches to Kloppenborg's redactional analysis of Q. Bart Ehrman's

---

[14]See Kloppenborg, *Formation*; F. Gerald Downing, *Christ and the Cynics: Jesus and Other Radical Preachers in the First-Century Tradition* (JSOT Manuals 4; Sheffield: JSOT Press, 1988); and Robert W. Funk, Roy W. Hoover, and the Jesus Seminar, *The Five Gospels: The Search for the Authentic Words of Jesus* (New York: Macmillan, 1993). For a combination of Kloppenborg's model and the Cynic hypothesis, see Mack, *Lost Gospel*. In *The Historical Jesus: The Life of a Mediterranean Jewish Peasant* (SanFrancisco: HarperSanFrancisco, 1991), John Dominic Crossan, co-chair of the Jesus Seminar with Funk, also draws on Kloppenborg's stratification of Q and, to a lesser extent, the Cynic comparison for Jesus.

[15]Mack, *Lost Gospel*, 105–30. Mack's reconstruction of the formative layer of Q differs from Kloppenborg's in several places. Also, Kloppenborg warns that his literary-historical conclusions should not automatically be used for tradition-historical conclusions (*Formation*, 244).

[16]Funk et al., *Five Gospels*, 4.

[17]James M. Robinson, "The Q Trajectory: Between John and Matthew via Jesus," in *The Future of Early Christianity: Essays in Honor of Helmut Koester* (ed. Birger A. Pearson et al.; Minneapolis: Fortress, 1991) 189, 194. See also Marcus J. Borg, "Portraits of Jesus in Contemporary North American Scholarship," *HTR* 84 (1991) 1–2.

[18]Even speaking of an eschatological consensus masks the lack of consensus throughout the century on this topic. Witness, for example, the proliferation of substantially differing qualifying adjectives to describe Jesus' (or early Christian) eschatology: apocalyptic, thoroughgoing, realized, futuristic, *sich realisierende*, inaugurated, fulfilled, proleptic, etc.

Jesus: Apocalyptic Prophet[19] counters reconstructions of the historical Jesus as a Cynic sage or a non-eschatological wisdom teacher. Luke Timothy Johnson's *The Real Jesus: The Misguided Quest for the Historical Jesus and the Truth of the Traditional Gospels*[20] makes it clear in the subtitle that his critique of the Jesus Seminar presents a defense of traditional approaches to the gospels. Examining recent debates over the apocalyptic and sapiential Q, or the eschatological and non-eschatological Jesus, reveals that they are part of long-standing theological debates that draw on reconstructions of the historical Jesus and Christian origins to authorize contemporary theological, ethical, and political perspectives.

Although this study is part of these ongoing debates, it is not framed by the kind of questions we might expect: "What is eschatology, and what is the eschatology of Q?"[21] Instead, it asks: "What interests and frameworks inform such questions, and what difference does it make for how we interpret Q? How does scholarship echo and even participate in contemporary public discourses about Christian identity?" What we will find is that the academic

---

[19]Bart D. Ehrman, *Jesus: Apocalyptic Prophet of the New Millennium* (Oxford: Oxford University Press, 1999).

[20]Luke Timothy Johnson, *The Real Jesus: The Misguided Quest for the Historical Jesus and the Truth of the Traditional Gospels* (San Francisco: HarperSanFrancisco, 1996).

[21]Several scholars have addressed various methodological and definitional problems with the category "eschatology." See, for example, Helmut Koester, "Early Christianity from the Perspective of the History of Religions: Rudolf Bultmann's Contribution," in *Bultmann, Retrospect and Prospect* (ed. Edward C. Hobbs; HTS 35; Philadelphia: Fortress, 1985) 59–74; Dieter Georgi, "Rudolf Bultmann's *Theology of the New Testament* Revisited," in ibid., 75–87; Burton Mack, *A Myth of Innocence* (Philadelphia: Fortress, 1988) 58–59; Cameron, "Anatomy"; Marcus Borg, "A Temperate Case for a Noneschatological Jesus," in his *Jesus in Contemporary Scholarship* (Valley Forge, Pa.: Trinity, 1994) 47–96; Elisabeth Schüssler Fiorenza, "The Phenomenon of Early Christian Apocalyptic: Some Reflections on Method," in *Apocalypticism in the Mediterranean World and the Near East* (ed. David Hellholm; Tübingen: Mohr/Siebeck, 1983) 295–316; William G. Doty, "Identifying Eschatological Language," *Continuum* 7 (1970) 546–61; J. Christiaan Beker, "Biblical Theology Today," in *New Theology No. 6* (ed. Martin E. Marty and Dean G. Peerman; London: Collier-Macmillan, 1969) 7–34. Some of these scholars have, for various reasons, called for a thorough overhaul or burying of the category altogether. See also G. B. Caird, *The Language and Imagery of the Bible* (Philadelphia: Westminster, 1980); Jean Carmignac, *Le mirage de l'eschatologie* (Paris: Letouzey et Ané, 1979); and Clayton Sullivan, *Rethinking Realized Eschatology* (Macon, Ga.: Mercer University Press, 1988). With regard to Q, see John S. Kloppenborg, "Symbolic Eschatology and the Apocalypticism of Q," *HTR* 80 (1987) 287–306; and Arland Jacobson, "Apocalyptic and the Synoptic Sayings Source Q," in *The Four Gospels, 1992: Festschrift for Frans Neirynck* (ed. Frans Van Segbroeck et al.; BETL 100; Leuven: Leuven University Press, 1992) 1:403–19.

debate on eschatology and Christian origins diversely but persistently places Jesus at the center of its inquiry. As in some popular Christian discourses, the primary interest of scholarly analysis is who Jesus was, why he was special or unique, and what he said and did. This emphasis on the identity of Jesus often results in understanding Q itself as similarly interested in articulating and defending Jesus' identity. As feminist critics have noted, when interpreters construct early Christianity as a response to the work and vision of one great man, they effectively mask the presence and interests of the men and women who shaped Jesus and lived alongside and after him.[22] This scholarly emphasis on Jesus resembles contemporary understandings of Christianity as individualistic and christocentric, and thus reinforces these views by giving them historical authority.

Are there alternatives to interpreting the gospels in terms of Jesus' identity? How would we interpret Q if we place the values and visions of *the community around Jesus* at the center of our inquiry? Clearly Jesus has a prominent place in Q. He is its central speaker and actor. But does Q assert and defend his unique and crucial—even, "eschatological"—identity? Or do Jesus' sayings and interactions in Q articulate the community's hopes and commitments? Whereas for many interpreters Q's rhetoric marks the lines of difference between the Q community and other groups who did not respond to Jesus' message or who did not recognize Jesus' unique identity, this book seeks to articulate the role that Q may have played in promoting group solidarity around a communal vision of the *basileia* of the God of Israel. In doing so, we multiply the historical reconstructions available to the contemporary discourses about Christian identity in a diverse and pluralistic world.

Entering the Debate

This book places an analysis of contemporary scholarly context and rhetoric into dialogue with an exegesis of Q, and thus moves away from traditional approaches that begin their investigations with the text and its problems. In this regard, this book on only a handful of verses from Q participates in the larger shifts in the field of biblical studies—shifts that are usually classified as part of a "postmodern"[23] turn that has been occurring in the field during the last several decades.

---

[22]Schüssler Fiorenza, *Politics*, 21.

[23]For an overview, see the collected essays in George Aichele, ed., *The Postmodern Bible* (The Bible and Culture Collective; New Haven, Conn.: Yale University Press, 1995);

Kathleen O'Connor provides a helpful summary of three postmodern shifts in the field of biblical scholarship,[24] each of which presents an epistemological challenge that this book attempts to take seriously. The first regards the role of interpreters. O'Connor rightly notes that "it is by now a cliché among academics to observe that no interpretation is 'objective' or context-free."[25] In the last several decades the voices of men and women from marginalized groups around the globe have proven the premise that what you see depends on where you stand. Secondly, we have become aware of the way that our texts are polysemous:

> Texts no longer appear as straightforward representations of past history. Instead they emerge as negotiations and renegotiations of symbolic systems and prior interpretations, designed to address concrete circumstances of a particular community, but always saying more than they intend. Because texts are complex amalgamations of competing voices, no interpretation exhausts meaning.[26]

This suggests that the meanings of a text are multiple—both synchronically and diachronically. Finally, many scholars now reject the notion that texts are windows onto the reality of the past. What is often called the "linguistic turn" or the "rhetorical turn" in biblical studies understands texts "not as descriptive and reflective" but as "rhetorical-communicative."[27] From this view, texts are political discourses that attempt to persuade their audiences to accept their constructions of reality, rather than records of

---

Walter Brueggemann, *Texts Under Negotiation: The Bible and the Postmodern Imagination* (Minneapolis: Fortress, 1993); David Jobling, Tina Pippin, and Ronald Schleifer, eds., *The Postmodern Bible Reader* (Oxford: Blackwell, 2001); and A. K. M. Adam, ed., *Handbook of Postmodern Biblical Interpretation* (St. Louis: Chalice Press, 2000). For feminist and liberationist perspectives on postmodern hermeneutics, see Elisabeth Schüssler Fiorenza, *Sharing Her Word* (Boston: Beacon, 1998) 75–104; Somer Bodribb, *Nothing Mat(t)ers: A Feminist Critique of Postmodernism* (Melbourne: Spinifex Press, 1992); Vincent Wimbush, "Reading Darkness, Reading Scriptures," in *African Americans and the Bible* (ed. idem; New York: Continuum, 2000) 1–43; and Fernando Segovia, "'And They Began to Speak in Other Tongues': Competing Modes of Discourse in Contemporary Biblical Criticism," in *Reading from This Place* (ed. idem and Mary Ann Tolbert; Minneapolis: Fortress, 1995) 1:1–34.

[24]Kathleen M. O'Connor, "Crossing Borders: Biblical Studies in a Trans-Cultural World," in *Teaching the Bible: The Discourses and Politics of Biblical Pedagogy* (ed. Fernando F. Segovia and Mary Ann Tolbert; Maryknoll, N.Y.: Orbis, 1998) 322–37.

[25]Ibid., 324.

[26]Ibid.

[27]Elisabeth Schüssler Fiorenza, *Rhetoric and Ethic* (Minneapolis: Fortress, 1999) 196.

things as they really were. "Because texts are embedded in the political, economic, social, and religious worlds that produced them, all texts serve the interests of their creators, just as all interpretations serve the interests of their producers."[28]

These epistemological challenges raise significant ethical questions. Recognizing that all history-writing is perspectival and selective, the postmodern historian asks: "Why is any history constructed as it is? Whose interests are served by any historical account? What material effects does this historical account have on people's lives, and what effects does it continue to have?"[29] Biblical scholars are asking similar questions. In his book *Ethics of Biblical Interpretation: A Reevaluation*, Daniel Patte recounts a series of experiences that brought him to reconsider his own ethics of biblical interpretation. He first understood ethical responsibility in biblical studies as "rigorously studying the text as a historical object by following strict critical methods . . . demanded by the Academy and the guild of biblical scholars."[30] By using thorough methodology, one could contain one's own interests and thus elucidate the true meaning of the text in its historical context. Comfortable in what he considered to be the inherently ethical nature of his scholarly work, Patte encountered difficult challenges from some of his colleagues and students, including Jews, African Americans, and Christian feminists. These confrontations brought Patte to the realization that the claim of ethical neutrality in historical-critical methodology served to insulate him from ethical accountability for his interpretations. This claim also served to deny the perspectival contributions of people who clearly articulate their location and interests:

> It is clear to me that we male European-American exegetes are not accountable to those who are affected by our work. The seriousness of the ethical problem that we have to confront is now fully apparent. Should we not question the integrity of exegetical practices that ultimately demand that Christian feminists, African Americans, third-world churches, Jews, and many other groups . . . renounce their own experiences and their own cultures, forsake their own identities, and deny the validity of their concerns and interests?[31]

---

[28]O'Connor, "Crossing Borders," 325.

[29]Fred W. Burnett, "Historiography," in Adam, *Handbook*, 111.

[30]Daniel Patte, *Ethics of Biblical Interpretation: A Reevaluation* (Louisville: Westminster/John Knox, 1995) 17.

[31]Ibid., 21.

Patte had always known the potentially liberating power of critical exegesis: there were many positive responses to his work, "including those who were liberated from the blinders their uncritical readings constituted."[32] But Patte's encounters with people different from himself also brought an awareness of the painful history of biblical interpretation. At the end of his book, he speaks to other male European-American exegetes:

> Even if my solutions do not convince you, I am sure you can recognize the seriousness of the problems. We cannot continue to promote apartheid, racism, sexism, oppression, and injustice in all its forms through our critical studies of the Bible. And this is what we are doing when we practice critical biblical studies as usual.[33]

If we accept that interpretation does not happen in a vacuum, that we are all shaped by our social locations, contexts, experiences, and commitments, then we are confronted with ethical questions. What are the effects of our interpretations? Whose interests have been and are being served in the texts and in our interpretations?

Ethics of Interpretation

To embrace these epistemological and ethical challenges means re-thinking my approach to the interpretation of biblical texts. Like many others, I do not characterize my methodology strictly within an overall framework of historical-critical exegesis.[34] Thus this book uses the tools of historical-criticism within a larger framework of an *ethics of interpretation*. By doing so, I seek to attend to the "meaning of the Bible but also the meaning-making of biblical studies."[35]

I have borrowed the expression *ethics of interpretation* from Elisabeth Schüssler Fiorenza, whose presidential address before the Society of Biblical Literature in 1988 issued a challenge to the guild to develop ethically

---

[32]Ibid., 18

[33]Ibid., 114–15.

[34]For example, Patte calls his approach androcritical multidimensional exegetical practice that is part of an ongoing process of the ethics of interpretation (ibid., 114–29). O'Connor proposes a three-step methodology geared at a "critical actualization of texts" ("Crossing Borders," 328). Schüssler Fiorenza has developed a Rhetorical-Emancipatory paradigm of biblical interpretation (for a summary, see *Wisdom Ways* [Maryknoll, N.Y.: Orbis, 2001] 43–49).

[35]Schüssler Fiorenza, *Politics*, ix.

accountable biblical scholarship.[36] In subsequent writings, Schüssler Fio-renza has classified this kind of scholarship under the rubric of an *ethics of interpretation*, that is, an

> area of critical reflexivity and research that studies the "pervasive and often only partly conscious set of value-laden dispositions, in-clinations, attitudes, and habits" of biblical studies as an academic discipline. Such a critical exploration of the ethos and morality of biblical scholarship, or of what it means to work scientifically and ethically, has as its goal scholarly responsibility and accountability as an integral part of the research process.[37]

Reflection on the "ethos and morality" of biblical interpretation informs all aspects of this study. An *ethics of interpretation* encompasses (1) an investigation of what we do and how we do it, (2) a set of ethically-grounded interpretive practices, and (3) a process by which we evaluate our ethics and practices. The concept of ethics also invokes the relationship between the individual and others (and the Other, in the sense of anything that is constructed as different).[38] Thus an ethics of interpretation naturally includes relational questions of accountability and responsibility.

This book contributes to an ethics of interpretation in Q studies with three intersecting kinds of practices: (1) *practices of critical reflexivity*; (2) *practices of textual re-reading*; and (3) *practices of public debate*. These are not methodical steps in a linear progression; they are mutually interacting practices that draw on and shape each other.

Practices of Critical Reflexivity

Throughout this book, we will reflect on the category of eschatology in Q studies as a scholarly construct that performs ideological work. Schüssler Fiorenza outlines the kinds of practices that characterize such critical reflexivity. She suggests that scholars "critically research the process of how interpretation is produced, authorized, communicated, and used." These practices include investigations of:

1. The area of questions and problem formulation
2. The "commonsense" assumptions and unarticulated presuppositions

---

[36]Elisabeth Schüssler Fiorenza, "The Ethics of Biblical Interpretation: Decentering Biblical Scholarship," *JBL* 107 (1988) 3–17; reprinted in eadem, *Rhetoric and Ethic*, 17–30.

[37]Ibid., 195.

[38]Patte, *Ethics*, 14.

3. The lenses of reading, patterns of interpretation, categories of analysis
4. The reconstructive models, analogies, and images
5. Which boundaries and limits are constructed and maintained by a scholarly discourse.[39]

This is not a wholly unfamiliar project for Q scholars. John Kloppenborg notes that since Q itself is a "product of hypothesis building, Q scholarship has become an important 'site' at which to understand the role of hypotheses and ideologically invested intellectual constructs within New Testament scholarship."[40]

Practices of critical reflexivity move back and forth between investigating how we read and analyzing how our readings shape and are shaped by our current contexts. Thus these practices have ethical-evaluative aspects: I not only ask what our patterns of interpretation are, but also what their effects are: "which questions are not admitted," "which arguments are silenced,"[41] whose interests are served by this interpretation? Daniel Patte includes this kind of reflection as a main feature of his own interpretive practice:

> The practice of this androcritical multidimensional exegesis necessarily confronts us with a moral choice when we ask each of the various legitimate interpretations the following questions: What is its relative value? Is it helpful? Is it harmful? Who benefits? Who is hurt? We have to assume responsibility for our choice of one reading as the most significant for us.[42]

Patte implies, however, that the moral choice or ethical evaluation only occurs after establishing a particular reading as legitimate. But practices of critical reflexivity also interrogate the methods by which we judge a reading legitimate or the categories that render certain ideas thinkable or unthinkable. In this book, practices of critical reflexivity inform both the analysis of interpretive practices and the ethical evaluation of the results of interpretation.

---

[39]Schüssler Fiorenza, *Rhetoric and Ethic*, 196–97.

[40]Kloppenborg Verbin, *Excavating Q*, 446. See, for example, Horsley and Draper (*Whoever Hears*, 15–45), who critique enlightenment theological frameworks that shape the interpretation of Q.

[41]Schüssler Fiorenza, *Rhetoric and Ethic*, 197.

[42]Patte, *Ethics*, 124–25.

We might hope that an investigation of the discourses on Q and eschatology would help to identify and *eliminate* underlying interests and frameworks prior to interpreting Q. Instead, this book seeks to identify and *articulate* competing interests that have a bearing on one's interpretation of Q. Like Elisabeth Schüssler Fiorenza and many other feminist and liberationist interpreters, my own interpretation begins with and is responsible to the ongoing struggle for equality for all people. This includes a keen interest in the ways that Christianity has been, is, and will be a social, political, and religious force for the empowerment, agency, and full citizenship of wo/men.[43] This interest requires a companion commitment to identify and describe the ways that Christianity has been, is, and will be a social, political, and religious force for domination, fragmentation, and violence. Locating our discussions of Jesus and Q in the larger contemporary debates about Christian identity in a diverse world is a practice of critical reflexivity. Recognizing this location challenges us to take active responsibility for the history we tell and for the role that such telling plays in the identity formation and meaning-making of our own time.

Practices of Textual Re-Reading

Perhaps the most challenging aspect of critical reflexivity for biblical exegesis is its tendency to unmask the discipline—and the exegete—as socially located. If our perspectives shape our interpretations, how do we adjudicate between readings? What makes my readings preferable to any others? The practices of critical reflexivity include reflection on the effects of interpretation. The two related practices we are considering—textual re-reading and public debate—also provide opportunities for adjudication. In this study, textual re-reading includes (1) evaluating the effectiveness of dominant readings of a text and (2) arguing for the

---

[43]Elisabeth Schüssler Fiorenza has proposed using the term "wo/men" rather than "women" in order to recognize that "wo/men are not a unitary social group but are fragmented by structures of race, class, ethnicity, religion, sexuality, colonialism, and age. The destabilization of the term 'wo/men' underscores the differences between wo/men and within individual wo/men. This writing is inclusive of subaltern men who in kyriarchical systems are seen 'as wo/men' and functions as a linguistic corrective to androcentric language use" (*Wisdom Ways*, 216). "Kyriarchical" is the adjectival form of "kyriarchy," a neologism coined by Schüssler Fiorenza and "derived from the Greek words for 'lord' and 'master' (*kyrios*) and 'to rule or dominate' (*archein*)" ibid., 210. The term is intended to replace the term patriarchy—which refers only to systems of domination based on gender—with a word that refers to such systems as complex and intersecting power relations based on many factors such as gender, class, race, etc.

plausibility of alternative readings. Historical-critical tools—such as text criticism, translation, word study, form criticism, redaction criticism, and rhetorical analysis—are valuable for both tasks. The exegetical chapters of this book (chapters 2–3 and 5–6) argue—through close textual work—that Q is most plausibly read not as an assertion of the singular significance of its central character, Jesus, but rather as a plea for the communal vision of the *basileia* of God.

To this end, chapters 2, 3, 5, and 6 present re-readings of two pairs of Q texts. The first pair, Q 7:18–35 (chapter 2) and Q 3:7–9, 16–17 (chapter 3), consists of Q's materials associated with John the Baptist. The second pair, Q 11:14–26 (chapter 5) and Q 11:16, 29–32 (chapter 6), depicts consecutive encounters between Jesus and people who accuse him of siding with Beelzebul, and people who demand a sign from him. The choice of texts is not arbitrary; they contain most of the lightning rods of the current debate over Q's eschatology: the *basileia* of God, the son of humanity (or "Son of Man"), and the so-called announcement of judgment on "this generation." Anticipating the practices of public debate, my selection of these texts intentionally places this book within the public discourse about Jesus, eschatology, and Q.

The dominant interpretations of these Q texts illustrate the intense scholarly focus on the identity of Jesus. This emphasis not only masks the presence of the men and women around Jesus; it also produces readings of Q that appear contrary to the rhetoric of the text and thus are ineffective for making sense of the rhetoric of Q. For example, most Q scholars approach Q 7:31–35 as a text that is part of what has been termed Q's "announcement of judgment on 'this generation.'"[44] Within this framework, "this generation" represents all of Israel[45] or that part of Israel that has rejected Jesus and his teachings as promoted by the Q community.[46] From this perspective, Q 7:31–35 criticizes "this generation" because they have rejected the messages of John and Jesus—the messengers of *Sophia*. This view aligns John and Jesus with the children in the simile who pipe and sing a dirge, and thus focuses on the response to John and Jesus as the central topic being addressed by the unit. Thus the children of *Sophia* are those who have

---

[44]For example, Lührmann, *Redaktion*; Kloppenborg, *Formation*; and Jacobson, *First Gospel*.
[45]Lührmann, *Redaktion*, 31.
[46]Kloppenborg, *Formation*, 167; Jacobson, *First Gospel*, 183. See also Tuckett, *Q*, 201; and Horsley and Draper, *Whoever Hears*, 299. Both Tuckett and Horsley attempt to deconstruct the dichotomy between the Q community and their fellow Jews, but they retain a dichotomy between insiders (the Q community) and outsiders (those who reject the community or the message).

responded positively to the message of Q, and the people of "this generation" are their contemporaries who have rejected the Q messengers. Within
this interpretive framework, Q 7:31–35 functions to establish boundaries
between competing groups of first-century Jews. Ironically, interpreting
the unit in this way results in a text that functions rhetorically to create the
very divisions it seeks to criticize.

A similar problem appears in interpretations of Q 11:14–20. The
theological expectation that Jesus must be unique vis-à-vis other Jewish
exorcists has played a significant role in the exegesis of 11:19, which
suggests that both Jesus and the "sons" of his accusers exorcize on the
side of God. There is a long tradition of exegetical wrangling over the fit
between 11:19 and 11:20, which relates Jesus' exorcisms with the *basileia*
of God. Scholars have tried to resolve the apparent equation of Jesus and
other Jewish exorcists by putting distance between the two verses with
arguments about redactional layers or by proposing alternative and more
theologically acceptable meanings for 11:19.[47] Despite the argument in
11:19, this pericope as a whole is regularly viewed as creating boundaries
between first-century Jewish groups by emphasizing the unique role of
Jesus in bringing the *basileia* of God. Thus many interpreters conclude
that the text functions rhetorically to assert the difference between the
Jesus movement and other Jewish groups. Once again, a social divide
is created rhetorically by a text that resists such divides both in its logic
and its imagery. My interpretations argue for the plausibility of reading
Q differently by showing how these re-readings make better sense of
Q's rhetoric.

Practices of Public Debate

The interpretive work of this study remains at the level of the rhetoric of the
text and thus represents only the beginning of the process of re-imagining
the traditions and interpretations of Q in light of an interest in focusing
our inquiry on the movement around Jesus. The success of this re-reading
of select Q texts requires ongoing methodological, historical, and textual
investigations. I expect that those who are not convinced by my interpretations of Q will offer public critique and alternative interpretations. It is
my hope that such readers also engage the methodological issues and the
analysis of scholarly discourse presented in this book. Biblical interpretation is not only a rarefied scholarly discipline; it is also part of the ongoing

---

[47]For discussion, see Kloppenborg, *Formation*, 123–24.

public discourse of our time. A quick search for "Q" on Amazon.com will prove the point. Books found there, including the academic scholarship read by lay people and clergy for education and insight, claim that Q presents "the original sayings of Jesus,"[48] or they defend the "truth of the traditional gospels."[49] This study engages in practices of public debate by paying attention to the public character and context of scholarly discourse and by intentionally entering into this conversation about the interpretation and value of the sayings source Q.

Interpreting the Sayings Source Q

By now it should be clear that this book proceeds from a feminist and postmodern perspective. But it is also a book about Q, and this raises particular problems. Isn't the critical reconstruction of Q based upon a series of scholarly assumptions about the diachronic and literary development of the Jesus tradition? The Q hypothesis itself emerged concurrently with various European and North American quests for the historical Jesus.[50] Why interrogate the Jesus-centered interpretations of Q and not the Jesus-centered hypothesis of Q? These are questions worth asking.

I agree that the production of the Two-Source hypothesis[51] and the reconstructed text of Q are valid and rich sites for an investigation of scholarly discourse and its theological and political interests:[52] the Q hypothesis—like any scholarly category, history, or theory—should always be subject to review both in terms of its persuasiveness and its effects. But for two primary reasons, this book accepts the methodological building blocks used to reconstruct Q as an early text that can be interpreted apart from the texts of Matthew and Luke. First, like many other scholars, I find the Two-Source hypothesis to be the most persuasive explanation offered to date of the literary relation-

---

[48]Mark Powelson and Ray Riegert, eds., *The Lost Gospel Q: The Original Sayings of Jesus* (Berkeley: Ulysses Press, 1996).

[49]Johnson, *Real Jesus*.

[50]See N. T. Wright, "Jesus, Quest for the Historical," *ABD* 3 (1992) 796–802.

[51]For a history of the growth of this hypothesis to its current status as enjoying a certain consensus, see Kloppenborg Verbin, *Excavating Q*, 11–54.

[52]See John S. Kloppenborg, "The Theological Stakes in the Synoptic Problem," in *The Four Gospels, 1992: Festschrift for Frans Neirynck* (ed. Frans Van Segbroeck et al.; BETL 100; Leuven: Leuven University Press, 1992) 1:93–120; and William Farmer, *The Synoptic Problem: A Critical Analysis* (New York: Macmillan, 1964).

ship between Matthew and Luke.[53] As Kloppenborg notes, because the Q hypothesis "offers the most economical and plausible accounting of the form and content of the Synoptic Gospels, it continues to be by far the most widely accepted solution to the Synoptic Problem."[54] *The Critical Edition of Q*, which was produced by the collaborative effort of a team of North American and European scholars through the International Q Project (IQP), represents our best guess at reconstructing the text of Q itself.[55] While the current study makes proposals for revising the current reconstruction of Q and the interpretation of Q, it does not conclude anything that necessitates rejecting the Q hypothesis altogether.

The second reason for working with the reconstructed text of Q is its presence in contemporary public debates. In order to investigate and contribute to the recent discussions of Jesus and eschatology, I have taken up one of the central texts in these discussions. In some sense, one could argue that whether or not Q *was* a text, it *is* a text. You can buy it at the bookstore and read commentaries and monographs on it. Along with the *Gospel of Thomas*, it has been at the center of recent controversies over the conclusions of the Jesus Seminar. Q is part of our contemporary popular and scholarly discourse. This book attempts to bring an ethically-reflective voice to this discourse and to offer persuasive alternatives to the interpretation of its meaning.

As in all areas of an academic discipline, Q scholars continue to debate several aspects of the hypothesis and the reconstruction of Q. There are a few contested issues that should be clarified at the outset. Richard Horsley and Jonathan Draper[56] have raised some important challenges to the prevailing assumptions about Q with their interpretation of Q as an orally-derived text.

---

[53]Christopher Tuckett (*Q*, 1–39) presents a thorough and systematic defense of the Q hypothesis.

[54]Kloppenborg Verbin, *Excavating Q*, 11. For an extensive analysis and a presentation of all alternative hypotheses, see E. P. Sanders and Margaret Davies, *Studying the Synoptic Gospels* (London: SCM Press, 1989). For defenses of the two leading alternatives, see Mark Goodacre, *The Case Against Q* (Harrisburg, Pa.: Trinity, 2002), for Mark without Q; and Allan J. McNicol et al., eds., *Beyond the Q Impasse: Luke's Use of Matthew* (Harrisburg, Pa.: Trinity, 1996), for the Griesbach hypothesis.

[55]For the members of the International Q Project and a review of Q scholarship in general, see Robinson, *Critical Edition*, xvii–lxxi. My presentation of the text of Q in chapters 2, 3, 5, and 6 depends upon the *Critical Edition of Q*. In order to retain the reconstructed nature of the text without too much sigla, I have used the unformatted text of Q with only the double square brackets that enclose probable but uncertain reconstructions. The translations are my own.

[56]Horsley and Draper, *Whoever Hears*.

However, the full implications and viability of this proposal have not yet been considered. For example, if Matthew and Luke each had textual scripts of performances of the Q "text," then on what grounds can we adjudicate the differences between Matthew and Luke's common material and thus reconstruct Q? Differences between Matthew and Luke could be explained under the rubric of different performances rather than according to redactional habits of Matthew and Luke. In addition, if Matthew and Luke each had a copy of a similar performance of Q, then we must presuppose a process of canonization of the oral performance and thus a limitation of the notion of multiple performances. At this point, the proposal that Q is an oral-derived text needs to be investigated further in terms of its compatibility with the highly text-based presuppositions and procedures essential to the Two-Source Hypothesis and the reconstruction of Q. This book, therefore, proceeds from the view that Q is a literary composition in Greek.[57]

Redaction-critical proposals for Q occupy a central place in the discourses on eschatology and Q that are the focus of this study. However, some of the tensions and discontinuities that interpreters perceive among the various elements of Q pericopes and themes are built into the assumptions and questions with which they approach the text. This book offers synchronic interpretations of the Q units in order to explore the rhetorical function of Q as a whole text.[58] This approach results in some challenges to the redaction-critical theories but, as I discuss in the conclusion, does not represent a wholesale refutation of them.[59]

---

[57]Scholars debate about whether there was an Aramaic predecessor for Q. It is my opinion that if we accept that Matthew and Luke shared a common source for the double tradition, and decide that this source can be reconstructed from the common material between Matthew and Luke, then the only text that can be reconstructed is a Greek text. For a discussion of proposals that there is an Aramaic *Vorlage* behind Q, and a defense of the view that Q was composed in Greek, see Kloppenborg Verbin, *Excavating Q*, 72–80.

[58]For redactional proposals, see Kloppenborg, *Formation*; Jacobson, *First Gospel*; and Allison, *Jesus Tradition*. For interpretations of Q as a whole text, see Tuckett, *Q*; Horsley and Draper, *Whoever Hears*; and Kirk, *Composition*. There is a great deal of disagreement about the provenance and date for the version of Q used by Matthew and Luke. I follow the general consensus that the final version of Q should be located in Syro-Palestine around the time of the Jewish war against Rome (66–73/74 C.E.). For a discussion, see Kloppenborg Verbin, *Excavating Q*, 80–87 and 171–75.

[59]Kirk (*Composition*) has provided the most thorough assessment to date of the compositional features and stylistic coherence of Q.

Interpreting the *Basileia* of God[60]

A final contested issue in Q studies is the meaning and rhetorical purpose of the expression ἡ βασιλεία τοῦ θεοῦ (the *basileia* of God). The expression appears in Q eleven times[61] but goes entirely without explication. This suggests that the term occupies the symbolic universe of Q to such an extent that its meaning is taken entirely for granted. By contrast, scholars show an intense interest in explicating the meaning, origin, and development of this expression. The classification and definition of the *basileia* often participates in larger genealogical arguments that attempt to locate the historical Jesus in a particular stream of ancient identity. A comparison of the treatment of the expression *basileia* of God in the first beatitude (Q 6:20b) will illustrate the point.

Q scholars are virtually unanimous that the position of the saying "Blessed are you poor for yours is the *basileia* of God" at the beginning of the inaugural sermon in Q gives it pride of place as a programmatic statement of Q's theology, ideology, or ethos. However, interpretations vary according to which kind of parallels scholars juxtapose to the beatitude, and whether they classify it as "eschatological" or "non-eschatological" in outlook.

---

[60]I have not translated the Greek term *basileia* for two reasons. First, the English term "kingdom" implies a territorial sense rather than God's kingly rule or reign, which most exegetes agree is the proper translation of the expression βασιλεία τοῦ θεου (see Dennis Duling, "Kingdom of God, Kingdom of Heaven," *ABD* 4 [1992] 50). Second, I agree with Elisabeth Schüssler Fiorenza's point that "most reviews of scholarship on the meaning of the expression '*Basileia* of God' do not even discuss its political significance in a context where people must have thought of the Roman Empire when they heard the word" ("To Follow the Vision: The Jesus Movement as *Basileia* Movement," in *Liberating Eschatology* [ed. Margaret A. Farley and Serene Jones; Louisville: Westminster/John Knox, 1999] 134). She recommends such terms as "empire" or "domain" in order to "underscore linguistically the oppositional character of the empire/commonweal of G*d to that of the Roman Empire" (ibid.). She notes that "such translation is generally not understood in an oppositional sense, however, but rather as ascribing to G*d imperial, monarchical power." Because of this she chooses to leave the word untranslated in order to "use it as a tensive symbol that evokes a whole range of theological meanings and at the same time seeks to foster a critical awareness of their ambiguity" (ibid.). I agree with Schüssler Fiorenza's assessment of the situation and have also left the term untranslated.

[61]See Kloppenborg, *Q Parallels*, 213. The expression "son of humanity" (traditionally translated "Son of Man") also appears eleven times in Q (ibid., 238). For a discussion of this phrase, see chapter 6 below.

In his book *Galilean Upstarts: Jesus' First Followers According to Q*, Leif Vaage suggests that the symbol "*basileia* of God" functions to explain how it is that the life of the "poor," a "life without political power or material prosperity was neither inevitably defeated nor depressed, but instead somehow 'blessed.'"[62] According to Vaage, what is at issue is what poverty means. The comparisons that follow support Vaage's position that some moral literature in antiquity challenged the commonplace idea that poverty was difficult and evil. Vaage quotes from the Cynic epistles: "Practice needing little, for this is nearest to God, while the opposite is farthest away";[63] and from Diogenes Laertius: "Socrates used to say that the fewer his needs, the nearer he was to the Gods."[64] For Vaage, the first beatitude enacts a similar challenge to the "customary understanding of misery and bliss."[65]

Vaage links his own understanding with Hans Dieter Betz's classification of the saying as an anti-macarism that is "consciously formulated in opposition to the conventional macarism and stands its values on its head."[66] Vaage juxtaposes this to the familiar interpretation of the beatitudes as a promise of eschatological reversal: "The dramatic 'reversal' of the usual categories of judgment habitually discerned here by NT scholars is nothing more and nothing less than this: in Nietzche's terms, an *Umwertung der Werte*; in those of Diogenes of Sinope, a 'defacing of the currency' of ancient beliefs about what made for the 'good life.'"[67]

Recourse to Betz's classification of the beatitudes as anti-macarisms is common whether one argues that Q 6:20b is eschatological or that it is non-eschatological. Few interpreters note that Betz locates such anti-macarisms in Greek philosophy, Jewish wisdom, and Jewish apocalyptic:

> Naturally, this "macarism of the wise man" is encountered frequently in Cynic and Stoic traditions. But it is also found in popular philosophy, collections of *gnomai*, and anecdotes on the lives of the philosophers. In this literature as well, the macarism can take on religious coloring. . . . In this secondary religious context the "macarism of the wise man"

---

[62]Vaage, *Galilean Upstarts*, 56.

[63]Ps.-Crates, *Ep.* 11 (Vaage's translation, ibid.).

[64]Diogenes Laertius, *Lives* 2.27 (Vaage, *Galilean Upstarts*, 165 n. 9). See Downing, *Christ and the Cynics*, 69.

[65]Vaage, *Galilean Upstarts*, 57.

[66]Hans Dieter Betz, *Essays on the Sermon on the Mount* (Philadelphia: Fortress, 1985) 33 (Vaage, *Galilean Upstarts*, 165 n. 13).

[67]Vaage, *Galilean Upstarts*, 57.

is also found in great numbers of Old Testament-Jewish Wisdom literature, in apocalyptic, and in early Christian literature.[68]

Betz's classification does not attempt to establish a singular genealogy of the anti-macarism, but rather to draw insights from its pervasiveness. Betz's work on anti-macarisms, however, is regularly used with recourse to only one category of parallels.

Christopher Tuckett in his book *Q and the History of Early Christianity*, examines the first beatitude in a section where he is concerned "to establish the more broadly-based eschatological framework of the Q material."[69] He suggests that the beatitudes as a whole are eschatologically oriented in that "those who are poor, hungry and mourning in the present are promised a reversal of their present suffering state in an eschatological future."[70] Tuckett reads the beatitudes in conjunction with Isaiah 61 and concludes that "the primary reference is most likely to be the fulfillment of Jewish eschatological hopes for the *relief* of *real* poverty and suffering."[71] Tuckett bases part of his argument against reading the Q sermon as sapiential on the fact that the beatitude form is multivalent and multi-contextual:

> As has often been pointed out, the beatitude form itself is multivalent, being usable—and used in a variety of different contexts. Thus, whilst clearly at home in a sapiential context to give ethical guidance, it is also used in an eschatological context to give assurance and encouragement to those presently suffering.[72]

Despite this recognition, Tuckett goes on to control the beatitude's meaning as eschatological by establishing its roots in the promises of Isaiah 61.

In both cases whether the saying is "eschatological" is determined less by its content or ideology and more by its genealogy. This points immediately to the larger issue at stake: identifying the eschatological or non-eschatological roots of the beatitude anchors Jesus within a stream of ancient identity—that is, Hellenistic philosophical discourse or Jewish biblical eschatological or prophetic expectations. Vaage locates the genealogy of this saying not in eschatological categories of reversal and judgment, but in the ideational reversals of Nietzsche and Diogenes. The classifications "eschatological" or

---

[68]Betz, *Essays*, 33.
[69]Tuckett, *Q*, 139.
[70]Ibid., 141.
[71]Ibid., 142 n. 9 (Tuckett's emphasis).
[72]Ibid., 142.

"non-eschatological" for the saying, therefore, can function to locate Jesus in a particular social and/or intellectual framework.

But the same must be said for the beatitude's eschatological genealogy. Tuckett's association of the beatitudes with Isaiah 61 leads to an assertion about the presentation of the figure Jesus:

> Q's Jesus thus starts with the programmatic claim that the promises of Isaiah 61:1ff are now being articulated afresh in his own preaching, Jesus himself is thereby implicitly being presented as the eschatological fulfillment of that text: he is the one anointed by the Spirit to evangelise the poor, i.e. the eschatological prophet.[73]

Thus the construction of the identity of Jesus in Q is based partially on the genealogy of this beatitude. In chapter 4, I discuss further how contemporary interests in the eschatology of Q are intertwined with interests in Q's christological claims and how they compare to the identity and self-understanding of the historical Jesus.

The constant point and counterpoint of the genealogical arguments about the *basileia* of God and the eschatology of Q suggest to me that we are caught up in a two-sided debate that distracts from the central feature of *basileia* language. Both Vaage and Tuckett understand this expression as language of reversal in relation to the present status quo, but this common ground is passed by in favor of competing genealogical arguments. I argue that parallels to the expression "*basileia* of God" should be marshaled not in order to establish genealogical roots but to seek out ideological kinship.[74] Vaage suggests that the "*basileia* of God" language in Q is part of the rhetorical production of ideology in the text. "Through repeated reference to another 'order' of things called the kingdom of God," Vaage says, "the Q people endeavored to imagine and construct an alternate reality to the dominant social institutions of their immediate context and its moral values."[75] This understanding of the rhetorical and ideological work of the *basileia* of God coincides with the rhetorical function of language classified as "eschatologi-

[73]Tuckett, *Q*, 226.

[74]Rasiah Sugirtharajah views the western historical-critical effort to fix the identity of Jesus as of little interest to Third World people. He notes that the "question that summarizes Third World yearning is not who Jesus is but where he is. . . . Is he with the poor, or is he with the rich? Is he with the oppressed, or is he with the oppressor?" ("'What Do Men Say Remains of Me?' Current Jesus Research and Third World Christologies," *Asian Journal of Theology* 5 [1991] 331–37).

[75]Vaage, *Galilean Upstarts*, 56.

cal" or "apocalyptic" insofar as such language imagines and constructs an alternative vision of reality and thus evaluates present political and ethical systems. The alternative reality envisioned by an "eschatological" *basileia* serves as a "symbolic subversion"—to use Vaage's term—to the present order of things.

Rather than deploy genealogical arguments about the *basileia* of God in order to enter the debate about Jesus' identity, I *presuppose* that this expression invokes a complex symbolic vision of an alternative "order of things" that stands in contrast to and contest with the dehumanizing and oppressive orders of the Roman imperial context. The *basileia* is communal or corporate imagery that draws on the socio-political realities of human life and imagines/projects the world and its power arrangements as if God rather than Caesar were in charge. The imagery of kinship with God, both as the children of Abraham (Q 3:7) and the children of *Sophia* (Q 7:35), carries a similar collective flavor but within a smaller socio-political frame of reference—the family unit. In both places, it is God not the King or the Lord (*kyrios*) who authorizes and judges proper human relationships and interactions. Throughout this study, we will explore how attention to the unique identity of Jesus can divert our attention from the *basileia* of God and other communal imagery in Q. The exegetical chapters in both sections of the book, therefore, place Q's communal visions at the center of our inquiry and thus at the center of Q's discursive interests.

A Note About the Book's Organization

Chapters 1 and 4 below present several interrelated hermeneutical reflections on the scholarly discourse about Jesus, Q, and eschatology. Each of these chapters is followed by two companion chapters that present alternative interpretations of select Q texts that have been central in the debates over the eschatological and/or apocalyptic outlook of Q. Although chapters 1 and 4 could have been combined and given pride of place at the beginning of the book, they are intentionally placed at beginning and midpoint in order to punctuate the book with reflections on scholarly debates and public discourses. This arrangement resists the temptation to review the scholarly literature up front so that we can turn, unencumbered, to the interpretation of the text. The book presses us to travel back and forth between contemporary debates and interpretations of texts so that we will not be lulled into thinking that when we engage the text we do so apart from contemporary rhetorical contexts and hermeneutical trends. Thus chapter 1 explains how interpreters regularly place the identity of Jesus at the center of Q's rhetorical interests. Chapters 2 and 3 then present re-readings of the John the Baptist material in Q (7:18–35 and 3:7–9, 16–17, respectively) in which the centrality of Q's rhetorical interests is not the identity of Jesus in relationship to John or "this generation," but is more generally the children of *Sophia* and the *basileia* of God. These three chapters form the first part of the book, which attempts to move our understanding of Q away from an interest in Jesus to an interest in communal visions and identity.

With chapter 4 we return to the contemporary debates in order to examine the way that uniqueness claims for Jesus participate in larger discourses about Christian identity in a pluralistic world. Chapters 5 and 6 then display how the expectation that Q primarily makes claims of Jesus' superlative value over and against his accusers results in the erasing of Q's argument for common cause in the Beelzebul and Sign of Jonah pericopes (Q 11:14–26 and 16, 29–32). Chapters 4 through 6 form the second part of the book, which recognizes Jesus' central place in Q but now as one among the children of *Sophia*. The re-readings in all four of the interpretive chapters (2–3 and 5–6) focus on the values and visions of the community around Jesus and argue that Q's rhetoric represents a call to solidarity across lines of difference. If these readings are persuasive, then they can be valuable in two ways. First, they raise new possibilities for how we historically reconstruct the Jesus movement and its relationship to other groups within Israel. And second, they enter into the public debate about Jesus, eschatology, and Q in a way that takes seriously the ethical consequences and possibilities of our reconstructions of Christian origins and identity.

CHAPTER 1

Eschatology and Identity: Q's Jesus and Christian Diversity

In the United States, it has become commonplace in the field of New Testament studies to say that early Christianity was diverse. We speak in terms of pluralities—of communities and Christologies and Judaisms of the first century C.E.[1] The reconstruction and interpretation of Q plays an important role in exploring the diversity of earliest Christianity. Some interpret Q as early evidence of " 'another kerygma'—one which had no special place for the death of Jesus and which, unlike Paul, did not view the vindication of Jesus through the apocalyptic metaphor of resurrection."[2] Some counter that "while Q may omit some things, it does not include anything really at odds with what Matthew or Luke held dear."[3] The lines in the debate over Q's "otherness" are drawn in terms of how scholars characterize Q's interpretation of Jesus. Was he remembered by Q as a Cynic-like teacher or an eschatological prophet? Just how different is Q's Jesus from the Jesus of the Synoptic Gospels or Paul's letters?

These debates over Q's Jesus take place within larger contemporary discourses about religious pluralism and Christian identity. We can catch a

---

[1] The discoveries of the Qumran and Nag Hammadi libraries have contributed a great deal to the development of diversity as a historical model for the reconstruction of ancient Judaism and Christianity. Much of the theoretical groundwork for this shift in the study of early Christianity was laid by Walter Bauer (*Orthodoxy and Heresy in Earliest Christianity* [German original, 1934; Mifflintown, Pa.: Sigler Press, 1996]), and James M. Robinson and Helmut Koester (*Trajectories Through Early Christianity* [Philadelphia: Fortress, 1971]).

[2] Leif E. Vaage and John S. Kloppenborg, "Early Christianity, Q and Jesus: The Sayings Gospel and Method in the Study of Christian Origins," *Semeia* 55 (1991) 6.

[3] Allison, *Jesus Tradition*, 45.

glimpse of this conversation about diversity by looking at any major news magazine just a few weeks before Easter, when they come out with their annual Jesus article. Such articles usually compare the views of everyday Christians with some scandalous theory put forth by biblical scholars about the resurrection never happening or the Gospels contradicting each other. The articles often construct a radical gulf between the scholarly study of the Bible and the beliefs of the faithful. In late March of 2000, *Newsweek* took a different tack. The cover headline reads, "Visions of Jesus: How Jews, Muslims, and Buddhists View Him." The article is titled "The Other Jesus"[4] and focuses almost exclusively on how the other world religions view Jesus. Although the article presents several images of Jesus, it controls this diversity with a prominently displayed quote from Pope John Paul II: "Christ is absolutely original and absolutely unique. If he were only a wise man like Socrates, if he were a prophet like Muhammad, if he were enlightened like the Buddha, without doubt He would not be what He is."[5] The gulf in this Easter article is not between the Jesus of secular scholars and the Jesus of believing Christians but between the Jesus of believing Christians and the Jesus of non-Christians.

For this article, the Gospels do not present diverse images of Jesus. "The Christ of the Gospels is certainly the best-known Jesus in the world," the article asserts. "For Christians, he is utterly unique—the only Son of God. . . . But alongside this Jesus is another, the Jesus whom Muslims since Muhammad have regarded as a prophet and messenger of Allah. And after centuries of silence about Jesus, many Jews now find him a Jewish teacher and reformer they can accept on their own terms as 'one of us.'"[6] This tension between a Christian understanding of Christ as unique and the appreciation of Jesus by other religious traditions culminates for the author not in a challenge to Christian claims of uniqueness at Eastertide but in a fundamental statement of difference: "Clearly," he says, "the cross is what separates the Christ of Christianity from every other Jesus." Thus the article claims that it is the crucified and resurrected Son of God that marks the uniqueness of Christ for Christians and non-Christians alike, affirming for Christians that the uniqueness of Christ—as the Pope asserts—is essential to Christian identity.

Rather than exploring the diverse understandings of Jesus within the Christian tradition, the *Newsweek* article responds to religious pluralism

[4]Kenneth L. Woodward, "The Other Jesus," *Newsweek* (March 27, 2000) 51–60.
[5]Ibid., 51.
[6]Ibid., 52.

by asserting a singular and unique identity for Jesus. Seen in this context, scholarship that reconstructs early Christianity as diverse poses a threat to a singular notion of Christian identity, because understanding the Christian tradition's view of Jesus as diverse has implications for seeing contemporary Christianity as diverse. In *Jesus: A Revolutionary Biography*, for example, John Dominic Crossan argues that the dialectic between multiple interpretations of the historical Jesus and multiple interpretations of the meaning of Christ "is at the heart of both tradition and canon, that it is perfectly valid, and that it has always been with us and probably always will be."[7] Crossan uses the diversity of early Christianity to authorize the diversity of modern Christianity. Historical-Jesus scholarship and Q studies, therefore, play a role in larger public discourses by defining a Jesus, produced through historical reconstruction, who shores up or challenges the dominant construction of Christian identity.

Because biblical scholarship participates in this larger social-religious discourse, an ethics of interpretation requires not only evaluating what we are saying about Jesus or Q, but also how we are saying it and to what ends. In the sections that follow we will explore four aspects of recent debates about Q and analyze their contribution to contemporary thinking about diversity and Christian identity. As we will see, although there is clear disagreement over how much Q's Jesus differs from other ancient Christian understandings of Jesus, the dominant methodological approach privileges Jesus' identity as the key to Christian identity and retains the notion that only one understanding of Jesus can be right, true, or accurate. In this sense, Q scholarship re-inscribes the rhetoric of *Newsweek* and its interest in shoring up Christian identity in the face of diversity rather than articulating ways to think about Christian identity that foster mutual respect and solidarity in the context of diversity.

Christian Origins and Christian Identity in a Diverse World

Reconstructing Christian origins is never only about reconstructing Christian origins.[8] As with the quest for the historical Jesus, Q scholarship is—perhaps quite surprisingly—quite conversant with and relevant to contemporary debates about Christian identity and religious and cultural diversity. For example, at the conclusion of *Honest to Jesus: Jesus*

---

[7]John Dominic Crossan, *Jesus: A Revolutionary Biography* (San Francisco: HarperSanFrancisco, 1995) 200.

[8]See a further discussion of Q and Christian origins in chapter 4 (pp. 115–30).

for a New Millennium, Robert Funk presents twenty-one implications of historical-Jesus research for contemporary understandings of Christianity. Number three asserts that the renewed effort to describe the historical Jesus "has serious ramifications for how we understand the Christian life."[9] Number four illustrates the historical value placed on Q—particularly a proposed first edition of Q—for reconstructing the historical Jesus: "The renewed quest points to a secular sage who may have more relevance to the spiritual dimensions of society than to institutionalized religion."[10] As with historical-Jesus research, the issue at stake in the debates over Q is Christian identity in a diverse and pluralistic world.[11] For example, Burton Mack concludes *Lost Gospel*[12] with a plainspoken epilogue that identifies the import of Q in terms of what he sees as the insufficiency of traditional forms of Christianity:

> Q enters the arena of public discourse at a time when all Christians are engaged in a turbulent quest to redefine commitments and re-arrange traditional Christian values. Christians are actively engaged in sorting through the rich archives of myths, teachings, and attitudes that have defined their religion, trying to locate the symbols that may constructively address the problems of our time. The quest is turbulent because the world has come alive with problems for which traditional clichés no longer work.[13]

Mack describes two problems that have arisen for "those concerned about the effective difference Christianity might make in a world where nations and cultures are struggling to find ways to work together."[14] The first is the Christian missionary impulse "with its implicit claim to know what is best for other people." The second is the recognition that the Christian tradition—particularly its "messianic vision of a powerful superhero to

---

[9]Robert Funk, *Honest to Jesus: Jesus for a New Millennium* (San Francisco: Harper-SanFrancisco, 1996) 302.

[10]Ibid.

[11]Elisabeth Schüssler Fiorenza argues that "the boom in Historical-Jesus publications is not so much about history as about identity" (*Politics*, 12). As one of the goldmines that feeds the boom, Q scholarship is equally engaged in the quest to reflect, construct, and prescribe identity. See also Vaage, *Galilean Upstarts*, 178 n. 1.

[12]I single out Mack's work in this chapter because it broadly reflects many of the same interpretive trends that I have found running through American Q scholarship. These trends are not often as boldly stated in other Q scholarship as they are in *Lost Gospel*.

[13]Mack, *Lost Gospel*, 254.

[14]Ibid., 255.

right the world's wrongs"—has done much to perpetuate systems of power that abuse and control rather than empower.[15] "The question before us," concludes Mack, "is what the Christian religion might have to offer as we rethink how to live in a multicultural world?"[16]

The importance of Q's Jesus for Christian identity in a multicultural world surfaces in the rhetoric of Mack's detractors as well. In a chapter entitled "Cultural Confusion and Collusion," Luke Timothy Johnson locates the vitriolic public debates in the 1990s over the historical Jesus in "diverse responses of Christians to the challenge posed by modernity."[17] Johnson describes a tension between two competing definitions of Christianity apparent in the contemporary debates over the historical Jesus. In the first, Christianity is defined internally, generally unified around a set of central beliefs, and authenticated by claims to ultimacy. In the second, Christianity is defined externally as one version of religiosity among multiple possibilities.[18] Although Johnson characterizes these two positions as incompatible, it is significant that both Johnson and Mack use "myth" and "symbol" to refer to something that is inherently false or constructed. Mack contrasts the ideally sagacious first Jesus followers with the "fantastic mythologies" of religion.[19] Johnson contrasts Christianity's "genuine experience of ultimate reality" with the "human construction of symbolic worlds" indicative of the world's religions.[20] The result in both cases is to render one's own understanding of ideal Christianity as inherently true (either rationally or metaphysically) over and against the mythic "other"—the world's religions for Johnson, and orthodox Christianity for Mack.

Like Mack, Johnson authorizes his own understanding of Christianity with historical and literary claims about the nature of early Christian literature: "Despite the obvious diversity in genre, perspective, and theme in the New Testament compositions, the coherence of their generative experiences and convictions can be glimpsed from their remarkable consistency concerning the image of Jesus and of discipleship."[21] Similarly, Dale Allison's critique of Mack takes the position that Q's Jesus is fully compatible with the Jesus

[15]Ibid., 255–56.

[16]Ibid., 257.

[17]Luke Timothy Johnson, *The Real Jesus: The Misguided Quest for the Historical Jesus and the Truth of the Traditional Gospels* (San Francisco: HarperSanFrancisco, 1996) 60.

[18]Ibid., 57.

[19]Mack, *Lost Gospel*, 5.

[20]Johnson, *Real Jesus*, 15.

[21]Ibid., 167.

of other New Testament literature. In the process, however, Allison points
to the problematic nature of the times:

> If in the past we have tended to find too much unity in the early
> church, perhaps now, as citizens of a pluralistic and fragmented
> society, we are going too far the other way. One may even wonder
> whether for its first decade or two early Christianity was not the
> complex thing modern scholars imagine but instead a very small
> movement with a few recognizable leaders who, as Paul tells us,
> agreed on quite a bit.[22]

Thus the lines are drawn: Q as "other" vs. Q as same; Q as another *kerygma*
vs. Q as just like Paul; Q as evidence of diversity vs. Q as evidence of
unity. Naturally, scholars on both sides of the debate analogize between
ancient and modern Christianity. For Mack, both contemporary and first-
century Christians are citizens of a pluralistic and fragmented society.
For Allison, modern and ancient Christianity is primarily a single, unified
movement.

Although Q scholars disagree on Q, therefore, they agree on the terms
of the debate. This includes the prevailing methodologies used to interpret
Q. Like many biblical scholars, most Q interpreters rely on rigorous historical, social scientific, and literary methods to "discover" things about Q.
Despite the persistence of a variety of interpretations of Q, we assume that
the goal is to produce one scientifically verifiable understanding of what Q
is, what it says, and what it means. Elisabeth Schüssler Fiorenza examines
this phenomenon in historical-Jesus research and identifies issues of authority at the heart of things. Despite the variety of scholarly interpretations of
Jesus, historical-Jesus scholarship presents itself as capable of discovering
an historically accurate—and therefore authoritative—Jesus. She suggests
that this scholarship "insists on the scientific character of its production of
knowledge as factual and historical. . . . [T]hey assert not theological revela-
tory positivism but historical positivism in order to shore up the scholarly
authority and scientific truth of their research portrayals of Jesus."[23] When
the reconstructed Q (or its first literary layer) is offered as the earliest gospel text, therefore, the battles over Q are fought out on the bloodied field
of authoritative and singular origins. In many ways, the dependence upon
methods and interests from the ongoing historical-Jesus debates moves Q

[22]Allison, *Jesus Tradition*, 45.
[23]Schüssler Fiorenza, *Politics*, 5.

studies toward arguing for diversity in which *one* form of the movement is still earlier (and thus considered more authoritative, whether theologically or historically) than the others.

Equating Jesus' Identity with Christian Identity

We can further utilize Burton Mack's forthright work to see another aspect of the contemporary discussions about Q, that is, how it places Jesus at the center of inquiry. In the prologue to *Lost Gospel*, Mack rightly points out that by ascribing teachings to Jesus, Q engages in what Mack calls "mythmaking" about Jesus. "Teachings attributed to Jesus were invested with programmatic status and cultivated as instruction" resulting in "the creation of a highly crafted and profoundly effective myth of origin."[24] This notion that every stage of the Jesus tradition reflects various attempts at persuasive interpretations of Jesus corresponds with Dieter Georgi's observation that interest in the life of Jesus—from the Gospels to historical-Jesus research—has centered around producing "the great individual Jesus, sufficiently human to allow identification with him, but also sufficiently lifted above the masses that he could be seen as a beacon."[25] Q scholarship similarly places Jesus' identity at the center of its inquiry and thus perpetuates a view of Jesus as the key to Christian identity.

For example, recognizing that Q (at any stage) is *arguing* for a central and singular significance for Jesus can facilitate a shift in focus from Jesus himself to reconstructing the interests and experiences of the movement that produced such arguments.[26] Mack sees a similar possibility:

> Q shows us that the notion of a pure origin is mythic and that the process of endowing Jesus with superlative wisdom and divinity was and is a mode of mythmaking. Q shifts the focus of conversation about Christian origins away from fascination with the many myths condensed in the New Testament and onto the people who

---

[24]Mack, *Lost Gospel*, 7.

[25]Dieter Georgi, "The Interest in Life of Jesus Theology as a Paradigm for the Social History of Biblical Criticism," *HTR* 85 (1992) 78.

[26]Although this shift takes different turns depending on the hermeneutical framework of interpreters, it can be seen in traditional historical-critical scholarship, such as Bultmann's interest in the *kerygmatic* community rather than the historical Jesus, and in feminist historiography and theology that focuses on wo/men in the early communities, such as the work of Elisabeth Schüssler Fiorenza and Antoinette Clark Wire.

produced them. Q lets us catch sight of real people struggling with a social vision.[27]

It is clear, however, that Mack links the identity of these "real people struggling with a social vision" directly to their understanding of Jesus' identity:

> The remarkable thing about the people of Q is that they were not Christians. They did not think of Jesus as a messiah or the Christ. They did not take his teachings as an indictment of Judaism. They did not regard his death as a divine, tragic, or saving event. And they did not imagine that he had been raised from the dead to rule over a transformed world. *Instead they thought of him as a teacher whose teachings made it possible to live with verve in troubled times.* Thus they did not gather to worship in his name, honor him as a god, or cultivate his memory through hymns, prayers, and rituals. They did not form a cult of the Christ such as the one that emerged among the Christian communities familiar to readers of the letters of Paul. The people of Q were Jesus people, not Christians.[28]

The Q people are presented as wholly "other" from the category "Christians" by means of an interpretation of Jesus as a "teacher whose teachings made it possible to live with verve in troubled times." Mack describes them as "Jesus people," creating an identity category that has Jesus as the center. In addition, Mack offers the category "Jesus people" to disrupt the dominant category "Christian."[29] Although Mack's interpretations of the first version

---

[27]Mack, *Lost Gospel*, 256.

[28]Ibid., 4–5 (my emphasis). Christopher Tuckett rightly points out that Mack's definition of "Christian" here would not apply to most NT texts: "Would Matthew think of Jesus as an indictment of Juda*ism* (as opposed to some Jews)? Does Luke regard Jesus' death as a 'saving event'? How many early Christians 'honored [Jesus] as a god'?" (*Q*, 107 n. 1, Tuckett's emphasis). Tuckett also implies that Mack's totalizing definition of "Christian" effectively violates the "now standard critical orthodoxy, [that] first-century Christianity was characterized by a rich diversity" (ibid.).

[29]Despite the role of diversity arguments in Mack's work—both in terms of the nature of the ancient sources and the exigencies of modern life—he repeatedly juxtaposes Q's Jesus-as-teacher over and against a totalizing characterization of "Christian" as all mythology and cultic practices associated with Jesus the Christ. In the end, his characterization of the "otherness" of Q must also be reined in to serve this totalizing notion of Christianity: "Q's story [that is, its redactional development] shows us that it was in no way different for any of the other Jesus movements, Christ congregations, or Christian churches at the beginning of the Christian tradition. Each took what they had in hand and coined new myths for new circumstances in the interest of compelling social visions" (*Lost Gospel*, 257).

of Q seek to turn Christian identity away from the "fantastic mythologies" of Jesus the Christ, they do not turn it away from Jesus the man.[30] Thus the "real people" that Mack seeks are effectively the real Jesus and his first (male) followers[31] free of the trappings of Christian mythologizing.

Fixing Jesus' Identity with Scholarly Taxonomy

Although the theme of diversity emerges regularly in scholarly discussions about Jesus and Q, the debates themselves are somewhat two-sided and often built upon recurring dichotomies. For example, debate over the eschatology of Q is often characterized by stark choices: Is Q's Jesus in line with the Pauline view of Jesus' death and resurrection as the salvific event that marks the dawning of a new age? Or is Q evidence of a different interpretation of Jesus whereby Jesus was a wisdom teacher who made no claims about the end of the world, had no aspirations to effect or mark the dawning of a new age, and no apocalyptically significant death? Much of the technical discussion of Q's Jesus is characterized by corresponding dichotomies such as the sapiential or apocalyptic genre of Q, the Hellenistic or Jewish context of Q, and the secular or religious worldview of Q. The persistence of these dichotomies in the discourse over Q's Jesus indicates the prevailing interest in fixing Jesus' identity through a series of antithetical taxonomies: he is x and not y, he is *this* and not *that*. For example, the effort to fix the identity of Q's Jesus as a Cynic-like teacher is often mirrored by historical-critical counterefforts to identify Q's Jesus as an eschatological prophet.[32] This rhetoric not only demands that Jesus'

---

[30]I do not only mean the "human" Jesus (as opposed to the divine Christ), but Jesus-the-man. Insofar as the identity of Jesus (as teacher or prophet or magician) is the center of historical-Jesus (and often Q) research, it continues to replicate the androcentrism of the text by placing "elite Man in the center of historical scientific discourses" (Schüssler Fiorenza, *Politics*, 11).

[31]Mack uses Cynic comparisons to early Q material in order to locate Q's Jesus as originally a Cynic-like teacher. Although Mack does point out that Cynics were notoriously independent (*Lost Gospel*, 121), the resulting identity formation for Jesus followers who remembered his sayings (and lived by them) is the school model of male teachers and students. See Schüssler Fiorenza, *Politics*, 24.

[32]See Tuckett, *Q*, 209–38; and Horsley and Draper, *Whoever Hears*, 292–310. Horsley and Draper present Jesus as in the prophetic tradition but not necessarily as an "eschatological" prophet. They also focus on Q as an oral-derived and thus repeatedly performed text. This has the effect of transferring Jesus' prophetic role to the Q people themselves as the text is

identity be something that can be fixed and that remains constant over time; it also continues to center Jesus-the-man (whether sage, prophet, or apocalypticist) as the key to Christian identity both for the Q people and for contemporary Christianity in a diverse world.

A North American discussion of the proper context in which to locate and interpret the "*basileia* of God" provides a good example of these taxonomies and their role in fixing the identity of Jesus. In 1986, the Jesus Seminar met at Notre Dame to discuss and evaluate the *basileia* of God sayings in Mark, Q, and the *Gospel of Thomas*. James Butts summarizes the "most significant developments" of the meeting in four propositions.[33] The first proposition is as follows: "For Jesus, the kingdom of God was *not* an eschatological nor an apocalyptic phenomenon."[34] In a paper written for this meeting, Mack argued that "Hellenistic wisdom" not "Jewish apocalyptic" provides the frame of reference in which to interpret Jesus' sayings about the *basileia* of God.[35] Mack is clear about how his classification of the *basileia* sayings of Q as *not* apocalyptic has implications for the historical Jesus: "There is now a great deal of evidence to the effect that Jesus' wisdom was not apocalyptic, but aphoristic."[36] The voting of the Seminar suggests that Mack's conclusions received support insofar as all of Mark's *basileia* sayings were voted to be inauthentic.

Edward Meadors's 1995 book on Q countered such conclusions in the very title of his book: *Jesus the Messianic Herald of Salvation*.[37] Meadors's approach to the classification of the *basileia* of God illustrates the sharp contrast between his view and that of scholars like Mack:

> *The kingdom of God cannot be separated from eschatology.* It is in its very essence an eschatological term. . . . Against those who interpret Q strictly against a Hellenistic background, we will see that the kingdom of God sayings—which establish the primary theme of Q—are dependent upon the background of Biblical Judaism.[38]

---

performed in community. This helps to de-emphasize the persistent interest in the identity of Jesus in these debates.

[33]James R. Butts, "Probing the Polling," *Foundations & Facets Forum* 3 (1987) 112–13.

[34]Ibid., 112 (Butts's emphasis).

[35]Burton L. Mack, "The Kingdom Sayings in Mark," *Foundations & Facets Forum* 3 (1987) 3.

[36]Ibid., 17.

[37]Edward P. Meadors, *Jesus the Messianic Herald of Salvation* (Tübingen: Mohr/Siebeck, 1995).

[38]Ibid., 149 (Meadors's emphasis).

Meadors's conclusions point to the direct relationship between such classifications and assertions about the historical Jesus whose "earthly acts and teachings implied his identity as the eschatological herald of salvation—the anointed wise Messiah, who had come to defeat Satan and gather God's people for salvation in the kingdom of God."[39]

Meadors clearly associates "eschatological" with "Biblical Judaism" and the unnamed "non-eschatological" or "sapiential" as "Hellenistic." Despite the fact that every historical-Jesus scholar (and Q scholar) asserts that Jesus is Jewish, the dichotomy of "Hellenistic" versus "Jewish" persists in much of the ongoing debate. William Arnal has usefully suggested that the controversy over the "Hellenistic versus Jewish" Jesus (or Q) is rooted in the dichotomy of "secular versus religious":

> The label "religious" is at the crux of the matter. At its heart are the debates concerning categories, idealism and the meaning of "religion." That is, the very self-evident and uncontentious statement, "Jesus was a Jew," is taken to mean, by advocates of the observant Jewish Jesus, that Jesus was a religious person in the tradition of Judaism.[40]

A Cynic-like Jesus is thus the Hellenistic and secular side of the coin. Arnal locates the interests of the proponents of a Cynic-like Jesus in the erosion of categories that characterize the postmodern situation. Thus contemporary scholars respond to the diffusion of postmodern identity in a practical way by "ignoring and even opposing conceptual archaisms such as 'religion,' and reifications thereof, including Judaism."[41] This important insight is an idealized conception in itself, however, in that it must overlook the persistence of these dichotomous categories (like secular/religious or Hellenistic/Jewish) in the actual discourses of proponents of the Cynic hypothesis. The designation "Cynic" still functions in the discourse over and against what it is not. What is most convincing in Arnal's analysis is his locating these debates in postmodernism's "corrosion of categories. . . . Of particular importance is the experience of fragmentation which is increasingly affecting the apprehension of what it means to be a subject, and how we conceive of our subjectivity."[42] Insofar as the Cynic hypothesis and

[39]Ibid., 325.

[40]William E. Arnal, "Making and Re-Making the Jesus Sign: Contemporary Markings on the Body of Christ," in *Whose Historical Jesus?* (ed. William E. Arnal and Michel Desjardins; Waterloo, Ontario: Wilfrid Laurier University Press, 1997) 310.

[41]Ibid.

[42]Ibid., 311.

most historical Jesus and Q scholarship remain interested in the identity of Jesus-the-subject, it serves to shore up "Christian" subjectivity rather than to face its fragmentation.

Theological Taxonomies and Christian Identity

Perhaps the dichotomies persist because they are doing work that we do not sufficiently recognize. In his recent book *Excavating Q*, John Kloppenborg describes Q studies' ever-present and much-debated adjectives "sapiential," "prophetic," and "apocalyptic" as *theological* taxonomies. This designation recognizes the role that these modern synthetic categories often play in characterizations of the worldview or theological orientation of a particular text, pericope, or saying.[43] These taxonomies synthesize texts, motifs, forms, genres, and ideas *in order to generalize* about their theology or ideology *and to compare* them to other theologies or ideologies. As Kloppenborg suggests, these taxonomies place Q "within the theological landscape of primitive Christianity."[44] Thus they serve to locate Q in a particular sector on the map of first-century Judaism. Scholarship has cordoned off such sectors as "sapiential" and "prophetic" by means of attendant sets of literature (wisdom literature, prophetic literature), ideological orientations (social accommodation, social critique), and social locations (elite, marginalized). The field of biblical studies relies upon these taxonomies to reconstruct the history (that is, to tell the story) of Jesus and early Christianity.

The extensive debate over these taxonomies, however, proves that they rarely make sense of the variety of forms, motifs, and rhetorical positions in any particular text. As Kloppenborg rightly points out,

> the debate about the *theological* taxonomy of Q—whether Q belongs to wisdom discourse, to prophecy, or to apocalyptic—is in one sense moot, since most contributors to the discussion, or recent contributors at least, are prepared to admit that Q does not fit neatly into any of the stereotyped synthetic categories used by modern theology.[45]

[43]Kloppenborg Verbin, *Excavating Q*, 381.

[44]Ibid., 383.

[45]Ibid., 395 (Kloppenborg's emphasis). It is curious that Kloppenborg here locates the use of these categories in "modern theology." This is hardly the case, if we are speaking of academic disciplines. These categories are pervasively defined, applied, and debated within biblical studies, both in historical criticism and biblical theology. Kloppenborg obviously

For Kloppenborg, therefore, identifying such terms as theological tax-onomies also marks them as theologically motivated categories and thus methodologically suspect for historical and literary work. For example, he points out that locating Christology as the "theological center" of Q drives the resistance to classifying the formative stratum of Q as sapiential.[46] In addition, the theological characterization of sayings in a particularly early text like Q serves an unstated interest in correlating Q as sapiential, prophetic, or apocalyptic with the historical Jesus as sage, prophet, or apocalypticist.[47]

Kloppenborg suggests, therefore, that work on the genre and composi-tional analysis of Q should *avoid* these theological terms so that "theological assumptions not determine the outcome of what are properly literary deci-sions."[48] He insists that

> the discussion of the genre of Q should proceed *not* on the basis
> of subjective judgments regarding contents, still less on a priori as-
> sumptions about theological or social history of the earliest Jesus
> movements. Instead, genre determination must proceed on the basis
> of more conceptually neutral features: framing devices; the domi-
> nant grammatical forms; the nature of argumentation (its warrants
> and methods); the nature of the authorial "voice"; and finally, the
> typical idioms and tropes.[49]

Thus he constructs a divide between more neutral literary analyses and theologically compromised taxonomies.[50] Although Kloppenborg contributes

---

agrees in that he does not discuss modern theologians here but Q scholars and biblical theologians such as Brevard Childs. While some biblical scholars define themselves as theologians, many do not and actively defend the academic boundaries between theologian and biblical scholar. Kloppenborg rightly exposes the fact that the categories sapiential and apocalyptic do theological work, but we should also recognize that they are often created and used by scholars who do not see themselves as theologians.

[46]Kloppenborg Verbin, *Excavating Q*, 388–91. He gives the example of the interest in emphasizing the link between Jesus and the coming son of humanity as the "*theologoumenon* that energizes Q" (p. 391). For a discussion of the christological interests inherent in the debates about eschatology, see chapter 4 below, pp. 115–30.

[47]Kloppenborg Verbin, *Excavating Q*, 381.

[48]Ibid., 381.

[49]Ibid., 380.

[50]This divide is marked strongly with evaluative language. Theological interests and presuppositions are said to "lurk beneath the surface" (ibid., 420, 422, 434). Confusing histor-ical and theological concerns is a "dangerous venture" that turns "historical explanation into apologetics" (p. 440).

much to elucidating the theological stakes of these debates, he reserves the privileged position for scholarship that eschews—rather than articulates—its theological interests and judgments.

This divide between theological (or ideological or ethical) interests and historical analysis depends upon an assumption that it is possible to isolate a scholarly practice such as literary analysis from the rhetorical strategies and ideological interests of biblical studies in general. The effort to determine the genre of Q depends not only upon the identification of the "more neutral features" mentioned by Kloppenborg above, but also upon the comparison of those features with those of other predetermined groups of literature—such as wisdom literature or prophetic literature—and the pronouncement of sameness or difference.[51] Much of the debate over the genre of Q ultimately serves the same locative function of such theological taxonomies as prophetic or sapiential or non-eschatological. That is, literary analyses—with varying degrees of nuance and methodological intensity—ultimately locate the producers of Q in a particular construction of ancient identity. Even arguments about literary genre must be contextualized, therefore, in the long-standing theological debates about the essence of Christianity and the purportedly value-neutral arguments that anchor that essence genealogically in its origins.

Insofar as they contribute to contemporary debates about Christian identity in a diverse world, these scholarly taxonomies are also evaluative. That is, they rhetorically construct a hierarchy of preferable options for locating Q or the earliest Jesus traditions. For example, Kloppenborg shows how the expectation that Q makes christological claims leads to a preference for classifying Q traditions as prophetic or eschatological over sapiential, which would supposedly result in Jesus as a "mere sage."[52] One's evaluation of the categories, however, depends on one's theological and ethical perspectives. It is not uncommon, for example, for either sapiential or prophetic to be preferred over apocalyptic. Returning to Robert Funk's twenty-one theses about the impact of historical Jesus research on contemporary Christianity,

---

[51]This process is a comparative one, which Jonathan Z. Smith (*Drudgery Divine* [Chicago: University of Chicago Press, 1990] 52) describes as "a disciplined exaggeration in the service of knowledge. [Comparison] lifts out and strongly marks certain features within difference as being of possible intellectual significance, expressed in the rhetoric of being 'like' in some stipulated fashion." The question is not *whether* literary analysis—as comparison in the service of knowledge—seeks to answer certain questions and interests, but *what* questions and interests it serves.

[52]Kloppenborg Verbin, *Excavating Q*, 398.

number twenty provides a forthright example of the negative evaluation of apocalyptic common in New Testament scholarship: "Exorcise the apocalyptic elements from Christianity. Apocalypticism at its base is world-denying and vindictive. . . . The desire to reward and punish in the next world is self-serving in its most crass, pathetic form. It is unworthy of the Galilean who asked nothing for himself, beyond his simplest needs."[53] Whether or not we agree, we can see that Funk employs his ethical evaluation of apocalyptic in order to critique modern Christianity. The scholarly construction of what counts as "apocalyptic" or "apocalypticism," however, rarely articulates the evaluative role that these taxonomies play in the reconstruction of Christian origins.[54]

Conclusion

Looking critically at the context and interests of Q scholarship does not mean that its questions are invalid or that its methods are faulty. Practicing critical-reflexivity presses us to examine the implications of our work in the ongoing and public process of biblical interpretation. This chapter suggests that the issue at stake in the debates over Q is Christian identity, which in the terms set by the debate is linked to Jesus' identity. The familiar taxonomic categories from biblical studies—apocalyptic vs. eschatological, prophetic vs. sapiential, Hellenistic vs. Jewish—often function to fix Jesus on a map of ancient identities. Although these categories are scholarly inventions, we rarely articulate the theologically evaluative role they play in our reconstructions of Christian origins. There is a general tendency in historical-Jesus research and Q studies to depend on scientific methodology to produce correct descriptions of Jesus and his first followers. This suggests that we are less interested in fostering diverse understandings of Christianity in contemporary discussions and more interested in countering a singular authoritative view of Christian identity with another singular authoritative version of Christian identity. If we argue that Christianity was and is diverse, then the question no longer has to do with which one

---

[53]Funk, *Honest to Jesus*, 314.

[54]Elisabeth Schüssler Fiorenza critiques the dichotomy often constructed between "eschatological" content and "apocalyptic" language or forms, which depends on an evaluation of "abstract philosophical language" as "theologically superior to imaginative language" ("The Phenomenon of Early Christian Apocalyptic: Some Reflections on Method," in *Apocalypticism in the Mediterranean World and the Near East* [ed. David Hellholm; Tübingen: Mohr/Siebeck, 1983] 304).

of the diverse meanings of Christianity is earliest or most accurate. The question has to do, rather, with which one is both textually persuasive and ethically preferable for thinking about Christian identity in a diverse world. The next two chapters attempt to take this question seriously by re-reading Q's texts about John and Jesus in a way that gives voice to communal traditions of solidarity in Q.

CHAPTER 2

Eschatology and Community:
Traditions of Solidarity in Q 7:18–35[1]

Q 7:18–35 offers a rich site for exploring the theological outlook and genre of Q. It contains most of the hotspots of the debates about Q: special appellations for Jesus ("coming one" and the "son of humanity") and references to "this generation," the *basileia* of God, and *Sophia*. Q 7:18–23 establishes Jesus as John's "coming one" from Q 3:16, and yet the description of his ministry (which echoes Isaiah) bears little resemblance to the figure who baptizes with fire and wields the winnowing shovel. Q 7:24–28 and 7:31–35 both seem to affirm John and yet relegate him to a secondary position to Jesus. These tensions lead interpreters to identify all of Q 3:7–7:35 as a compositional effort to "mediate conflicts between John's characterization of the 'coming one' and Jesus' enactment of that role."[2] Arland Jacobson has dubbed this first section of Q, "John and Jesus."[3]

Q 3:7–7:35 clearly features John and Jesus, but this does not necessitate the conclusion that Q's primary rhetorical interest in Q 7:18–35 is establishing Jesus' identity in relationship to John or John's preaching. Q commonly links materials that share similar themes into larger discourses. Q 7:18–35

---

[1] A revised version of portions of this chapter entitled "Bridging the Gap to 'This Generation': A Feminist Critical Reading of the Rhetoric of Q 7:31–35" appears in *Walk in the Ways of Wisdom: Essays in Honor of Elisabeth Schüssler Fiorenza* (ed. Shelly Matthews, Cynthia Briggs Kittredge, and Melanie Johnson-DeBaufre; Harrisburg, Pa.: Trinity, 2003) 214–33 (reprinted by permission).

[2] Kirk, *Composition*, 380; and bibliography at ibid., n. 396.

[3] Jacobson, *First Gospel*, 77–129.

contains three "rhetorically autonomous yet interlinked units"[4] that concern John and Jesus.[5] In addition, Q 3:7–9, 16–17 and 7:18–35 form an *inclusio* of John material around Q 4:1–7:10. Because John's question about the "coming one" in 7:18 alludes to the figure mentioned by John in 3:16 (ἐρχόμενος), interpreters often emphasize Q's interest in whether Jesus is the "coming one." But there is another intertextual link between the children (τέκνα) of Abraham in Q 3:8 and the children of *Sophia* (τὰ τέκνα αὐτῆς) in Q 7:35.[6] Abraham's children appear before John's "coming one," and the children of *Sophia* are referenced after John's question to Jesus. Thus the theme of the children of Abraham and/or *Sophia* forms the widest *inclusio* around the entire section. Q 7:31–35 functions as the crowning argument to the unit's linear progression. As Alan Kirk points out, "In the opening unit John had raised the question of the true identity of the 'children (τέκνα) of Abraham.' By the time we reach the climax of the culminating unit, this question has been answered: they are the children (τέκνα) of Wisdom, the followers of John and Jesus."[7] I will argue that Q's primary rhetorical interest is not so much in clarifying the community's understanding of Jesus as in shaping the community's self-understanding as unified around a common vision. This chapter also identifies the way scholarly interest in the identity of Jesus often precludes alternative readings of Q 7:18–35. Placing Jesus' identity at the center of our inquiry produces interpretations of Q as similarly interested in the identity of Jesus. By focusing on Q as a communal text that seeks to shape its audience, we can begin to reconstruct the values and struggles of the people who shaped the movement(s) attributed to John and Jesus.

The following discussion begins with an interpretation of Q 7:31–35 and proceeds to 7:18–23 and 7:24–28. Reading Q 7:31–35 first and on its own terms removes much of the traditionally recognized opacity of Q 7:31–35. For example, Christopher Tuckett begins with 7:18 and the "question of the identity of the figure predicted by John," asserting that all of "Q 7:18–35 [is]

[4]Kirk, *Composition*, 370; and bibliography at ibid., n. 356.

[5]The three smaller units are: (1) John's question about the "coming one" in 7:18–23; (2) Jesus' evaluation of John in 7:24–28; and (3) the simile of the children in the marketplace in 7:31–35. As is common in Q, each of the three parts of Q 7:18–35 ends with an aphoristic saying (7:23; 7:28; and 7:35) (Piper, *Wisdom*, 64; see also Kirk, *Composition*, 264–65).

[6]Sevenich-Bax, *Konfrontation*, 463; Allison, *Jesus Tradition*, 9; Jacobson, *First Gospel*, 128.

[7]Kirk, *Composition*, 377; see also Tuckett, *Q*, 178–79: "The section [7:31–35] serves as the literary climax, and serves to provide the interpretative key, for the passage as a whole."

devoted to the relationship between Jesus and John."[8] In his discussion of Q 7:35, however, it is unclear whether the text is about Wisdom's children or about Jesus and John as messengers to "this generation":

> It is hard to see how John and Jesus alone as "acknowledging Wisdom to be in the right" really fits the context. Much better is the idea of Wisdom's children as those responding to Wisdom's call (cf. Prov 8:32; Sir 4:11; 15:2) so that Wisdom's children provide the antithetical parallel to the people of this generation who have not responded. The saying in v. 35 thus provides a polemical thrust at the end of the pericope, *implying* that "this generation" do not comprise the true children of Wisdom by their rejection of the calls of Jesus and John. *Implicit* here is the idea that Jesus and John are messengers of Wisdom, and hence acceptance of their message is acceptance of Wisdom.[9]

For Tuckett, the saying's apparent focus on a wider group that justifies Wisdom cannot stand as the conclusion to Q 7:18–35 because the purpose of the composition has already been marked out as clarifying the "relationship between John and Jesus." Therefore John and Jesus (and their perceived opponents in 7:31, namely, "this generation") must be related to 7:35 *by implication*. When Tuckett concludes his discussion, the larger group—so apparent in the saying—has receded in favor of the *implied* foci: "The thrust of the small section in 7:31–35, and derivatively of the wider unit in 7:18–35, is thus that Jesus and John appear in parallel as messengers of Wisdom but shunned by this generation."[10] The previously noted emphasis on a communal meaning for "children of *Sophia*" has largely disappeared. As I will show, however, beginning with Q 7:31–35 results in interpretations of this section of Q as interested in promoting group solidarity rather than negotiating the relationship between John and Jesus.

Sophia is Vindicated by All Her Children: Q 7:31–35

Q 7:31–35 consists of (1) a simile that compares "this generation" with children sitting in the marketplace (7:31–32); (2) an application that gives a parallel comparison of the reception of John and Jesus (7:33–34); and

---

[8]Tuckett, *Q*, 125.
[9]Ibid., 178 (my emphasis).
[10]Ibid., 179.

(3) a concluding aphorism (7:35). The text is reconstructed by the International Q Project (IQP)[11] as follows:

Q 7:31 τίνι . . . ὁμοιώσω τὴν γενεὰν ταύτην καὶ τίνι ἐ‹στ›ὶν ὁμοί‹α›;

To what am I to compare this generation and what is it like?

Q 7:32 ὁμοία ἐστὶν παιδίοις καθημένοις ἐν ⟦ταῖς⟧ ἀγορ⟦αῖς⟧ ἃ προσφωνοῦντα ⟦τοῖς ἑτέρ⟧οις λέγουσιν· ηὐλήσαμεν ὑμῖν καὶ οὐκ ὠρχήσασθε ἐθρηνήσαμεν καὶ οὐκ ἐκλαύσατε.

It is like children seated in the market-places, who, addressing the others,[12] say: We fluted for you, but you would not dance; we sang a dirge,[13] but you would not cry.[14]

Q 7:33 ἦλθεν γὰρ Ἰωάννης μὴ . . . ἐσθίων μήτε πίνων, καὶ λέγετε· δαιμόνιον ἔχει.

For John came, neither eating nor drinking, and you say: He has a demon!

Q 7:34 ἦλθεν ὁ υἱὸς τοῦ ἀνθρώπου ἐσθίων καὶ πίνων, καὶ λέγετε· ἰδοὺ ἄνθρωπος φάγος καὶ οἰνοπότης, τελωνῶν φίλος καὶ ἁμαρτωλῶν.

The son of humanity came eating and drinking, and you say: Look! A person [who is] a glutton and drunkard, a friend of tax collectors and sinners.

Q 7:35 καὶ ἐδικαιώθη ἡ σοφία ἀπὸ τῶν τέκνων αὐτῆς.

But *Sophia* is vindicated by [all][15] her children.

---

[11]Robinson, *Critical Edition*, 140–49.

[12]See p. 52 n. 31 below.

[13]I translate θρηνέω as "sing a dirge" (LSJ first definition) rather than the IQP "wail" (LSJ second definition) in order to make the element of musical performance in the second phrase more apparent.

[14]The IQP selects Luke's ἐκλαύσατε (LSJ: "to cry, wail, lament") rather than Matthew's ἐκόψασθε (LSJ: "beat one's breast or head through grief"; also "mourn," but usually with an accusative object). Adopting the Matthean version would make both verbs in the second half of each line actions that involve moving the body. The evidence is strong either way. Whichever verb was in Q, the other verb choice may have been inspired by a line in the poem in Ecclesiastes 3 LXX about there being a time for everything: "a time to weep [κλαῦσαι] and a time to laugh; a time to mourn [κόψασθαι], and a time to dance [ὀρχήσασθαι]" (Eccl 3:4). This may indicate Q's having κόπτω (which is more parallel to Ecclesiastes) or Matthew's changing Q to make it adhere more closely with Ecclesiastes. If Luke found the verb κόπτω unseemly, as Olof Linton argues ("The Parable of the Children's Game," *NTS* 22 [1975–1976] 162), then the verse in Ecclesiastes may have provided the alternative κλαίω.

[15]Although the IQP prefers Luke's τέκνων to Matthew's ἔργων, it leaves aside Luke's

Scholars often puzzle over the relationship between the three components of Q 7:31–35. As Jacobson notes, "The problems with this pericope have less to do with reconstructing the Q text than with understanding the inter-relationships of the various elements in the pericope."[16] The aphorism in 7:35 introduces elements that do not appear in the first two parts (such as *Sophia*, and τέκνα rather than παιδίον).[17] In addition, debate persists about whether the simile in 7:31–32 is properly applied[18] to John and Jesus in 7:33–34.[19] As Cameron summarizes:

> Are the uncooperative children those addressed by John and Jesus? Or do the children represent "this generation," calling unsuccessfully to John and Jesus? Does "this generation" represent *two* groups of children each calling to the other yet refusing to respond? Or are John and Jesus identified with one group which calls, and "this generation" with another which rejects their summons?[20]

Thus, "although it seems apparent that the parable and its interpretation criticize 'this generation,' the *tertium comparationis* is far from clear."[21]

As shown in the following pages, however, the difficulty of the relationship between the simile, the application, and even the concluding aphorism is overstated. There is complete structural similarity between the bipartite speech of the children in the marketplace and the sayings about John and Jesus. The introduction to the parable in 7:31 makes it very clear that "this generation" resembles children who *address* "the others." How could the

---

πάντων as Lukan. In the context of this chapter's interpretation of 7:31–35, Luke's πάντων reflects well the rhetorical interests of the Q passage.

[16]Jacobson, *First Gospel*, 120.

[17]Kloppenborg, *Formation*, 110; and bibliography at ibid., n. 37.

[18]It may be more useful to describe 7:33–34 as an argument "from example" as Ron Cameron does ("'What Have You Come Out To See?': Characterizations of John and Jesus in the Gospels," *Semeia* 49 [1990] 60). This would function to substantiate the truth of the simile by giving a concrete example from the realm of human behavior.

[19]This perceived lack of fit has been a primary factor in the routine classification of the interpretation (7:33–34) as secondary. See Hoffmann, *Studien*, 227; Schulz, *Q*, 380–81.

[20]Cameron, "'What Have You Come Out to See?'," 40 (Cameron's emphasis). This kind of list also appears in Kloppenborg, *Formation*, 111; and Wendy J. Cotter, C.S.J., "The Parable of the Children in the Market-Place, Q (Lk) 7:31–35: An Examination of the Parable's Image and Significance," *NovT* 29 (1987) 294. For a helpful elaboration of these interpretive options as they appear in scholarship before 1975, see Dieter Zeller, "Die Bildlogik des Gleichnisses Mt 11:16f./Lk 7:31f.," *ZNW* 68 (1977) 252–57.

[21]Kloppenborg, *Formation*, 111.

children in the marketplace also represent Jesus and John addressing "this generation"? Although John and Jesus are the subjects of verses 33–34 (along with "you" plural), they are not the subjects of 7:31–32.[22] As we shall see, much of the opacity of the relationship between vv. 31–32, 33–34, and 35 results from interpreting this pericope as part of Q's "announcement of judgment" against "this generation" for its rejection of Jesus' and John's messages. The proposal that all of the John materials in Q were part of Q's redaction, characterized by the "Announcement of Judgment,"[23] should not preclude an effort to make the best sense of each unit in its Q context.[24] By bracketing the interpretation of "this generation" as the monolithic recipient of Q's announcement of judgment, other interpretive possibilities for Q 7: 31–35, and 7:18–35 as a whole, come into view. Let us consider one such re-reading, and then we will return to a discussion of "this generation" in Q at the end of this chapter.

[22]Cotter, "Parable of the Children," 295. Tuckett (*Q*, 177 n. 35) critiques Cotter for placing too much weight on the introduction to the simile. Tuckett's alternative, however, is to bracket the introduction altogether: "The initial comparison, likening this generation to the children in the market place, need not necessarily imply that the people of this generation are to be equated with the children in the parable who call to others. The comparison may be a much more general one, equating the situation of this generation with (aspects of) the whole picture painted in the parable. Thus the people of this generation are not necessarily to be identified with the calling children, but rather with the other, non-responding children. 'This generation' is thus accused of failing to respond to the different messengers and messages given to it by Jesus and John" (ibid., 176–77). This preempts the analysis of the simile with the conclusion that the real comparison is between the recalcitrant children and "this generation." Tuckett does not deal with the fact that Cotter's interpretation of the simile and the application smooths many of the problems that Tuckett tries to sidestep.

[23]See Lührmann, *Redaktion*, 24–48; Kloppenborg, *Formation*, 102–15.

[24]While it is possible that the application (vv. 33–34) was created to interpret a previously independent simile (Bultmann, *History*, 172; Kloppenborg, *Formation*, 111), it is not possible to say what the meaning of the independent simile was, given that we have no other context for interpreting it except for the one created by Q. Arnold Ehrhardt ("Greek Proverbs in the Gospels," in *The Framework of the New Testament Stories* [ed. idem; Cambridge, Mass.: Harvard University Press, 1964] 44–63) suggests that the first stanza of the simile resembles Herodotus's use of one of Aesop's *Fables* (27b) in Cyrus's reply "to the Ionian cities, which had applied for treatises after his conquest of the Lydian kingdom" (p. 51): "A flute-player saw the fish in the sea and played his flute believing that they would come to land. Finding, however, that he was mistaken, he took a net and enclosed a great many of the fish, 'Stop dancing, for you did not come to dance when I played for you'" (Hdt. *Hist.*, 1:114). Sirach 7:34 proverbially points to the importance of doing the right thing at the right time: "Do not avoid those who weep, but mourn with those who mourn." While both of these parallels may resemble Q 7: 31–32, neither can fix a singular meaning for the simile as an originally independent unit.

Rather than assuming a dissonance between 7:32 and 7:33–34, it is instructive to note the parallel structure of each subunit and the similarities between them. In terms of the central verbal structure, verses 33–34 are strikingly parallel in their construction:

John	came	*not* eating and drinking	and you say	"He has a demon"
	ἦλθεν	ἐσθίων μήτε πίνων	καὶ λέγετε	
Son of humanity	came	eating and drinking	and you say	"Look, a glutton and a drunk . . ."

The two verses speak about two people, each being negatively evaluated. They share two elements of similarity: (1) both have particular eating habits; and (2) both are evaluated negatively. The difference is the nature of the eating habits.[25] Thus the text constructs Jesus and John as two sides of the same coin. Whether or not they eat and drink, they are evaluated negatively by "you" (plural).

The children's speech in 7:32 attests a similar structure:

We fluted for you	but you would not dance
ηὐλήσαμεν ὑμῖν	καὶ οὐκ ὠρχήσασθε
ἐθρηνήσαμεν	καὶ οὐκ ἐκλαύσατε
We sang a dirge	but you would not cry

As in 7:33–34, there are two similarities between the parts: (1) both speak of musical performance; and (2) both receive a negative response. As in vv. 33–34, the first action in v. 32 is both similar and different: they both perform musically but one evokes celebration and one evokes mourning.

---

[25]Jesus also uses the expression "son of humanity" to refer to himself. There is some dispute over whether this alone elevates Jesus over John in 7:31–35. Given its recurrence throughout Q, this expression does function to mark Jesus' significance for the audience. Like the references to the "*basileia* of God," however, its meaning throughout Q is assumed rather than explicated. It is my contention that Jesus' identity as the "son of humanity" is not a central interest for Q in the way that it is for scholars.

Thus they are opposites—two sides of the same coin—in precisely the same way that Jesus and John eat and do not eat.

Recognition of the symmetry between 7:32 and 7:33–34 results in the simple conclusion that the two elements of the application correspond to the two elements of the parable. There are two possibilities for their structural relationship: (1) *a*, *b*, *a'*, *b'* (lefthand column); or (2) *a*, *b*, *b'*, *a'* (righthand column):

a	"We fluted for you	but you would not dance"	*a*
b	"We sang a dirge	but you would not mourn"	*b*
a'	John came neither eating nor drinking	and you say, "He has a demon"	*b'*
b'	The son of humanity came eating and drinking	and you say, "He is a glutton and a drunkard . . ."	*a'*

The second option (righthand column) creates a parallel between John's not eating and drinking and the children's singing a dirge, and a parallel between Jesus' eating and drinking and the children's fluting.[26] Although the details are not always pressed, this is the most common interpretation of the relationship between the simile and the application.[27] Because Jesus and John become associated with the active children in the simile, this interpretation requires that "this generation" (v. 31) represents the nonresponsive children. However, linking "this generation" to the passive children renders the introduction in v. 31 unintelligible, since it directly links "this generation" to the active children who pipe and sing a dirge.[28]

[26]Linking John with singing a dirge and Jesus with piping a dance has long been theologically attractive to interpreters who contrast John and Jesus as respectively dour and joyous. I suggest that Q both constructs this dichotomy and seeks to undermine it.

[27]See, for example, Mack, *Lost Gospel*, 157–58; Jacobson, *First Gospel*, 123; and Majella Franzmann, "Of Food, Bodies, and the Boundless Reign of God in the Synoptic Gospels," *Pacifica* 5 (1992) 17–31. Although Séan Freyne ("Jesus the Wine-Drinker: A Friend of Women," in *Transformative Encounters* [ed. Ingrid Rosa Kitzberger; Leiden: Brill, 2000] 162–80, at 172) describes the structure as "*a,b-a',b'*," his interpretation clearly depends on the *a,b-b',a'* structure; he has reversed the order of John and Jesus in 7:33–34. Not all interpreters suggest that this structure exists. Some conclude more generally that Jesus and John must be the ones who act and that "this generation" aligns with those who are nonresponsive. See, for example, Tuckett, *Q*, 177.

[28]So also Linton, "Children's Game," 171–72; Cotter, "Parable of the Children," 295.

Moreover, the *a, b, b', a'* pattern must twist the simile to fit the application. The seemingly straightforward statement that the people of "this generation" are like children addressing other children in the marketplace is ruled out on account of predetermined roles for John/Jesus and "this generation." For example, Kloppenborg argues that:

> The interpretive saying (vv. 33–34), which has to do with the response of opponents to John and Jesus, seems to exclude the final alternative [that "this generation" is both groups calling to one another] for the parable as it existed in Q. The identification of John and Jesus with the children who do the calling, and "this generation" with those who refuse to respond, seems the most natural interpretation, especially since v. 35 characterizes John and Jesus as children (τέκνα) of Sophia.[29]

Such a reading aligns "this generation" with the addressees in both the simile and the application ("you" plural): they neither dance nor mourn, and they call John a demoniac and Jesus a glutton. But the second offense, calling John and Jesus names, corresponds with the charge that "this generation" is like children *addressing* other children in the marketplace—a reading excluded by the association of Jesus and John with the musicians in 7:32.

This compounding fog dissipates with two interpretive moves: (1) identifying the structural relationship between the parts not as *a, b, b', a'* but as *a, b, a', b';*[30] and (2) distinguishing the antecedent of "you" in the simile from the "you" in the sayings about John and Jesus. The children's first taunt claims that "we" ("this generation") played the flute and "you" (other children)

---

[29]Kloppenborg, *Formation*, 111; and bibliography at ibid., n. 39.

[30]Verses 33–34 do function as an application of the elements of the parable to the situation of the audience rather than an allegorizing of the parable. However, even the allegorical interpretations attached to parables in the Synoptics follow a similar progressive structure (rather than a ring structure). See, for example, Mark 4:3–9 and 14–20. Kloppenborg (*Formation*, 110) describes 7:33–34 as an "attempt at allegorization of the parable," which nonetheless gets the procedure wrong insofar as "the interpretation, which refers to John first and then the Son of Man, does not accord with the order of the verbs in vv. 31–32 (αὐλέω. . .θρηνέω)." Kloppenborg confirms that the expected structure should be *a, b, a', b'*, but sees a poor fit between the parable and allegory because he expects that John and Jesus should correspond to the active children in the parable. In a later article, Kloppenborg similarly notes that if John and Jesus were meant to correspond to the active children in the parable, then they would do so in an *a, b, a', b'* pattern ("Jesus and the Parables of Jesus," in *The Gospel Behind the Gospels* [ed. Ronald A. Piper; Leiden: Brill, 1995] 291).

would not dance. Its application declares that, indeed, John (one of the other children) would not dance (came fasting), but "you" ("this generation") say he has a demon. Similarly, in the second taunt, "this generation" complains that they sang a dirge and the other children did not cry. Then its application concedes the point: Jesus did not mourn (he came feasting), and "you" ("this generation") say he is a glutton. The result of this interpretation is that Jesus and John correspond to the "other" children in the parable.[31] The *tertium comparationis* lies in the criticisms—of the unresponsive children and of John and Jesus.[32] "This generation" is a judgmental generation. It judges John and Jesus because they do not play along.[33]

---

[31]This conclusion renders the choice between Matthew's τοῖς ἑτέροις ("to the others") and Luke's ἀλλήλοις ("to each other") in Q 7:32 insignificant for interpretation of the simile (*pace* Jacobson, *First Gospel*, 121). The IQP puts double square brackets around its choice of Matthew's τοῖς ἑτέροις indicating that it ranks its decision as "probable but uncertain, {C}" (Robinson, *Critical Edition*, lxxxii). The stylistic arguments can go either way. Cotter chooses Matthew's formulation and cites literature that points to Luke's stylistic preferences ("Parable of the Children," 291). Linton for the most part accepts the common view that Matthew's version is the Q version, but relativizes his position with a footnote that shows how Matthew's version can be interpreted as particularly Matthean ("Children's Game," 162 and n. 1). See also Sevenich-Bax, *Konfrontation*, 216–17. Jacobson (*First Gospel*, 122) rightly notes that in this case "word statistics are ambiguous and cannot decide the matter." What is most significant in the decision is the common perception that the meaning of the simile is influenced by the decision: "[D]o the children in the marketplace call to others within their own group (ἀλλήλοις, so Luke) or to another group of children from whom they are separate (ἑτέροις, so Matthew)" (Tuckett, *Q*, 176)? See also Linton, "Children's Game," 162; and Jacobson, *First Gospel*, 121. This is a red herring. Since ἀλλήλοις has a reciprocal meaning (to each other) and τοῖς ἑτέροις a dual meaning (to the others [of two]) (Smyth, *Greek Grammar*, §§1271 and 1278), it is clear that both words point to children addressing other children. Matthew's version identifies the interlocutors as "other" children with a pronominal adjective that agrees in person and number with the initial group of children (παιδίοις). Luke's version helps to clarify what is only implied in Matthew's version by using the reciprocal pronoun. Since Luke has a penchant for making his sources more specific, Matthew's version is probably the Q version. But this does not exclude the conclusion that there are two groups of children (who are nonetheless both children).

[32]Zeller ("*Bildlogik*," 254) argues that this cannot be the case because early Christians would not associate John and Jesus with stubborn children.

[33]This interpretation also retains the notion that vv. 33–34 have some allegorical relationship to the parable. The allegory is commonly made between the fluting and Jesus' ministry; the wailing and John's ministry. My interpretation, however, links "not dancing" with John and "not mourning" with Jesus. There are clear parallels between the two-sided music and the two-sided approach to eating. Where interpreters have gone wrong is in the need to understand John and Jesus as the actors and subjects rather than as those who are acted upon.

As Wendy Cotter has shown, the sting of the parable lies in the image of the children itself. She notes the peculiar vocabulary associated with the children's behavior. Although the content of the taunts implies childlike games, the children are "seated" (καθημένοις) and formally "addressing" (προσφωνοῦντα) "the others" in the marketplace. This vocabulary is consistently used for adults who sit as judges in civic courts in the agora.[34] Thus "no matter how these 'children' adopt dignified behavior, it is plain from the content of their objections, that they are, after all, only shallow children."[35] In the application of the parable, therefore, the judgments made against John and Jesus are equally childish in that they are now spoken by children play-acting at being grown-up in the agora.

It makes the most sense to retain the meaning of the unit's introduction that "this generation" is like children sitting in the marketplace addressing other children (represented in the application by John and Jesus). It is common, however, to portray these two groups of children as active and passive players: "this generation" plays the flute and wails, and "the others" just sit and are judged for not playing along. There is, however, another possibility. What if "this generation" is two groups of children in the marketplace calling to each other? What if the groups of children each call and each reject the other? If this is the case, then the structural relationship between the parable and the interpretation can be further nuanced. With this approach, the two parts of the children's taunts (and the criticisms of John and Jesus) are spoken by opposing groups (represented in the chart by *italics* and **bold**):

a	"*We* fluted	and **you** did not dance"
b	"**We** sang a dirge	and *you* did not mourn"
a'	For **John** came not eating and drinking	and *you* say he has a demon"
b'	The *son of humanity* came eating and drinking	and **you** say he is a glutton and a drunk"

One side (the italics group) calls to the other (the bold group) and accuses them of not dancing when the italics group piped. Then the bold group retorts that they sang a dirge and the italics group did not mourn. The application then applies this image of the judgmental and uncooperative children to those who judge John and those who judge Jesus on the basis

---

[34]Cotter, "Parable of the Children," 295–302.
[35]Ibid., 302.

of their eating practices. "Indeed," Jesus says to the italics group, "John came not dancing and you ostracize him." "Indeed," Jesus says to the bold group, "the son of humanity (I) came not mourning and you criticize him (me)." In addition to the alternating structure (*a, b, a', b'*), there now is a chiastic relationship within each pair: the italics group both plays the flute and does not mourn, and the bold group both refuses to dance and sings a dirge (*a, b*); the bold group (represented by John) does not eat/drink and says that he who does is a glutton, and the italics group (represented by the son of humanity) eats/drinks and says that he who does not has a demon (*a', b'*).

There are several textual and interpretive indicators that make this inter-pretation possible. (1) If Matthew's τοῖς ἑτέροις was in Q 7:32, then Luke's ἀλλήλοις indicates at least that the author of Luke understood the simile as referring to two groups of children calling to each other. Matthew's version does not say whether the second group of children is addressing the other group as well. It is possible that Luke sought to fix and sharpen this already implied meaning. (2) Cotter has shown well that the image of the parable plays on the juxtaposition of childish judgments and adults sitting in court in the agora. Cotter does not explain, however, why children would be doing that at all. Sitting around pretending to make serious judgments of other children who are not doing anything is hardly a game worth playing for very long. Interpreting the children as play-acting at court and judging each other with equal and opposite childishness lends even more vitality to the image.[36] (3) Scholars have long recognized that there seems to be some correspondence between the polar opposites of John's and Jesus' eating behavior and that of the children who sing dirges and play the flute, respectively. But here-tofore, Jesus/John could only correspond to *either* the pipers/wailers *or* the unresponsive mourners/dancers. The former (identifying them only with the pipers/wailers) wreaks havoc with the relationship between the parable and its interpretation. The latter (identifying them only with the unresponsive mourners/dancers) is better but must leave aside the correspondence between

---

[36] As Richard Horsley argues (Horsley and Draper, *Whoever Hears*, 123–27), our ways of reading are formed by the print culture in which we live. Unlike oral-based cultures, we often read in silence rather than perform texts. Imagining the two criticisms as spoken by opposing groups is easier in the context of a dramatic reading of the text. At the literal level of the text, we have no indicator that "we" in each stanza might refer to different groups. If someone was performing this text, that reading might have emerged as a natural reading because it is inherently more dramatic.

the similar-but-opposite pairs: piping/wailing and eating/not eating. Interpreting the children (and John and Jesus) as two groups, addressing and judging each other, accounts for both parallels. This creates the long sought-after symmetry between the parable and application that has eluded interpreters.

The parable and the application make a case to the audience of Q that when they judge John or Jesus on the basis of their different eating practices, they are like children in the marketplace foolishly judging *each other*. It has long been recognized that there is no rivalry in 7:31–35 between John and Jesus.[37] They are affirmed equally against their critics. What is unexpected, however, is the possibility that there is also no divide between "this generation" and John/Jesus, and thus no divide between "this generation" and the audience of Q.[38] The text argues for the equal legitimacy of John's practices and Jesus' practices *within the larger group which they represent*[39] *and of which they are both a part*. This interpretation places Jesus, John, and the audience in the same category as "this generation." Jesus asks, "What is this generation like?" To recast this question colloquially, Q's Jesus now asks, "What are the people of our time like? What's wrong with us?" The answer stings: we are like children sitting in the marketplace judging each other on the basis of our differences.

The aphorism in Q 7:35 functions as concluding aphorisms do: it reverses "characterizations set up earlier in the unit."[40] Although "this generation" is characteristically factional and divisive along lines of difference, *Sophia*

[37]Kloppenborg, *Formation*, 112; Jacobson, *First Gospel*, 122; Allison, *Q*, 34; Tuckett, *Q*, 131; Piper, *Wisdom*, 126; Mack, *Lost Gospel*, 157; Vaage, *Galilean Upstarts*, 110 (for vv. 33–34 only); idem, "More Than a Prophet, and Demon-Possessed: Q and the 'Historical John,'" in *Conflict and Invention: Literary, Rhetorical, and Social Studies on the Sayings Gospel Q* (ed. John S. Kloppenborg; Valley Forge, Pa.: Trinity, 1995) 183.

[38]Several interpreters make a move similar to Kloppenborg (*Formation*, 112), who sets aside the view that Q 7:31–35 deals with the opposition between John and Jesus in favor of an opposition between John/Jesus and "this generation." He writes, "Q 7:31–35 looks in retrospect at the careers of John and Jesus and at their lack of success with 'this generation.' . . . Q 7:31–35 does not oppose John to Jesus, but both to 'this generation'" (ibid.). See also, Lührmann, *Redaktion*, 30; Jacobson, *First Gospel*, 122; Allison, *Jesus Tradition*, 17, 53; Tuckett, *Q*, 135; Mack, *Lost Gospel*, 157; Vaage, *Galilean Upstarts*, 109.

[39]The plural "you" in 7:32 does not contradict the reference to John and Jesus in the application, since the criticisms of John and Jesus are presented as representative examples of the tendency of "this generation" towards factionalism.

[40]Kirk, *Composition*, 375. "The appending of a concluding aphorism reversing characterizations set up earlier in the unit makes 7:31–35 parallel to 7:18–23 and 7:24–28" (ibid.). See also Cameron, "'What Have You Come Out To See?'" 61.

is vindicated by all her children.[41] Wisdom's children are *all* children who vindicate her, that is, who prove her right or "acknowledge her to be right."[42] Without the divide between John/Jesus and "this generation," it is possible to read the aphorism in the way that we expect, that is, as affirming *both* John and Jesus and, therefore, all the "children" who pipe a dance and sing a dirge, as children who vindicate Wisdom. Their differences are insignificant given their common ground as children of Wisdom. Thus "this generation" can be like children in a marketplace or like children of *Sophia*. Those like the former are judgmental of each other, those like the latter recognize that Wisdom is vindicated by all her children.[43] The problem here is judgmentalism among diverse members of one larger group. It is not rejection of John and Jesus as messengers.

The verb ἐδικαιώθη carries a forensic flavor[44] and, therefore, reverses the childish judgments made in the simile and application. Both John's and Jesus' eating habits vindicate *Sophia*. In the first-century B.C.E. *Psalms of Solomon*, δικαιόω appears frequently. The righteous person vindicates God by practicing God's instruction and accepting God's judgments (when he/she "stumbles"):

> The righteous remember the Lord all the time, by acknowledging and *proving the Lord's judgments right*. The righteous does not lightly esteem discipline [or instruction] from the Lord; his desire is [to be] always in the Lord's presence. The righteous stumbles [or offends] and *proves the Lord right*; he falls and watches for what God will

[41]The shift from παιδίον to τέκνον may be because the aphorism in 7:35 was a well-known proverb (Lührmann, *Redaktion*, 29). Given the deliberateness of the composition of 3:7–7:35, the link of the children of Abraham in 3:8 and the children of *Sophia* in 7:35 facilitates a larger compositional role for 7:35 as the conclusion not only to 7:18–35 but also to 3:7–7:35.

[42]Piper, *Wisdom*, 168.

[43]Patrick Hartin ("'Yet Wisdom Is Justified by Her Children' [Q 7:35]: A Rhetorical and Compositional Analysis of Divine Sophia in Q," in *Conflict and Invention: Literary, Rhetorical, and Social Studies on the Sayings Gospel Q* [ed. John S. Kloppenborg ; Valley Forge, Pa.: Trinity, 1995] 155) notes that "it is important to stress this wider conception of the children of Sophia because there is the tendency to see the notion in a very individualistic way as relating to only John and Jesus." While I agree, Hartin does not explain how he distinguishes Jesus and John, who vindicate *Sophia* as her messengers, from the community, which vindicates *Sophia* by responding positively to John and Jesus. The saying has only two characters: *Sophia* and her children. The children of *Sophia* should recognize their common ground, not respond positively to John and Jesus.

[44]Lührmann, *Die Redaktion*, 30–31; Schrenk, "δικαιόω," *TDNT* 2 (1964) 177–255; and Tuckett, *Q*, 178.

do about him; he looks to where his salvation comes from. . . . The righteous constantly searches his house, to remove unintentional sins. He atones for (sins of) ignorance by fasting and humbling his soul, and the Lord will cleanse every devout person and his house. (*Pss. Sol.* 3.3–8)[45]

In Luke 7:29–30, the Lukan redactor of Q understands the reception of John's baptism as vindicating God:

And when they heard this all the people and the tax collectors vindicated [ἐδικαίωσαν] God, having been baptized with the baptism of John; but the Pharisees and the lawyers rejected the purpose of God for themselves, not having been baptized by him.[46]

In Proverbs and Sirach, Wisdom's children are called to keep her ways and accept her judgment and discipline (Prov 8:32; Sir 6:23).[47] The aphorism declares that John's and Jesus' eating practices, which are representative examples of the contentious differences among "this generation," both vindicate Wisdom. It attempts to move the audience to recognize this common ground.

The emphasis on righteous practice vindicating *Sophia* makes sense of the focus on John's and Jesus' eating practices. In light of the motif of

---

[45]"I thought about the judgments of God since the creation of heaven and earth; I proved [acknowledged] God right in God's judgments in ages past" (*Pss. Sol.* 8:7). See also *Pss. Sol.* 2:15; 4:8; 8:23, 26; and 9:2.

[46]The critical edition of Q places Matt 21:28–32//Luke 7:29–30 in square brackets, indicating the IQP's judgment that its presence in Q is indeterminate (see Robinson, *Critical Edition*, 138–39). The only agreement between the two passages is "the tax collectors" (οἱ τελῶναι) and "John." The IQP provides a reconstruction based primarily on the common structures of Luke and Matthew: [[<<For John came to you>> . . . the tax collectors and . . . <<responded positively>>, but <<the religious authorities rejected>> him.]] If this verse was in Q, then there is a parallel between Jesus' eating with tax collectors and John's baptizing tax collectors. In addition, the lack of specificity of the collective noun "all the people" in 7:29 is instructive. Despite the fact that "all the people" vindicated God by being baptized, Luke singles out the Pharisees and lawyers for critique. There is a tension between the statement that "all the people" were baptized and the assertion that some of the people were not. "All the people" responded to John; therefore, he and they are presumed to be in social relationship to each other. What separates some from others is how they evaluate him. The same phenomenon may be present in the collective appellation "this generation." John, Jesus, and all the people of their time are in relation to each other. What divides them from each other is their judgmental evaluations of each other.

[47]See also Sir 4:11; 15:1–2; and Prov 2:1.

Sophia sending prophets in Q 11:49–51, interpreters expect the affirmation of John and Jesus to be an affirmation of their identities and their messages (as prophets and messengers of *Sophia*). Kloppenborg concludes that "only with the addition of 7:35 with its connections with deuteronomistic theology does it become clear that John and Jesus are *preachers*; the rejection of the two in vv. 33–34 is apparently not based upon their preaching, but upon their respective life styles."[48] He does not specify, however, how John and Jesus being *preachers* becomes apparent from the saying in 7:35. The saying rejects the in-fighting characterized by the negative judgments of John and Jesus. Thus the defense of John and Jesus does not aim at establishing who John and Jesus were in contrast to each other (as Q 7:18 may lead us to believe) or in contrast to "this generation," but rather at affirming their common ground as children of *Sophia*. The children of *Sophia* do not quarrel like children in the marketplaces, but rather recognize the many who vindicate her.

But what common ground do these factions share? Both sides are among the children of *Sophia*. But they are also different, insofar as John—and anyone like John—characteristically fasts (and metaphorically sings a dirge), and Jesus—and anyone like Jesus—characteristically feasts (and metaphorically pipes a dance). The text does not suggest that these differences should be erased nor clearly state why both practices vindicate *Sophia* and are worthy of being recognized as such. In some ways, the aphorism simply declares by fiat that they both vindicate *Sophia* and calls the audience to act in accordance with that recognition.[49]

[48]Kloppenborg, *Formation*, 111. Tuckett's conclusion to his analysis of 7:35 indirectly makes a similar point: "Implicit here is the idea that Jesus and John are messengers of Wisdom, and hence acceptance of their message is acceptance of Wisdom. Thus this saying fits well with the other Q sayings examined so far: Jesus and John constitute part of the series of Wisdom's messengers, though their specifically 'prophetic' status is not spelt out here" (*Q*, 178). Jacobson (*First Gospel*, 125) also imports too many characters into 7:35: *Sophia*, Jesus and John as messengers of *Sophia*, and the "children" who vindicate *Sophia* by responding positively to John and Jesus. The saying is bipartite. The only characters here are *Sophia* and her children.

[49]The juxtaposition of fasting versus feasting cannot be seen as inferring that John was somehow more religious or more Jewish than Jesus. As Linton points out ("The Children's Game," 175), fasting and feasting are both affirmed in Jewish tradition. The issue may be refusing to participate properly in one on account of over-valuing the other. The evaluation of people's eating practices was not peculiar to Judaism or any other ancient social identity. As Leif Vaage has shown, the Cynic philosophers were the target of dichotomized and equally criticized eating practices (*Galilean Upstarts*, 102; see also Cameron, "'What Have You Come Out to See?'," 42). But this shows that eating practices are significant across social identities, not that Jesus and John were or were not remembered as Cynics. Vaage ("More

But perhaps there is more. Both criticisms attempt to marginalize the other, to place them at society's margins. Those like John criticize Jesus as a "glutton and a drunk"; he is a friend of tax collectors and sinners. According to the charge, Jesus' characteristic feasting leads to the slander that he is excessive in his consumption and a friend of disreputable people. Although the words φάγος and οἰνοπότης are translated as "glutton" and "drunkard,"[50] the English may emphasize the quantity of the eating and drinking over the quality of the crowd with which one eats and drinks.[51] Proverbs 23:20–21 LXX warns: "Do not be among winebibbers [οἰνοπότης], or among gluttonous eaters of meat [ἐκτείνου συμβολαῖς κρεῶν τε ἀγορασμοῖς]; for the drunkard and the glutton will come to poverty, and drowsiness will clothe them with rags."[52] It may follow from Jesus' being a "glutton and a drunk," therefore, that he keeps company with those looked down upon by society.[53] It may be significant, then, that the few words that do overlap in Luke 7:29 and Matt 21:31 are "John" and "tax collectors." Both state that it was these kinds of people who received John's baptism.[54] If John's fasting is related to his call to

---

Than a Prophet," 191) over-interprets the Cynic analogy and concludes that "at the level of Q's formative stratum, John was remembered as one more of those 'doggone' philosophers."

[50]These are *hapax legomena*. They may reflect the context of Deut 21:18–21 although the Greek is substantially different (LXX: συμβολοκοπῶν οἰνοφλυγεῖ). Kee ("Jesus: A Glutton and a Drunkard," *NTS* 42 [1996] 374–93, at 390) argues that not enough attention has been paid to the deuteronomic context of the rebellious son who is threatening to both his parents and the community.

[51]Vaage ("More Than a Prophet," 189) sees a sharp contrast between the depiction of Jesus in 7:34 and the "messianic aura" of the previous portrait of Jesus' activities in Q 7:22. "Any scandal provoked by Jesus' person in 7:34 will not be due to eschatological surprise and wonder, but the direct result of his low-life associations." This view overlooks the fact that the "eschatological wonders" invoked in 7:22 *also* suggest association with society's "low-life," that is, the sick and the poor.

[52]Freyne ("Jesus the Wine-Drinker," 164 n. 4) notes that Polybius (*Histories* 20.8.2) "describes Antiochus the Great as a 'wine-drinker and rejoicing in drunkenness' by way of explaining his infatuation with a young virgin from Chalcis."

[53]Vaage (*Galilean Upstarts*, 88) makes the common assumption that the criticism "glutton and drunk" means that "according to Q 7:34, [Jesus] apparently ate and drank well and often enough to be suspected of overindulgence." Vaage identifies the elements of 7:34b as two different criticisms of Jesus. This rules out the possibility that the extravagant criticism in Q 7:34b is generated not by excessive eating but by Jesus' keeping company with tax collectors and sinners.

[54]Matthew's additional parable in 21:28–31a also confirms that the reputation of those who went out to John's baptism was a point of contention. Matthew's version also speaks of prostitutes who were baptized by John.

"bear fruit worthy of repentance" (Q 3:7–9), then John may be surrounded by the wrong people. The aphorism in Q 7:35, therefore, would not only argue that John and Jesus vindicate *Sophia* (as all her children should), but that the socially undesirable people around them are children of *Sophia* as well—by virtue of the criticisms of John and Jesus being reversed by the aphorism.[55] There may be some irony here in that the common ground between these two factions is precisely staked out among the people whose marginalization provides the sting of the slander flying between them.

If the link between John's baptism and tax collectors (Luke 7:29//Matt 21:31b) appeared in Q, then the accusation against Jesus may be a deliberate rhetorical effort to assert John's and Jesus' similarity.[56] The criticisms of John and Jesus in Q 7:33b and 34b are not parallel. While the slander against Jesus lampoons his eating practices, the charge against John is more extreme[57] and the relationship to his fasting is unclear.[58] This may indicate that there is some interest here in refuting the marginalization of John (and those like him).[59] As discussed below, the two units in Q 7:18–28 also show an interest in affirming John by making him parallel to Jesus. James Robinson has noted that "it is striking, and calling for some explanation, that the opening of Q would have been more suited to John's followers than to those of Jesus."[60] As we will discuss in chapter 3, however, this affirmation of both John and Jesus and those like them stands in tension with Q's representation of Jesus

[55]Piper (*Wisdom*, 168–69) argues that Luke 7:29 was in Q and thus strengthens his interpretation of 7:35 as including anyone who accepts Jesus and John as children of *Sophia*.

[56]As suggested below, there are several indications throughout Q 7:18–35 that Q creates parity between John and Jesus. If Luke 3:10–14 was in Q, this would be another case of the same phenomenon. Luke 3:10–14 is a speech attributed to John that summarizes Jesus' teachings in the inaugural sermon. A few scholars argue that this passage is non-Lukan and should be considered as in Q (see Kloppenborg, *Q Parallels*, 10). In Luke 3:12 John speaks to the tax collectors who have come to be baptized.

[57]Indeed this charge is made repeatedly against Jesus in the gospel of John (7:20; 8:48, 52; 10:20, 21). In Mark 3:21, Jesus is accused of being "out of his mind" and then of being possessed by Beelzebul after he does not eat because of the gathering of the crowds.

[58]Linton mentions that some people thought demons needed no food ("Children's Game," 176). Vaage discusses how Cynics were commonly called insane (*Galilean Upstarts*, 88).

[59]Hartin argues that 7:33b and 34b function primarily to vindicate Jesus' practices: "Because the accusations against John are so unwarranted, the same conclusion is drawn with regard to Jesus. These statements demonstrate the unreasonable rejection of John and Jesus" ("Wisdom," 154).

[60]Robinson, "The Sayings Gospel," 362. Robinson is referring to John's speech in 3:7–9 and its lack of christological reflection. The same can be said about the repeated rhetorical efforts in 7:18–35 to affirm John by making him parallel to (not less than) Jesus.

as the central figure in the present and future of the people. To some extent, John's status in Q as a child of *Sophia* fades in the light of Jesus' position in Q as the son of humanity who stands at the judgment. However, the status of society's marginalized as children of *Sophia* is rendered completely *invisible* if we presuppose that Jesus' identity and his relationship to John is the only issue on Q's rhetorical horizon. If John's case is being made here, it is on behalf of those in the community or "this generation" being slandered by those who prefer to follow Jesus' example.

The elements of the Q text hang together when John/Jesus and "this generation" are understood as (parts of) the same group rather than as foes. The entire unit critiques the addressees (and thus the audience) as a faction-ridden group by comparing them all to mutually uncooperative children.[61] It also affirms them by concluding that they all have or are able to vindicate *Sophia*. Thus it argues for solidarity in the group across differences. The emphasis on *this* generation—that is, all the people in the present of the text—points to a sense that *now* is the crucial time to recognize the common ground between John and Jesus (and thus those who are like them).

This interpretation of Q 7:31–35 makes sense of the passage as it stands in Q. While many of the pieces have been considered and argued, this comprehensive interpretation has not been proposed before now because our expectations about the meaning and goals of the text have removed this interpretation from the range of possible meanings.[62] Two presuppositions have ruled this interpretation out of court: first, that there is a fundamental

---

[61]Freyne, Kee, and Franzmann all suggest that the slander against Jesus in 7:34b derives from Jewish religious leaders' "efforts to vilify the Jesus movement as being not just unobservant in regard to purity but as being un-Jewish in its basic affiliation" (Freyne, "Jesus the Wine-Drinker," 175). This interpretation views the central conflict in this text as a conflict with *religious* authorities over *religious* identity. However, this interpretation must pass over the text's assertion that John is also defended from the slanderous evaluation of his eating practices. If the issue is proper religious rigor, why would the ascetic John be criticized as having a demon? Why would a text like Q seek to defend John's practices as equally vindicating *Sophia*? Kee suggests that "strict adherents to ritual, cultic and ethnic limits for participation in . . . the people of God" would regard Jesus as rebellious and seditious like the son in Deut 21:18–21 ("A Glutton," 391). But Kee has attributed this same approach to defining the "people of God" to John (ibid., 381) and thus does not explain why Q would equally defend John's practices in the context of this passage. Unfortunately, Franzmann's interpretation ("Food," 20–21) creates a sharp dichotomy between Jesus' inclusive Christian table-fellowship and John's exclusive and boundary-setting Judaism. This does not take into account the common ground between John and Jesus created by the structure and content of 7:31–35.

[62]Schüssler Fiorenza, *Rhetoric and Ethic*, 197.

difference between John/Jesus and "this generation"; and second, that this pericope seeks to clarify the identity of Jesus in relationship to John. These expectations rest on an underlying interest in the identity of Q's Jesus vis-à-vis John and "this generation." In the context of 7:31–35, Q places special value on Jesus only by presenting him as an authoritative speaker and through his self-designation as the "son of humanity." Regardless of what this appellation meant to Q's audience, its recurrence throughout Q establishes it rhetorically as marking the significance of Jesus for those who remember him. There may be some tension between the assumption of Jesus' central significance and an emphasis on the communal vision of the *basileia* of God. We will explore this question in the next chapter.

Should We Expect Another? Q 7:18–23

As we just saw, the concluding saying of Q 7:18–35 affirms as children of *Sophia* a variety of people who vindicate her, and thus the self-understanding of the community as a whole is in view rather than the identities of John or Jesus. Can the prior subunits, Q 7:18–23 and 7:24–28, be interpreted as similarly reflecting the values of the community? While both units identify their subjects as figures who fulfill expectation (Jesus in 7:23 and John in 7:28), both units also locate the significance of that fulfillment in the communal vision of the *basileia* of God.

The scene[63] between John's disciples and Jesus and the question they pose to him is a return in Q to materials about John both in terms of the re-entry of John as a character in the progression of the text[64] and in light of the reference to ὁ ἐρχόμενος whom John mentions in Q 3:16. The IQP reconstruction[65] is as follows:

Q 7:18 . . . ὁ . . . Ἰωάννης ⟦ἀκούσας   And John, on hearing about all these
περὶ πάντων τούτων⟧ πέμψ⟦ας⟧ διὰ   things, sending through his disciples,
τῶν μαθητῶν αὐτοῦ

---

[63]Bultmann (*History*, 23) identifies Q 7:18–23 as an apophthegm. Kirk (*Composition*, 370) calls it a *chreia*.

[64]John's opening speech at the beginning of Q 3:7–9, 16–17 is followed by Jesus' testing, the inaugural sermon, and the encounter with the centurion.

[65]Robinson, *Critical Edition*, 118-26. I have adopted the IQP English translation for much of this section.

Q 7:19 ⟦εἶπεν⟧ αὐτῷ· σὺ
εἶ ὁ ἐρχόμενος ἢ ⟦ἕτερ⟧ον
προσδοκῶμεν;

said to him: Are you the coming one,
or are we to expect someone else?

Q 7:22 καὶ ἀποκριθεὶς εἶπεν
αὐτοῖς· πορευθέντες ἀπαγγείλατε
Ἰωάννῃ ἃ ἀκούετε καὶ βλέπετε·
τυφλοὶ ἀναβλέπουσιν καὶ χωλοὶ
περιπατοῦσιν, λεπροὶ καθαρίζονται
καί κωφοὶ ἀκούουσιν, καὶ νεκροὶ
ἐγείρονται καὶ πτωχοὶ εὐαγγελί-
ζονται·

And in reply he said to them: Go
report to John what you hear and
see: The blind regain their sight and
the lame walk, the skin-diseased are
cleansed and the deaf hear, and the
dead are raised, and the poor are
given good news.

Q 7:23 καὶ μακάριός ἐστιν ὃς ἐὰν
μὴ σκανδαλισθῇ ἐν ἐμοί.

And blessed is whoever is not offended by me.

The reconstruction of vv. 22 and 23 is straightforward.[66] Although Matthew
and Luke agree in the basic content of vv. 18–19 (John, his disciples, and
the question), the reconstruction of the precise wording is very difficult
given their divergence from each other. Matthew and Luke do agree on
enough to get a clear sense of the scene in Q. John sends his disciples
to ask Jesus a question:[67] "Are you the coming one or are we to expect
someone else?"

John's question comes to Jesus through John's disciples and serves to
establish a connection between Jesus and the "coming one" of 3:16.[68] In the
context of 7:18, ὁ ἐρχόμενος is someone that John and his disciples expect
(προσδοκέω; also "to wait for," "to look for"). At this point in the text, John
inquires whether they should keep waiting or whether Jesus understands
himself as meeting that expectation. Jesus does not answer directly but
rather sends John's disciples to report to John a series of events that they

[66]There is practically verbatim agreement between Matthew and Luke on both verses. The
only differences are that Matthew has ἀκούετε and βλέπετε ("hear" and "see") in 22a while
Luke has εἴδετε and ἠκούσατε ("have seen" and "have heard"). The IQP prefers Matthew's
verb choice and tense as well as Matthew's order (hear, see). The IQP also prefers Matthew's
repetition of καί throughout the clauses to Luke's version. These differences are very minor
and do not effect the Q reconstruction in any significant ways.

[67]Jacobson, *First Gospel*, 111.

[68]Allison (*Jesus Tradition*, 6 n. 32) notes that "because there is no evidence that 'the
coming one' was a recognized title [in first-century Judaism], the article in Q 7:19 ('*the* coming
one') is probably anaphoric: it refers back to 3:16."

see and hear (7:22). In the concluding macarism, Jesus seems to answer in the affirmative, but his reply is similarly indirect: "Blessed is whoever is not offended by me."

The list of events in 7:22 echoes the language of the prophet Isaiah but does not reproduce any text verbatim.[69] The closest parallel is Isa 61:1 LXX:

Πνεῦμα κυρίου ἐπ' ἐμέ, οὗ εἵνεκεν ἔχρισέν με· εὐαγγελίσασθαι πτωξοῖς ἀπέσταλκέν με, ἰάσασθαι τοὺς συντετριμμένους τῇ καρδίᾳ, κηρύξαι αἰχμαλώτοις ἄφεσιν καὶ τυφλοῖς ἀνάβλεψιν.	The spirit of the Lord is upon me, because he has anointed me. He has sent me to preach good news to the poor, to heal those whose hearts are broken, to proclaim release to the captives and sight to the blind.

This accounts for the first and last elements of 7:22 but in reverse order.[70] Although it is possible that the healing of the lame, lepers, deaf, and dead stand as elaborations[71] on "heal those whose hearts are broken," it is more likely that 7:22 is highly intertextual and echoes several Isaiah texts such as 26:19 (dead rise, healing), 29:18–19 (deaf hear, blind see, poor rejoice), and 35:5–6 (blind see, deaf hear, lame walk).

Throughout the Isaiah passages, these events characterize God's saving power on behalf of the people of Israel. Although the construction of the

[69]Bultmann's focus on the "eschatological consciousness" inherent in Q 7:22 denies its dependence on Israelite scriptural tradition. "In so far as this eschatological consciousness is something new in distinction from Judaism, . . . these beatitudes [Lk 6:20–21] [are] in any case unJewish. Similarly the immediacy of eschatological consciousness is given such emphatic expression in . . . Lk 7:22f that it is impossible for any Jewish tradition to provide an origin" (*History*, 126). For the presence of Israelite traditions in Q, see Horsley and Draper, *Whoever Hears*, 94–122. For a discussion of Christian uniqueness arguments as they are mediated by the category eschatology, see chapter 4 (pp. 115–30).

[70]Robinson ("Sayings Gospel," 363) points out that the beginning and the end of 7:22 are from Isa 61:1 LXX, but in chiastic order.

[71]This list of events raises questions about how much of the Jesus tradition was available in the "Q community." So far in the reconstructed Q, Jesus has healed the centurion's boy (which is only implied) and proclaimed that the poor are blessed. None of the other events have been spoken of or demonstrated. In the rest of Q, the followers of Jesus are instructed to "heal the sick" in 10:9, and Jesus performs an exorcism in 11:14. What is remarkable is how well this list corresponds with the miracle stories associated with Jesus in the Synoptics. This may attest to an ongoing oral tradition in the Q community well beyond what is inscribed in Q. The presence of the cleansing of lepers in 7:22 also points to a mixture of Isaianic allusions and the Jesus tradition since the cleansing of lepers occurs in none of the Isaiah texts (Jacobson, *First Gospel*, 112).

scene in Q rhetorically focuses on Jesus as the key player in the fulfillment of that expectation, the activities listed in Q 7:22 are not restricted to Jesus' activity in Q as a whole. The disciples are sent out to heal the sick (and say "the *basileia* of God has come near" in 10:9) and, as discussed below in chapter 5, the sons of the accusers in the Beelzebul pericope (11:14–20) are affirmed in their ability to exorcize with the power of God.[72] Although there is no reference to the *basileia* of God in Q 7:22, it can stand as a summary of the manifestation of the *basileia* of God among the people as much as a summary of Jesus' ministry. Indeed, Q directly links the *basileia* of God with the blessing of the poor (6:20b), healing (10:9), and exorcism (11:20).

Although interpreters presume that the question posed to Jesus in 7:18 focuses on the issue of Jesus' messianic identity, Q 7:22 employs the prophetic images of Isaiah to authorize its interpretation of what is happening among the people, and thus also redirects the focus of the question away from the identity of Jesus as John's "coming one" to God's saving actions on behalf of the poor and sick.[73] This redirection is often interpreted as a realignment of the apocalyptic image of John's "coming one" to fit Jesus better.[74] However, this presupposes that the text's redirection results primarily from a lack of fit between John's "coming one" and Jesus' activity. There is also a lack of fit, however, between the events listed in 7:22 and what Jesus *actually does* in Q. So, what if one interprets the lack of fit as the discontinuity between emphasis on the manifestations of the *basileia* of God among the people and the emphasis on the expectation of a figure of singular significance?[75] If this

[72]Q 10:13–15 speaks of the "wonders done" (αἱ δυνάμει αἱ γενόμεναι) in the cities of Chorazin and Bethsaida. The verb is intransitive, but in the context of the mission speech (Q 10:2–16), the followers of Jesus are going from town to town, performing healings, and saying that the *basileia* has come near.

[73]For example, Kloppenborg describes the contrast as one between John's expectations of a messiah and the depiction of Jesus as a miracle-worker (*Formation*, 107). In Q, however, the type of events described in Q 7:22 are not performed exclusively by Jesus. Indeed Luke may have corrected precisely this problem by adding Luke 7:21 before 7:22: "In that hour he cured many of the diseases and afflictions and evil spirits, and to many who were blind he granted sight."

[74]For example, Tuckett (*Q*, 126) observes that "the answer, referring to Jesus' credentials as a preacher and miracle worker fulfilling the expectations of the Isaianic prophecies, and the question, referring to John's expectation of an apocalyptic End-time judging figure, seem quite tangential to each other." See also, Jacobson, *First Gospel*, 113; and Hoffmann, *Studien*, 209. Jesus' answer in 7:22, however, does not refer to Jesus at all but to the saving acts of God among the people, not performed exclusively by Jesus in Q.

[75]Kirk (*Composition*, 370) notes that *chreia* "challenge and revise preconceived notions

is the case, then 7:22 redirects the question about the identity of Jesus onto the manifestations of the *basileia* among the people.[76]

Q 3:16–17 implies that the moment of crisis is in the future of the text (albeit soon); in 7:22–23, however, Jesus affirms John's expectation of a "coming one" by directing the attention of John's disciples to what is currently happening around them (in the present time of the text). This is similar to Jesus' efforts to redirect the question about the coming of the *basileia* of God in Q 17:20–21:[77] "The *basileia* is not coming," he implies; "It is among you." There is a parallel contrast between an expectation of a "coming" *basileia* and figure, and the presence of the *basileia* (among you) or the evidence of the figure's identity (happening around you). In this sense both the *basileia* and the "coming one" are not things that are coming; rather, they are all around, and hence they are located "among us."[78] Thus, the events of the *basileia* are among the people, as the disciples of John can attest with their eyes and ears. So also, in Q 10:23–24 the people around Jesus are blessed because of what they have seen and heard (βλέπετε and ἀκούετε).[79]

The concluding saying returns the focus to the person of Jesus. In this sense Q 7:18–23 places Jesus at a crucial location, that is, as a key enactor of God's saving action among the people. While in content the saying resembles the proverbial saying in Mark 9:40 ("Whoever is not against us is for us"),[80] it is

---

and questionable opinions. In this case it counters John's opening question with a challenge to reconsider the premises and stereotypes which generated it." Kirk assumes with most other interpreters that the *chreia* counters John's understanding of the "coming one" as an apocalyptic judge (p. 371). See also Cameron, " 'What Have You Come Out To See?'," 53.

[76]Although he retains a focus on the singular significance of John and Jesus, Horsley (*Whoever Hears*, 86) points to the communal implications of Q 7:18–35: "[This section of Q] deals not merely with Jesus, John, and 'this generation' but with the significance of what is happening with John and Jesus, the fulfillment of expectations and prophecies of personal and societal renewal."

[77]I follow Koester (*Ancient Christian Gospels*, 155–56) that this Lukan text derives from Q.

[78]This spatial understanding of *basileia* may also be useful for understanding the charge to the disciples in 10:9 to say to those they heal and visit: "The *basileia* of God has come near."

[79]Hoffmann (*Studien*, 210–12) makes a similar comparison but holds that 10:23–24 is an earlier tradition. At the level of Q, however, both John's disciples and the people around Jesus see and hear the events of the *basileia*. See also Tuckett, *Q*, 127.

[80]This same saying appears in Q 11:23, but because of the context of Q 11:14–26, it is formulated in the negative: "Whoever is not with me is against me." See the discussion below in chapter 5, pp. 131–68.

important to note that in the context of the scene Jesus gives this answer to John's disciples and thus Q applies a general saying to the issue at hand.[81] The scene echoes the tension between factions lampooned in the simile about the children in the marketplace. In response, the macarism in 7:23 casts the net wide and confirms that anyone who is not scandalized by Jesus is blessed.[82] In this sense, the answer in 7:23 is similar to 7:35: loyalties to John or Jesus are unimportant in comparison to what is happening among the people.[83]

If 7:22 represents the vision of the *basileia* of God, what values are inherent in that vision? What alternative to the present is imagined for the community? In God's *basileia*, the sick are healed and the poor receive good news. As in the opening of the sermon in 6:20–23, the *basileia* of God is imagined as a *basileia* of justice for those who have no justice, as a vision of inclusion for those who are excluded. The entire sermon then provides guidelines for enacting that justice in the social and economic relationships of the community. As discussed in chapter 3 below, John's preaching in Q 3:7–9 and the parables of judgment in Q 13:26–27 similarly center on enacting justice as the primary and necessary characteristic of the people of God.

[81]Vaage (*Galilean Upstarts*, 108; "More Than a Prophet," 189) argues that Q 7:18–23 "magnifies Jesus at John's expense." However, Q 7:27 also identifies John as a "coming one" by similarly identifying John as the fulfillment of prophecy.

[82]Jacobson assumes that the potential for scandal lies in the disparity between John's prophecy of a coming apocalyptic judge and Jesus' ministry in 7:22. He concludes, therefore, that the "beatitude affirms those who see no problem claiming that Jesus was nevertheless the 'coming one' announced by John" (*First Gospel*, 114). This interpretation is unnecessary if one locates the shift not from one type of superlative figure to another, but from a focus on a superlative individual to a communal focus.

[83]Kloppenborg also interprets Q 7:23 as inclusive of John's disciples but adds that it "warns against rejecting Jesus" and establishes that John is inferior to Jesus (*Formation*, 108). He notes that, "there is no polemic here, but John's inferiority to Jesus is obvious. It is as if John is 'on the outside looking in,' seeking the fulfillment of his own prophecy rather than actively engaged in the events of the kingdom" (ibid.). It is unclear how this interpretation follows from these verses. Q 7:23 speaks only of the *positive* result of recognizing the fulfillment of prophecy among the people and in Jesus. In addition, the passage confirms that Jesus is the "coming one" predicted by John and thus Q does not tacitly undermine John but rather actively authorizes him as a legitimate prophet whose prophecies are being fulfilled in observably verifiable ways. For a similar point, see Tuckett, *Q*, 127. For a discussion of the legitimizing function of verifiable prophetic signs, see chapter 6 below, pp. 178–90.

The Least in the *Basileia* are Greater: Q 7:24–28

Insofar as Q 7:18–23 clarifies the relationship between John's prophecy of a "coming one" and the manifestations of God's reign among the people, so Q 7:24–28 clarifies John's own relationship to the *basileia* of God. As we have seen in other units, Matthew and Luke are nearly in verbatim agreement on the wording of the dialogue in the pericope. The IQP reconstructs[84] the passage as follows:

Q 7:24b τούτων δὲ ἀπελθόντων ἤρξατο λέγειν τοῖς ὄχλοις περὶ Ἰωάννου· τί ἐξήλθατε εἰς τὴν ἔρημον θεάσασθαι; κάλαμον ὑπὸ ἀνέμου σαλευόμενον;

And when they had left, he began to talk to the crowds about John: What did you go out into the wilderness to look at? A reed shaken by the wind?

Q 7:25 ἀλλὰ τί ἐξήλθατε ἰδεῖν; ἄνθρωπον ἐν μαλακοῖς ἠμφιεσμένον; ἰδοὺ οἱ τὰ μαλακὰ φοροῦντες ἐν τοῖς οἴκοις τῶν βασιλέων εἰσίν.

If not, what did you go out to see? A person arrayed in finery? Look, those wearing finery are in kings' houses.

Q 7:26 ἀλλὰ τί ἐξήλθατε ἰδεῖν; προφήτην; ναὶ λέγω ὑμῖν, καὶ περισσότερον προφήτου.

But <<then>> what did you go out to see? A prophet? Yes, I tell you, even more than a prophet!

Q 7:27 οὗτός ἐστιν περὶ οὗ γέγραπται· ἰδοὺ [[ἐγὼ]] ἀποστέλλω τὸν ἄγγελόν μου πρὸ προσώπου σου, ὃς κατασκευάσει τὴν ὁδόν σου ἔμπροσθέν σου.

This is the one about whom it has been written: Look, I am sending my messenger ahead of you, who will prepare your path in front of you.

Q 7:28 λέγω ὑμῖν· οὐκ ἐγήγερται ἐν γεννητοῖς γυναικῶν μείζων Ἰωάννου· ὁ δὲ μικρότερος ἐν τῇ βασιλείᾳ τοῦ θεοῦ μείζων αὐτοῦ ἐστιν.

I tell you: There has not arisen among women's offspring <<anyone>> who surpasses John. Yet the least significant in God's *basileia* is more than he.

---

[84]Robinson, *Critical Edition*, 128–37. The English translation for this section of Q is also from the *Critical Edition*.

This unit can be broken down into three sections: (1) a series of rhetorical questions concerning John (vv. 24–26);[85] (2) a scripture quotation affirming the answer to the third question (v. 27); and (3) a saying relating John to the least in the *basileia* of God (v. 28).

Q links the first and second units of Q 7:18–35 with a narrative transition: "And when they [John's disciples] had left, he [Jesus] began to talk to the crowds about John" (24a).[86] Now it is Jesus who asks the question about John: "What did you go out into the wilderness to look at?" Just as John's disciples ask Jesus who he is, so Jesus asks the crowd who they think John is. Thus both 7:18–23 and 7:24–28 deal with the relationship between certain expectations and the manifestations of the *basileia* of God.

The text locates John in the wilderness and depicts the crowds who are listening to Jesus as also having gone out to see John.[87] Thus, the inscribed audience both listens to Jesus and went out to see John. Jesus does not tell them *not* to go out to see John; the unit rather seeks to clarify precisely what the crowds see when they encounter John. Thus it focuses on elaborating a characterization of John, just as 7:18–23 elaborated a characterization of Jesus as the "coming one" by drawing attention to God's saving acts among the people.

The first question, "What did you go out into the wilderness to look at?" is answered by a rhetorical question providing an initial answer: "A reed shaken by the wind?" Since 7:26 eventually answers one of the six questions affirmatively (ναί), it is likely that each of the preceding questions presuppose a negative answer. John is not a reed shaken by the wind, but no explanation is given as to why that is the case. The natural image of a reed that bends with the wind implies pliability—someone who is susceptible to the blowing of the wind.[88] In a parallel from Lucian of Samosata's *Herotimus*

---

[85]Jacobson (*First Gospel*, 114) notes that the address to the crowd, the use of rhetorical questions, and the use of λέγω ὑμῖν ("I say to you") in 7:26 and 28 recalls John's speech at the beginning of Q (3:7–9, 16–17).

[86]The genitive absolute creates the connection between the scene in 7:18–23 and 7:24–28. Cameron, "'What Have You Come Out To See?'," 38.

[87]Q creates a locative separation of John and Jesus. In 3:7, the crowds come to the Jordan to be baptized by John. Jesus is led out into the wilderness to be tempted (Q 4:1–13). The centurion comes to Jesus in Capernaum (7:1–10). John sends his disciples to speak to Jesus (7:18). The crowds listening to Jesus have also gone out to the wilderness to see John (7:24).

[88]The only thing that we can know surely from this metaphor is that on ancient riverbanks, reeds bent with the wind. The reed imagery may point to location but scholars are divided as to whether reeds would appear in the outlying wilderness areas of the Jordan valley or whether

(160–180 C.E.), the metaphor is deployed as a critique of a person who does not carefully choose the right philosophical school and/or teacher:

> [Failing to make the right choice, Herotimus is told, means] that nothing will save you from being dragged by the nose . . . or from following a leafy branch in front of you as sheep do; you will be like water spilt on a table, running whithersoever someone pulls you by the tip of his finger, or indeed like a reed [καλάμῳ] growing on a river bank, bending to every breath of wind, however slight the breeze that blows and shakes [διασαλεύσῃ] it.[89]

In this context, the image may be one of "accommodating pliability."[90] In another parallel, God punishes king Ptolemy like wind tosses a reed: "He shook him on this side and that as a reed is shaken by the wind, so that he lay helpless on the ground."[91] In this context, Q 7:24b rejects a characterization of John as one who is victim to the blowing of the wind.

John also does not wear fine clothes or live in palaces.[92] The second version of the question, "If not, what did you go out to see?" (ἀλλὰ τί ἐξήλθατε ἰδεῖν;) is answered with an image from the realm of human life: "A person arrayed in finery?" Again, the implicit answer is "No," but here there is an explanation for the answer: "Look, those wearing finery are in kings' houses." This answer plays on the reference to John's location and reminds the audience that it is in kings' houses—not the wilderness—that one finds people in finery. The comparison locates John in terms of social-political allegiances. He is not among those who mingle with the ruling class.[93]

---

even the riverbanks of the Jordan might be understood as wilderness (see Vaage, *Galilean Upstarts*, 182 n. 50).

[89]*Herotimus* 68; reference and quotation from Cameron, "'What Have You Come Out to See?'," 45.

[90]Cameron, "'What Have You Come Out To See?'," 45.

[91]3 Macc 2:21. See also 3 Kgdms 14:15.

[92]Several interpreters (for example, Horsley and Draper, *Whoever Hears*, 265) suggest that the image alludes to Herod Antipas's palace in Tiberius, which Galileans looted and burned in 66 C.E. See Josephus, *Life* 64–65.

[93]Piper, *Wisdom*, 125. There are several citations in the Cynic epistles that suggest that royal palace living and luxurious clothing was often criticized by the Cynics as a "soft" lifestyle. See Cameron, "'What Did You Go Out to See?'," 43. See Pseudo-Crates, *Ep.* 29; Pseudo-Diogenes, *Eps.* 28 and 12. Cameron and Vaage (*Galilean Upstarts*, 98–100) use these comparisons to fix Q 7:24–26 as interpreting John as Cynic-like. By arguing that 7:24–26 and 7:33 were part of the formative stratum of Q, Vaage ("More Than a Prophet," 194) suggests that the "historical" John remembered by Q was "rather like a Cynic." While Cameron and Vaage are correct that

The final two questions get to the issue of John's significance: "If not, what did you go out to see? A prophet?" Jesus finally answers his own question: "Yes, I tell you, even more than a prophet!"[94] Since the two previous questions assume a negative answer, the presence of ναί signals that the inscribed audience has finally gotten it right.[95] But even then they are corrected, as the explanatory remark goes on to say "even more than a prophet!" Thus the progression of the argument is: (1) "What did you expect? A reed? [That's wrong.]"; (2) "What did you expect? A person in finery? [That's wrong.]"; (3) "What did you expect? A prophet? [Yes, but not what you expected—more.]"[96]

The theme of expectation in the previous unit is amplified by the explanation of 7:26b in 7:27. Verses 27 and 28 provide two explanations of 7:26b in that they both give content to the notion of being "more than a prophet."[97]

Q 7:24–26 depicts John as a wilderness-located critic of the dominant systems of power, it is unclear why the characterization "prophet" (given to John in 7:26) does not fit this culturally-critical profile. Vaage (*Galilean Upstarts*, 101) speaks of the prophets of Israel as champions of "traditional values" over and against the monarchy of Israel. Doesn't this dichotomy also pit the figure of the prophet against the ruling and powerful? Indeed, Mack (*Lost Gospel*, 114) speaks of the Cynics as "the Greek analogue to the Hebrew prophets." The problem seems to lie in the association of the prophets of Israel with a "religious" critique and Cynic philosophy with a "secular" critique aimed at the "reigning culture as such" (Vaage, *Galilean Upstarts*, 101; Mack, *Lost Gospel*, 120). The Cynic comparison is often used in order to understand early Christianity as a "cultural" phenomenon. This dichotomizes Judaism as the "religious" or "mythologizing" opposite to Cynicism. Of course, all religion (and philosophy) in antiquity was thoroughly cultural, social, and ideological. Thus the Jewish prophetic tradition and Cynic philosophy are equally likely sites of social-critical perspectives. Consequently the presence of that perspective in Q 7:24–26 cannot adjudicate the identity-driven debate over the Cynic-like Jesus and John.

[94]Vaage's argument that Q 7:24–26 points to John as a Cynic-like cultural critic is labored when it must argue that 7:26 does not confirm the crowd's expectation that John is a prophet. Vaage (*Galilean Upstarts*, 182 n. 56) takes the particle ναί as part of the "emphatic introductory expression," ναὶ λέγω ὑμῖν, rather than as an affirmative answer to the question in 7:26a. While the phrase may be emphatic, it still confirms the initial claim: Indeed, I tell you, a prophet. It is unclear how Vaage can move from "indeed a prophet" to "not a prophet."

[95]For ναὶ λέγω ὑμῖν as confirming the crowd's expectation of John as a prophet, see Sato, *Q und Prophetie*, 240; and Tuckett, *Q*, 129 n. 79; *pace* Cameron, " 'What Did You Go Out to See?'," 41; and Vaage, *Galilean Upstarts*, 97.

[96]Cameron (" 'What Did You Go Out to See?'," 55) describes this section as "questioning the issue of preconceived expectations."

[97]Ibid., 39.

Verse 27 is a biblical citation that elides Exod 23:20 LXX and Mal 3:1.[98] The citation is introduced by a traditional formula (γέγραπται, "it has been written") and identifies John (οὗτός ἐστιν, "This is the one") as God's messenger. The citation incorporates different elements of each passage:

Q 7:27b ἰδού ἐγὼ ἀποστέλλω τὸν
ἄγγελόν μου **πρὸ προσώπου σου**,
ὃς κατασκευάσει *τὴν ὁδόν σου*
ἔμπροσθέν σου.

Look, I am sending my messenger
before your face, who will prepare
your way in front of you.

Mal 3:1 LXX ἰδοὺ ἐγὼ ἐξαποστέλλω
τὸν ἄγγελόν μου, καὶ ἐπιβλέψεται
ὁδὸν **πρὸ προσώπου μου**,

Look, I am sending out my
messenger, and he will look upon *a*
way **before my face**.

Mal 3:1 MT   הִנְנִי שֹׁלֵחַ מַלְאָכִי
                      וּפִנָּה־דֶרֶךְ לְפָנָי

Here, I am sending my messenger,
and he will prepare *a way* **before
me**.

Exod 23:20 LXX Καὶ ἰδοὺ ἐγὼ
ἀποστέλλω τὸν ἄγγελόν μου **πρὸ
προσώπου σου**, ἵνα φυλάξῃ σε ἐν
τῇ ὁδῷ.

And look, I am sending my
messenger **before your face**, to
guard you on *the way*.

The first clause of the Q version most resembles the first clause of Exod 23: 20 LXX. The second clause shows several similarities to the second clause in Mal 3:1 LXX.[99] The most striking accomplishment of this amalgamation of Scripture verses in Q is the shift in the identification of the one before whom the messenger goes from "me" (in Mal 3:1 LXX and MT) to "you" (in Q and Exod 23:20 LXX). This is also accomplished by adding σου after τὴν ὁδόν and after ἔμπροσθέν.[100] God is the speaker in all versions of the

[98]This exact formulation is used to interpret John in Mark 1:2, but there it is incorrectly identified as being from the prophet Isaiah. This could point to Mark having had Q, or to the wide circulation of proof-texts associated with different figures in the Jesus tradition.

[99]The verb tense is the same and is followed by ὁδόν. The last phrase in Q (ἔμπροσθέν σου) accommodates πρὸ προσώπου μου in Mal 3:1 LXX, which has already appeared in the Q version in the first clause.

[100]The second σου stands out, in that the parallel construction to replace the missing phrase from Mal 3:1 LXX should be πρὸ προσώπου **μου**.

Hebrew Bible citations. Thus, the Mal 3:1 reference to "me" suggests that it is God before whom the messenger will go. Indeed, the rest of chapter 3 in Malachi speaks of God's coming in judgment after God's messenger has refined the priests of Levi (as in a refining fire).[101]

This shift from "me" to "you" removes God as the one before whom John has come. Who is indicated by σου in the context of Q is difficult to determine. In Exod 23:20 LXX, the singular pronoun is used but in the context of a long series of covenant stipulations that apply to the people of Israel as a whole.[102] In Q the audience may be in sight, but in 7:26 the crowds are just referred to as ὑμῖν.[103] The rest of the verse of Malachi may provide the key:

Mal 3:1 LXX ἰδοὺ ἐγὼ ἐξαποστέλλω τὸν ἄγγελόν μου, καὶ ἐπιβλέψεται ὁδὸν πρὸ προσώπου μου, καὶ ἐξαίφνης ἥξει εἰς τὸν ναὸν ἑαυτοῦ κύριο, ὃν ὑμεῖς ζητεῖτε, καὶ ἄγγελλος τῆς διαθήκης, ὃν ὑμεῖς θέλετε· ἰδοὺ ἔρχεται, λέγει κύριος παντοκράτωρ.	Behold, I send my messenger, and he will look upon the *way* **before my face**, and the Lord, whom you seek, will come suddenly into his temple. And the messenger of the covenant, whom you desire—**Look, he is coming**, says the Lord almighty.[104]

The messenger in Malachi is someone who "is coming" (ἔρχεται). This may be echoed in Q 7:18, where John's disciples inquire whether Jesus is the "coming one." If so, now John himself is also a "coming one." But unlike the context of Malachi, he is not coming before God's coming but presumably before the coming of Jesus himself.[105] Thus the shift in

[101]Mal 3:5: "Then I will draw near to you for judgment." See chapters 3 and 4 of Malachi for images of judgment fire, dividing the righteous and the wicked, and the removal of crops/ trees that are the evildoers. See especially 4:1 for an image that looks a lot like the cutting down of the trees in Q 3:7–9 (but with fire).

[102]The first verse of the "Book of the Covenant" (Exod 20:22–23:33) declares: "The Lord said to Moses: Thus you shall say to the Israelites . . ." (Exod 20:22). Exod 21:1 introduces the laws with the following: "These are the ordinances that you shall set before them." Throughout the Book of the Covenant, the laws are given in direct address to a singular "you."

[103]Of course the citation of scripture hardly necessitates a one-to-one correspondence between the actors in the original version and the citation. It is clear that this citation is used to interpret John. It is noteworthy, however, that God is not retained as the one to come after John.

[104]Greek text from *Septuaginta* (ed. Alfred Rahlfs; 2 vols.; 4th ed.; Stuttgart: Privileg. Württ. Bibelanstalt, 1935).

[105]Although the verb ἔρχομαι is not used, Mal 3:1 and 5 speak of God's coming suddenly (ἐξαίφνης ἥξει) and drawing near (προσάξω) in judgment. Mal 4:5–6 use second aorist forms

pronouns has a specific purpose: to ensure that it is Jesus who is preceded by John, not God.

This citation serves as an authoritative explanation of 7:26: "But <<then>> what did you go out to see? A prophet? Yes, I tell you, even more than a prophet!" But the citation does not speak of John as a prophet but as a messenger who prepares the way for someone else. The link may again be found in the Malachi allusion. In Mal 4:5–6 the messenger of 3:1 is identified as "the prophet Elijah," whom God will send before the "day of the Lord." Thus, Q's John is the messenger, who is coming, who is also the prophet Elijah.[106] The reference to "more than a prophet" in this case may refer to the particularly high estimation of Elijah in Israelite tradition due to his being translated to heaven in 2 Kings 2. Indeed, Sir 48:1–11 praises Elijah as a "prophet like fire" (48:1). Praising Elijah's wondrous deeds, Sir 48:4 inquires: "Whose glory is equal to yours?"[107] Of course, the answer to such a question is an implied "No one's glory is equal." This echoes Jesus' answer, "and more than a prophet." Sirach also alludes directly to Mal 4:5–6 and speaks of Elijah as a figure whose return is associated with God's judgment: "At the appointed time, it is written, you are destined to calm the wrath [ὀργήν] of God before it breaks out in fury, to turn the hearts of parents to their children, and to restore the tribes of Jacob" (48:10).[108]

It is possible that the identification of John as a prophet and "more than a prophet" is driven primarily by the citation of Mal 3:1 LXX and the allusion to Elijah returned. The parallel in the *Gospel of Thomas* to Q 7:24–25 suggests that this unit was known independently of the third question and answer:

> Jesus said, "Why have you come out to the countryside? To see a reed shaken by the wind? And to see a person dressed in rich clothing,

---

of ἔρχομαι to refer to the day of the Lord and God's coming (both preceded by the messenger now identified as the prophet Elijah). It is worth noting that Mal 4:6 points out that if Elijah is effective, then the Lord *will not* come and "strike the land with a curse." This reflects the same kind of parenetic function for judgment language as Q 3:7–9.

[106]This link between Elijah and John (or Jesus) is attested throughout the gospels. It is noteworthy that in the fourth gospel (John 2:19–25), John the Baptist denies that he is Elijah (or the Messiah, or a prophet) and claims rather that he is the "voice crying in the wilderness" from Isa 40:3. Mark 1:2–3 elides the quotations from Mal 3:1 and from Isa 40:3 and says they are both from Isaiah.

[107]Sir 48:9: "You were taken up by a whirlwind of fire, in a chariot with horses of fire."

[108]The compatibility between the vocabulary (wrath, fire) and the themes (judgment, repent and avoid judgment) of Q 3:7–9, 16–17 and Sir 48:1–11 are striking.

[like your] rulers and your powerful ones? They are dressed in rich [clothing], but they cannot understand truth. (*Gos. Thom.* 78)

It is significant that the parallel in the *Gospel of Thomas* does not associate this saying of Jesus with John. With the genitive absolute (τούτων δὲ ἀπελθόντων) in 7:24, as well as the expansion of the reed saying of Jesus to reach its climax with the identification of John as the prophet Elijah, the careful composition of the Q unit comes into view. Now both Jesus and John are "coming ones." Just as 7:18–23 accepts that Jesus is one who has fulfilled expectation about God's saving work, so 7:24–28 affirms John as one who has fulfilled expectation. What is significant about this move is that the link between Jesus and the "coming one" has an effect on the significance of John. John is "more than a prophet" and the greatest of human beings (7:28). But he is still a precursor—not to God's coming, but to Jesus himself.[109] Thus, there is some tension here between the aspects of Q 7:18–35 that affirm John's significance and the aspects that subordinate him to Jesus.[110] Given the presentation of both Jesus and John as figures who fulfill expectation, however, it is not a surprise that Q uses ἦλθεν (7:33–34) for both John and Jesus in the crowning unit of the argument (7:31–35).

The second explanation of 7:26b's "more than a prophet," offered in verse 28, also speaks of John in superlative terms: "I tell you: There has not arisen among women's offspring <<anyone>> who surpasses John. Yet the least significant in God's *basileia* is more than he."[111] Q 7:28 affirms that

---

[109]Hoffmann, *Studien*, 218–19.

[110]This may also occur in Jesus' self-reference as the son of humanity in 7:34. Q uses what is clearly one of its special appellations for Jesus in a context that otherwise thoroughly asserts Jesus' and John's parity.

[111]This is a two-part saying that is also attested as referring to John in *Gos. Thom.* 46: "Jesus said, From Adam to John the Baptist, among those born of women, no one is so much greater than John the Baptist that the person's eyes should not be averted. But I have said that whoever among you becomes a child will know the kingdom, and will become greater than John" (Kloppenborg, *Q Parallels*, 55). This version specifies the range of humans (from Adam to John the Baptist) for comparison to John and suggests that no one is "so much greater" than John "that the person's eyes should not be averted." Thus, some human beings are greater or as great as John but should still avert their eyes (and thus honor him). This teaching is then confirmed by the second saying, which says that if one becomes like a child, he or she will become greater than John. Thus it is both possible and desirable for someone to be greater than John. The *Thomas* passage emphasizes the paraenetic possibilities of a comparison with John, where Q 7:28 emphasizes a deliberative focus on the significance of John in relation to the *basileia*.

(1) among human beings, no one is greater than John, but adds the caveat that (2) the least in the *basileia* of God is greater than he.[112] Q interpreters traditionally read Q 7:28 (a and/or b) as appended to 7:27 in order to limit the overly positive evaluation of John in 7:26.[113] This is possible in that Q attests a tension between the positive evaluation of John and the subordination of him to Jesus. It is significant, however, that 7:28b is not speaking of Jesus but of the least in the *basileia* of God.[114] The relationship between 7:28a and b, therefore, should not be read in terms of the relationship between John and Jesus but between John and the least in the *basileia* of God.[115]

Q scholars also traditionally read 7:28b as indicating that John is outside of the *basileia* of God.[116] According to this argument, the saying sets up a contrast between John and the *basileia* of God; therefore, it locates John as one who is not in the *basileia* of God. This interpretation builds upon the view that 7:28b corrects (by contradicting) the affirmation of John in 7:26 and 7:28a. But there has been little negation of John in this entire unit.[117] Indeed only the implication that John is the "coming one" who precedes Jesus serves to limit the affirmation of his significance by Q. But even this point

[112]Sevenich-Bax (*Konfrontation*, 228) understands 7:28 as presenting a paradox. See also Kirk, *Composition*, 373.

[113]Kloppenborg, *Formation*, 109; Jacobson, *First Gospel*, 116; Lührmann, *Redaktion*, 27; Schulz, *Q*, 233–34; Hoffmann, *Studien*, 218 and 230; Vaage, "More Than a Prophet," 186.

[114]Some scholars have argued that "the least in the *basileia*" refers to Jesus (see Kloppenborg, *Formation*, 109 n. 32). Kloppenborg interprets 7:28 as emphasizing the "greatness of the kingdom of God by asserting that even the greatest representative of the old order, John, paled in comparison with it" (*Formation*, 109). Indeed, Q does not compare John to Jesus in Q 7:28. The comparison, however, is not between John's greatness and the *basileia's* greatness, but rather between John's greatness and the greatness of *the least* in the *basileia*. While Horsley (*Whoever Hears*, 265), Allison (*Jesus Tradition*, 34), and Kirk (*Composition*, 375) do not see any tension between 7:28a and b, they all make a similar mistake in seeing a contrast here between the greatness of John and the greatness of the *basileia* or everyone in the *basileia* (rather than the *least* in the *basileia*).

[115]"The least in the *basileia* of God" (ὁ μικρότερος ἐν τῇ βασιλείᾳ τοῦ θεοῦ) can refer to any person of low status or age. Three of the LSJ meanings for μικρός are possible here: small (1) of stature; (2) of significance; or (3) of age. Vaage ("More Than a Prophet," 197 n. 21) recognizes that all three units (7:18–23, 7:24–28, and 7:31–35) conclude with a communal focus but insists that the first two passages still are concerned primarily with the respective identities of Jesus and John. He dismisses the "least" as "a new group of 'politically correct' persons associated with the kingdom of God."

[116]For example, Cameron ("'What Have You Come Out to See?'," 59) argues that 7:28 is a statement from an authority (that is, Jesus) that juxtaposes John and the community of Q. See also Kloppenborg, *Formation*, 109.

[117]Tuckett, *Q*, 132–33.

is mitigated by Q 7:31–35, which places John and Jesus on equal footing as children of *Sophia*. If Q 7:28 can be read as an affirmation of John in its entirety, it would better fit the flow of the argument in Q. These three points should be taken into account when interpreting Q 7:28: (1) 7:28b concerns the least in the *basileia* of God (and not Jesus); (2) Q 7:31–35 does not treat John as outside the *basileia*; and (3) 7:28 best serves as an explanation of 7:26b ("more than a prophet") if it does not undermine John.

The key to interpreting 7:28 in this way lies in the interest that Q's Jesus shows in groups of people who might be understood as "the least":

> "Blessed are you poor [οἱ πτωχοί], for God's reign is for you. Blessed are you who hunger [οἱ πεινῶντες], for you will eat your fill. (Q 6:20b–21a)

> At that time he said, I thank you father, lord of heaven and earth, for you hid these things from the sages and learned, and disclosed them to babes [νηπίοις]. (Q 10:21)

> It is necessary for enticements to come, but woe to the one through whom they come! It is better for him if a millstone is put around his neck and he is thrown into the sea, than that he should entice one of these little ones [τῶν μικρῶν τούτων]. (Q 17:1–2)

Indeed, in Q 7:22 the events that Jesus speaks of are ones that bring relief and inclusion to the blind, lame, lepers, and poor. Although Jesus is the "coming one," God's *basileia* is for society's marginalized. So also with John: although he is the greatest of human beings, the least in God's *basileia* are greater, that is, they are more significant in the *basileia* of God. This does not mean that John is outside the *basileia*, but that in the *basileia*, the world is turned upside down—the least are the greatest. Thus, John's greatness is relativized in relationship to the values of the *basileia*.[118] Q 7:28b does not reverse its affirmation of John in 7:26b or 7:28a; it reverses the notion of greatness in the *basileia* of God. John is the greatest human being, but in the *basileia* of God, the least are greater.

---

[118]The theme of reversal is common in the Jesus tradition. It appears twice in Q (17:33 and 13:30). Its most familiar formulation is in Q 13:30: "The last shall be first and the first shall be last."

Rethinking "This Generation"

Resisting both an emphasis on the identity of Jesus and John and dichotomous assumptions about Jesus/John and "this generation," this chapter
proposes an interpretation of the rhetoric of Q 7:31–35 that raises new
possibilities for interpreting the simile and its application as well as for
the preceding two units in Q 7:18–28. Interpreters often see a jumble of
contradicting assertions about John's role and identity in relation to Jesus'
role and identity in Q 7:18–35. An interpretation that centers the values,
visions, and struggles of the community, however, can give voice to an
affirmation of John (and his followers) that is part of an extended argument
for solidarity and common cause among all of Wisdom's children. In the
first two units, the significance of Jesus (7:18–23) and of John (7:24–28)
is explicated in relationship to the visions and values of the *basileia* of
God (7:22, 7:28b). The implication that each figure is a "coming one"
culminates, in the progression of the text, with the assertion that they
have come (ἦλθεν). This does not result in an affirmation of one over the
other, however, but rather an exhortation to a quarreling generation that
Sophia is vindicated by all her children. Throughout all three units, it is
society's weak and marginalized—not its great individuals—that occupy
the center of the communal vision. Regardless of their eating practices,
Sophia is vindicated when her children heal the sick, value the least, and
recognize the tax collector as a child of Wisdom.

It may be necessary, therefore, to reconsider the traditional interpretation of "this generation" in Q. Since the work of Dieter Lührmann, scholars
interested in the redactional history of Q have paid special attention to the
expression "this generation." In his small but highly influential 1969 book,
Die Redaktion der Logienquelle, Lührmann argues that the announcement of
judgment against "this generation" is a "characteristic feature for determining
the theology of Q."[119] For Lührmann, "this generation" stands for all of Israel,
and the conflict between Jesus and "this generation"[120] reflects the conflict
between the Q community and Israel. Citing the work of Max Meinertz,[121]
Lührmann views "this generation" as a pejorative *terminus technicus*, which

[119]Lührmann, *Redaktion*, 93.

[120]Ibid., 31.

[121]Max Meinertz, "'Dieses Geschlecht' im Neuen Testament," *BZ* 1 (1957) 283–89.
Lührmann does not treat the term itself in any length. Evald Lövestam has pointed out that
Meinertz de-emphasizes the temporal aspects of "this generation" in favor of its negative
moral characteristics because of his interest in Mark 13:30 ("The ἡ γενεὰ αὕτη Eschatology in

points to the people of Israel as chronically unrepentant and stubborn. According to Lührmann, "the announcement of judgment against this generation creates a decisive opposition between Jesus and the community on the one hand and Israel on the other: for Israel there remains only judgment."[122]

Kloppenborg builds on Lührmann's redactional insights in *The Formation of Q*. His own analysis results in the conclusion that the redactional structures of Q point to "the conflict between the Q group and their Jewish contemporaries over the preaching of the kingdom."[123] Drawing on the work of O. H. Steck,[124] Jacobson links Q's use of "this generation" to its use of the deuteronomistic tradition to make sense of the rejection of Jesus and the Q community by their fellow Jews. This theologizing reaches its climax in Q 11:49–51, where Wisdom declares that "this generation" will have to pay for its murder of the prophets. According to Jacobson, "The situation has reached crisis proportions; there seems to be not even a shred of hope for the conversion of Israel, for its reawakening. The polarization of 'this generation' and Wisdom's children seems to be understood in terms of God's judgment, in terms of the separation even now of those who respond from those blind ones who remain in darkness."[125]

The language about "this generation" in Q, therefore, is understood as polemical language that rhetorically reflects and constitutes boundaries between competing identity groups—particularly between the Q community and other Jews. Both Tuckett and Horsley have criticized Lührmann's understanding of "this generation" as all of Israel. They likewise identify "this generation" as a polemical expression, but argue that it has a more limited horizon in Q. For Tuckett, it points to "simply the non-responsive part of the Jewish people."[126] For Horsley, it refers to the scribes and Pharisees in particular, and in general to the elite Jerusalem leaders who oppose Q's

---

Mk 13, 30 parr.," in *L'Apocalypse johannique et l'Apocalyptique dans le Nouveau Testament* [ed. Jan Lambrecht; Louvain: Leuven University Press, 1980] 403–13). Lövestam proposes that "this generation" derives from Jewish reflection on special 'generations' in the history of Israel. The flood generation and the wilderness generation, for example, are characterized as demanding signs and ignoring the preaching of repentance, and suffering the wrath of God as a result. Given the persistent emphasis in Q on the crucial significance of the present situation, Lövestam's proposals should be explored for their value in interpreting "this generation" in Q.

[122]Lührmann, *Redaktion*, 93.

[123]Kloppenborg, *Formation*, 167.

[124]Odil Hannes Steck, *Israel und das gewaltsame Geschick der Propheten* (WMANT 23; Neukirchen-Vluyn: Neukirchener Verlag, 1967).

[125]Jacobson, *First Gospel*, 183.

[126]Tuckett, *Q*, 201.

local program for the renewal of Israel.[127] Both Tuckett and Horsley attempt to deconstruct the dichotomy between the Q community and Judaism that is implied by Lührmann's interpretation of "this generation" in Q, but they retain a dichotomy between insiders (the Q community) and outsiders (those who reject the community or the message).

The interpretation of 7:31–35 proposed in this chapter supports the conclusion that the rhetoric of the unit does not announce irretrievable judgment on "this generation." Rather it diagnoses the problem with "this generation" and seeks to correct it. "This generation" is like children who refuse to play together because different groups compete to set the rules of the game. The concluding aphorism urges the solidarity of all the children of *Sophia*. Tuckett makes a similar observation about this passage: " 'This generation' is compared with grumbling children, but Wisdom is justified by her children: hence the message to the audience is not a statement about a judicial decision already made—rather, it is a call to the audience to stop behaving like the grumbling children of the parable."[128]

According to Tuckett, however, the audience can become Wisdom's children "by responding positively to Wisdom's envoys John and Jesus."[129] As discussed above, this view aligns Jesus and John with the children who pipe and sing a dirge and focuses on the response to John and Jesus as the central problem being addressed by the unit. However, the problem being addressed is not resistance to John and Jesus but the judgmental in-fighting between their followers who play a divisive game when they judge each other on the basis of different eating practices. This interpretation assumes a common identity horizon among Jesus, John, and "this generation," and thus depends upon a rhetorical situation not of insider vs. outsider but rather of insider vs. insider. In addition, this interpretation suggests that the rhetoric of the text is not aimed at creating group boundary lines between insiders (as one might expect for intra-Jewish debate) but rather at persuading those groups to recognize their common cause.

This interpretation of Q 7:18–35 raises some important possibilities for the interpretation of "this generation" in Q 11:16, 29–32 and Q 11:49–51. Despite the increasingly negative tone of these units, "this generation" in Q may point to the self-reflection of the Q community as representative of the larger collective identity of "Israel," rather than a polemical critique of some Jewish "others" who have rejected the Q mission.

[127]Horsley and Draper, *Whoever Hears*, 299.

[128]Tuckett, *Q*, 203.

[129]Ibid. Horsley also interprets 7:31–35 as reflecting aggressive resistance to the movement (*Whoever Hears*, 270).

CHAPTER 3

Eschatology and Theology:
The Judgmental Jesus and John's Opening Speech in
Q 3:7–9, 16–17

Chapter 2 argues that Q 7:18–35 attempts to persuade Q's audience to solidarity around the vision of the *basileia* of God; this chapter examines the relationship between John's opening speech in Q 3:7–9, 16–17 and the values of this communal vision. So much emphasis has been placed by scholars on the alleged discontinuities between John's preaching of judgment and apocalyptic doom and Jesus' positive ethical preaching that Q itself is often understood as attempting to mediate and account for that difference. Once again, the questions that we ask of the text shape our understanding of its rhetorical aims and effects. If we begin with questions about the relationship between Jesus and John or their preaching, then these issues will dominate our interpretation of Q. However, by examining how Q's judgment language relates to the communal vision of the *basileia* of God, we can understand how the rhetoric of God's judgment underlines the crucial importance of the movement of which both John and Jesus are a part. Before presenting an interpretation of Q's opening speech, we will address two preliminary issues: (1) the reconstruction of the beginning of Q; and (2) several ways that traditional approaches to John's speech focus the interpreter's attention on the person of Jesus and his relationship to judgment language.

John at the Beginning of Q

In his article on the reconstruction of Q's beginning, Harry Fleddermann comments that "we often probe the beginning and end of a literary work for clues to its meaning."[1] Although the very beginning of Q is probably beyond our reach,[2] both Matthew and Luke identify the speaker of Q 3: 7–9 as John by placing the sayings immediately after he is introduced (see Matt 1:1–6 and Luke 3:1–6, both of which depend heavily on Mark 1: 2–6). This suggests that Q also must have identified the speaker of 3: 7–9 as John, since it is unlikely that both Matthew and Luke would have independently linked the sayings with Mark's story about John. The IQP, therefore, reconstructs Q 3:2–3 as containing something that sets the scene, that is, introducing John and his geographic location.[3] Based on the minor agreement between Matthew and Luke against Mark, the IQP text includes "all the region of the Jordan" in Q 3:3.[4]

Unlike the very beginning of Q, John's speech in 3:7–9, 16–17 is as well-attested as any unit in Q.[5] The IQP reconstructs the text as follows:[6]

Q 3:7 [[εἶπεν]] τοῖς [[ἐρχ]]ομένο‹ι›ς [[ὄχλοις]] βαπτισ[[θῆναι]]· γεννήματα ἐχιδνῶν, τίς ὑπέδειξεν ὑμῖν φυγεῖν ἀπὸ τῆς μελλούσης ὀργῆς;

He said to the crowds coming to be baptized: Brood of vipers! Who warned you to flee from the coming wrath?

[1]Harry Fleddermann, "The Beginning of Q," *SBLSP* (1985) 153–59.

[2]For attempts and discussion, see David Catchpole, "The Beginning of Q: A Proposal," *NTS* 38 (1992) 205–21; and John S. Kloppenborg, "City and Wasteland: Narrative World and the Beginning of the Sayings Gospel (Q)," *Semeia* 52 (1990) 145–60. See also Robinson, *Critical Edition*, 2–7.

[3]Q 7:24 also locates John in the wilderness. Horsley and Draper (*Whoever Hears*, 252–53) suggest that both "the region of the Jordan" (Lk 3:3) and "wilderness" (Matt 3:1) set the scene of John's preaching in the wilderness. This evokes the wilderness wanderings of the Exodus generation and the tradition of renewal and entrance into the promised land. As I discuss below, Kloppenborg argues that "all the region of the Jordan" functions in Q to evoke the story of Lot and the destruction of Sodom ("City and Wasteland," 150). Kirk points out that "wilderness has strong associations with liminality, for it designates and symbolizes space outside human culture and society" (Alan Kirk, "Liminality and Transformative Wisdom in Q," *NTS* 45 [1999] 9).

[4]Kloppenborg, *Q Parallels*, 6; idem, "City and Wasteland," 149–50.

[5]The speech in Q 3:7b–9 is remarkable in its literary agreement between Matthew and Luke. Chrisopher Tuckett comments that, "this section comprises one of the stock examples of almost verbatim agreement between the Greek texts of Matthew and Luke so that a Greek *Vorlage* is almost demanded" (Tuckett, *Q*, 109–10).

[6]Robinson, *Critical Edition*, 8–16.

Q 3:8 ποιήσατε οὖν καρπὸν ἄξιον τῆς μετανοίας καὶ μὴ δόξητε λέγειν ἐν ἑαυτοῖς· πατέρα ἔχομεν τὸν Ἀβραάμ. λέγω γὰρ ὑμῖν ὅτι δύναται ὁ θεὸς ἐκ τῶν λίθων τούτων ἐγεῖραι τέκνα τῷ Ἀβραάμ.

Therefore bear fruit worthy of repentance, and do not presume to tell yourselves: We have Abraham as a father! For I tell you: God can produce children for Abraham out of these rocks!

Q 3:9 ἤδη δὲ ἡ ἀξίνη πρὸς τὴν ῥίζαν τῶν δένδρων κεῖται· πᾶν οὖν δένδρον μὴ ποιοῦν καρπὸν καλὸν ἐκκόπτεται καὶ εἰς πῦρ βάλλεται.

And the ax already lies at the root of the trees. So every tree not bearing healthy fruit is to be chopped down and thrown on the fire.

Q 3:16b ἐγὼ μὲν ὑμᾶς βαπτίζω ⟦ἐν⟧ ὕδατι, ὁ δὲ ὀπίσω μου ἐρχόμενος ἰσχυρότερός μού ἐστιν, οὗ οὐκ εἰμὶ ἱκανὸς τ⟦ὰ⟧ ὑποδήματ⟦α⟧ ⟦βαστά⟧σαι· αὐτὸς ὑμᾶς βαπτίσει ἐν πνεύματι ⟦ἁγίῳ⟧ καὶ πυρί·

I baptize you in water, but the one who is coming after me is more powerful than I, [in comparison with whom] I am not worthy to wear sandals.[7] He will baptize you in holy spirit and fire.

Q 3:17 οὗ τὸ πτύον ἐν τῇ χειρὶ αὐτοῦ καὶ διακαθαριεῖ τὴν ἅλωνα αὐτοῦ καὶ συνάξει τὸν σῖτον εἰς τὴν ἀποθήκην αὐτοῦ, τὸ δὲ ἄχυρον κατακαύσει πυρὶ ἀσβέστῳ.

His winnowing shovel[8] [is] in his hand, and he will clear his threshing floor and gather the wheat into his granary, but the chaff he will burn on a fire that can never be put out.

[7]The IQP translation is "whose sandals I am not fit to take off." My translation follows Paul Bretscher (" 'Whose Sandals'? [Matt 3.11]," *JBL* 86 [1967] 81–87) who makes the case that the traditional translation of Matt 3:11 does not account for the οὗ as a genitive of comparison, which is its function in all of the parallels (Mark 1:7; Luke 3:16; John 1:27; and Acts 13:25). This decision to translate οὗ in relationship to ἱκανός rather than as a possessive that identifies the sandals as belonging to the "more powerful one," has implications for the translation of τὰ ὑποδήματα βαστάσαι. Bretscher argues that since Matthew [and Q] lack the αὐτοῦ to identify the owner of the sandals (present in Mark 1:7; Luke 3:16), "the sandals are to be understood as those of the nearest personal antecedent of τὰ ὑποδήματα. That antecedent is the subject of the verb εἰμί: John the Baptist himself" (p. 83). This translation points to an allusion in 3:16 to Exod 3:5 and Josh 5:15, where Moses and Joshua respectively must remove their shoes before one more powerful. This accords with the traditional interpretation of John's sayings in 3:16–17 as referring to the coming of the God of Israel. Bretscher's proposal has not been widely accepted, but in light of the sense that it makes of the Q passage, it should be reconsidered.

[8]Robert Webb ("The Activity of John the Baptist's Expected Figure at the Threshing Floor [Matthew 3.12 = Luke 3.17]," *JSNT* 43 [1991] 103–11) convincingly distinguishes between

This is the only speech delivered by John in Q. In it he calls his addressees a "brood of vipers" and inquires: "Who warned you to flee from the coming wrath?" This polemical address and unanswered rhetorical question establish both the negative tone of the speech and John's negative evaluation of the addressees. They are the offspring of snakes and they do not deserve the warning they have received. Yet John goes on to instruct them on how to avoid the coming wrath: bear fruit worthy of repentance.

Unfortunately, it is difficult to identify the addressees in Q 3:7a. The IQP's translation places Luke's "crowds" in square brackets and thus prefers Luke's version to Matthew's "Pharisees and Sadducees." Matthew's version may make better sense of the rhetorical question in that it might polemically ask of a particular group: "Who warned *you* to flee?" But Matthew's reading has little else to support it. Matthew's redactional linking of Pharisees with "brood of vipers" is attested in the other occurrences of the uncommon expression in Matt 12:34 and 23:33. Neither of these uses of "brood of vipers" appears in the IQP text, primarily because they are not attested in Luke and the polemic against the Pharisees is pronounced in Matthew. Matthew's introduction to John's speech, therefore, is particularly Matthean in both its content and style. Fleddermann suggests that both Luke's "crowds" and Matthew's "Pharisees and Sadducees" are redactional. He concludes that Q must have contained no addressees, only "John said."[9] The other option, unmentioned by Fleddermann, is that the Q version is lost. Kloppenborg points out that Matthew and Luke agree on placing John's speech in a chreiic (anecdotal) scene and thus rightly concludes that Q must have mentioned someone who came out to hear John.[10] One's arguments about who that someone is, however, depend on how one interprets Q's announcement of judgment as a whole.

---

the winnowing fork (θρῖναξ) and the winnowing shovel (πτύον): "The actual winnowing of the grain, that is separating the wheat from the straw and chaff by throwing it up into the wind, was accomplished by means of the winnowing fork and not the shovel. The shovel was used to heap up the grain before winnowing as well as to gather the wheat and straw into piles after the winnowing was completed. It was also used for the final clearing of the threshing floor and for moving the wheat in the granary" (p. 107).

[9]Fleddermann, "Beginning," 154.

[10]Kloppenborg, "City and Wasteland," 149.

The Judgment and the Interpretation of Q 3:7–9, 16–17

Two observations dominate much of the interpretation of John's speech in Q. First, the speech's tone is "bitter and reproachful";[11] and second, the speech attests a futuristic or apocalyptic eschatology. These seemingly common sense characterizations of John's speech are often juxtaposed with the presentation of Jesus in Q. For example, one might ask how John's vituperative speech compares with the mild-mannered blocks of Jesus' teaching such as the inaugural sermon (6:20–48) or the speech about basic needs (12: 22–32).[12] Or, how the apocalyptic outlook of John's speech resembles or contrasts with the temporal horizon of Jesus' sayings.[13] Both comparisons maintain a basic interest in characterizing Q's Jesus in relationship to John and the judgment themes in Q.

The interpretation of Jesus in comparison to John resembles larger contemporary discourses that theologically evaluate the apocalyptic tradition in Christianity and attempt to locate it in relationship to Jesus' own theology. For example, in *Jesus and Judgment*, Marius Reiser charges that in North American New Testament scholarship "certain aspects of eschatology, including judgment, [have been] silently dropped from consideration."[14] He links this "vanishing judgment" to theological interests:

> In preaching and catechesis within the churches today, the general consensus is that Jesus' message was *good news, not grim news*, as the handy formula would have it. A Jesus who threatens a city with "you will be brought down to Hades!" [Q 10:15] does not fit the popular picture of Jesus, the friend of humanity, who proclaimed a God who forgives without measure. . . . But it is not only in preaching that the serious side of Jesus' message is neglected; it also receives little attention among scholars.[15]

---

[11]Kloppenborg, *Formation*, 106. This characterization of the speech is pervasive regardless of one's approach to the question of the stratigraphy of Q.

[12]See, for example, Wendy Cotter, C.S.J., "Prestige, Protection and Promise: A Proposal for the Apologetics of Q²," in *The Gospel Behind the Gospels: Current Studies on Q* (ed. Ronald A. Piper; NovTSup 74; Leiden: Brill, 1995) 117–38; and David Seeley, "Futuristic Eschatology and Social Formation in Q," in *Reimagining Christian Origins: A Colloquium Honoring Burton L. Mack* (ed. Elizabeth A. Castelli and Hal Taussig; Valley Forge, Pa.: Trinity, 1996) 144–53.

[13]Tuckett, *Q*, 139–63.

[14]Marius Reiser, *Jesus and Judgment: The Eschatological Proclamation in Its Jewish Context* (trans. Linda M. Maloney; German original, 1990; Minneapolis: Fortress, 1997) 3.

[15]Ibid., 1 (Reiser's emphasis).

John Dominic Crossan's epilogue to *The Birth of Christianity*, however, shows that there is more at stake in the debates over the apocalyptic tradition in Christianity than just producing a comfortable Jesus:[16]

> I ask emphatically whether apocalypticism, be it in Judaism or in Christianity, is about divine justice or divine revenge. Justice and revenge dwell close together in the human heart. When we examine our conscience, we usually find them happily wedded and bedded together. We find it hard, therefore, not to project their amalgam onto God. When Judaism imagines apocalyptic consummation, what will happen to the pagans; and when Christianity imagines apocalyptic consummation, what will happen to the Jews? If, confronted with the blinding glory of God, all convert freely *not* to Judaism or Christianity *but* to justice and righteousness, then all is well with our religious imagination. But if we await a divine slaughter of those who are not Jews or those who are not Christians, then we are the killer children of a Killer God. It is a question, once again, of character. Is your God a God of justice or revenge?

For Crossan, the theological issue (What is the character of your God?) is inextricably linked with contemporary ethical issues (such as, What is the character of Christianity in a pluralistic world?). Thus, identifying when, how, and why apocalyptic theology entered the Christian tradition is a historical question for Crossan, because it is also a pressing ethical question for him.

It is not surprising, therefore, that the "vanishing judgment" in contemporary North American scholarship is accomplished primarily through the "historical" judgment that much of the apocalyptic material in the gospels is not authentic.[17] Reiser takes issue with the theologically invested methodology of scholars like Crossan, but in the process reveals his own theological interests. For example, he criticizes Crossan's depiction of Jesus as a "Jewish Cynic and his proclamation of the reign of God as a kind of party program. . . . Only by means of violent reinterpretations," protests Reiser, "can one present Jesus as a socially engaged politician in a modern format."[18] For Reiser, the problem with Crossan's "non-apocalyptic" Jesus, therefore, is not only that he is comfortable for contemporary religious consumption, or

---

[16]John Dominic Crossan, *The Birth of Christianity* (San Francisco: HarperSanFrancisco, 1998) 586 (Crossan's emphasis).

[17]Reiser, *Jesus and Judgment*, 3.

[18]Ibid., 4.

that he is produced with unacceptable methodologies, but that he is political and secular rather than properly apolitical and religious.

The question of Jesus' relationship to John, therefore, participates in adjudicating the larger question of Jesus' identity. Insofar as Jesus' "location" on the theological and social map of first-century Galilee and Judea can be pinpointed through a statement of his likeness to or difference from John, scholars can also locate Jesus in relationship to the theologically contested theme of God's fiery judgment. An examination of two approaches to John's speech illustrates the issues at stake in the interpretation of the beginning of Q. The first is the redactional approach; the second is the process of doctrinal classification.

A Judgmental Jesus and the Redaction of Q

The history of Q scholarship attests a long-standing interest in the relationship between the seemingly positive and ethical-oriented sayings of Jesus (such as the Inaugural sermon) and the ostensibly negative and "apocalyptic" sayings of Jesus and John (such as Q 12:39–59 and Q 3:7–9, 16–17). In 1972, Siegfried Schulz produced the first comprehensive effort to interpret Q redactionally.[19] Although his methodology is based on literary analysis, his resulting proposal accounts for these two kinds of material in Q. Schulz argued that an early layer in Q represented a Palestinian Jewish-Christian community steeped in apocalyptic fervor. As Q developed, its apocalyptic enthusiasm was hellenized and applied to the life of the church with an emphasis on universal ethical teachings. The most recent proposal for the redaction of Q represents a reversal of Schulz's literary trajectory whereby a collection of instructional sayings is expanded with material that emphasizes traditionally apocalyptic themes such as an announcement of judgment against "this generation."[20] According to this paradigm, the apocalyptic and judgmental themes are redacted into Q as a response to the rejection experienced by the Q community.

Much of the recent work on Q 3:7–9, 16–17 participates in this larger debate over the redaction of Q and the formative genre of Q, broadly construed

---

[19]Schulz, *Q*; see also Hoffmann, *Studien*.

[20]Kloppenborg, *Formation*. Several scholars have adopted (and revised) Kloppenborg's proposal. For example, William E. Arnal, *Jesus and the Village Scribes* (Minneapolis: Fortress, 2001); Mack, *Lost Gospel*; John Dominic Crossan, *The Historical Jesus: The Life of a Mediterranean Jewish Peasant* (San Francisco: HarperSanFrancisco, 1991); idem, *Birth*; Vaage, *Galilean Upstarts*; Cotter, "Prestige."

as the choice between a prophetic book and a wisdom book.[21] As discussed in chapter 1, regardless of the intentions of the scholars who propose them, these literary analyses often participate in larger and ongoing debates about the historical Jesus as prophet or sage, the *basileia* of God as at home in Jewish apocalyptic thought or Hellenistic (and/or Jewish) wisdom ideas, and the original Q community as a prophetic Jewish movement or an association of Cynic-like (Jewish) philosophers. Thus they are part of the contemporary discourse on Christian identity and how that identity might be constituted by interpretations of Jesus' identity.

A review of recent treatments of Q 3:7–9, 16–17, however, also illustrates how the contemporary interest in the relationship between Jesus and a judgmental or apocalyptic theology is negotiated through redactional interpretation. For example, interpretations based on Kloppenborg's redactional proposal create an increasing gulf between the Jesus of the first literary version of Q (referred to as Q[1]) and the judgmental Jesus and John of Q[2], the proposed redactional layer of Q. According to Kloppenborg, the addition of John's speech to the beginning of Q realigns the interpretation of Jesus in Q[1] in such a way that "John in effect stands together with Jesus (and the Q preachers) in proclaiming the coming judgment upon Israel."[22] Thus the introduction of the theme of judgment and Jesus as the "coming one" in John's speech makes it possible for Q to imagine Jesus as a preacher of apocalyptic judgment against the Galilean cities (10:13–15) or against unbelieving Israel (11:29–32). Since this is identified as a redactional process, the Jesus of Q[1] is set apart from the Jesus of Q[2] through the latter's association with John.

---

[21]The major works representing each side of the discussion are Migaku Sato, *Q und Prophetie* (WUNT 2.29; Tübingen: Mohr/Siebeck, 1988) and Kloppenborg, *Formation*. Both Sato and Kloppenborg take a diachronic approach and attempt to identify Q's original genre and the generic trajectory of its growth. Alan Kirk takes a synchronic approach (*Composition*). Kirk agrees with Kloppenborg, however, insofar as he identifies Q as entirely within the genre of wisdom instruction and interprets prophetic and apocalyptic motifs and forms as comfortably incorporated (and subsumed) into the overall framework and interests of that genre. Tuckett (*Q*) and Allison (*Jesus Tradition*) argue that genres cannot be so clearly delineated, insofar as sapiential, apocalyptic, and prophetic forms and motifs appear across Second Temple Jewish literature. They do not offer alternative genre classifications for Q. Horsley and Draper (*Whoever Hears*) reject the literary classification project and argue that Q is an oral-derived text. Their interpretation of Q as a script for the performance of popular and (antiscribal) covenant renewal enacted by the prophets John and Jesus, however, still attempts to adjudicate the classification of Q as prophetic/apocalyptic or sapiential.

[22]Kloppenborg, *Formation*, 105.

For example, Wendy Cotter argues that Jesus' association with John in Q[2] "means that Jesus' denouncement of Israel and his promise of a displacement by the Gentiles can in no way be attributed to him as personal and private notions."[23] Thus Q[2]'s Jesus is associated with John. This allows us to disassociate another "Jesus" from Q[2]'s themes of judgment. It is unclear in Cotter's statement whether the Jesus she speaks of is Q[1]'s Jesus or the historical Jesus, or whether she equates the two.

The gulf between the Jesus of Q[1] (and/or the historical Jesus) and the judgmental preaching of Q[2] widens even further when interpreters separate the historical John from the John of Q[2]. For example, William Arnal argues that because John's opening speech in Q so strongly reflects the redactional interests of Q[2], it must be a fabrication of the Q community. Arnal separates the historical John from Q's John by distancing Q's John from the John of the synoptics and Josephus: "John's preaching in Q is vituperative, polemical, and threatens a 'coming wrath' that is to be effected by an apocalyptic thresher-figure. Not one of these ideas is even alluded to in the other gospel materials or in Josephus."[24] Thus the responsibility for the apocalyptic judgment language of John's speech is transferred from Jesus to John, and then from John to the Q community.[25]

Although interpreters generally are content to leave the unwanted apocalypticism in the hands of the Q community,[26] there is one more subtle transfer

[23]Wendy J. Cotter, "Yes, I Tell You, and More than a Prophet: The Function of John in Q," in *Conflict and Invention: Literary, Rhetorical, and Social Studies on the Sayings Gospel Q* (ed. John S. Kloppenborg; Valley Forge, Pa.: Trinity, 1995) 138.

[24]William Arnal, "Redactional Fabrication and Group Legitimation: The Baptist's Preaching in Q 3:7–9, 16–17," in Kloppenborg, ed., *Conflict and Invention*, 169. See also Ron Cameron, "'What Have You Come Out To See?' Characterizations of John and Jesus in the Gospels," *Semeia* 49 (1990) 35–69; and Leif Vaage, "More Than a Prophet, and Demon-Possessed: Q and the 'Historical' John," in Kloppenborg, ed., *Conflict and Invention*, 181–202.

[25]If interpreters find Arnal's argument persuasive, this provides a different answer to the challenge of James Robinson that any theory of Q must make sense in the trajectory from John the Baptist to Matthew ("The Q Trajectory: Between John and Matthew via Jesus," in *The Future of Early Christianity: Essays in Honor of Helmut Koester* [ed. Birger A. Pearson et al.; Minneapolis: Fortress, 1991] 173–94). Robinson's own answer is that Jesus (or at least Q[1]'s Jesus) represents a "sapiential deviation" (p. 190) from an otherwise apocalyptic trajectory. Although Arnal is not so explicit, his proposal points toward a non-apocalyptic origin (for both the historical John and Jesus) followed by an increasingly apocalypticized tradition represented by Q[2].

[26]According to Uro, "the gloomy message of John" belongs to the Q community itself ("John the Baptist and the Jesus Movement: What Does Q Tell Us?," in Piper, *Gospel*, 233).

that may result from the framework within which recent redactional critics of Q are working. Following Steck and Lührmann, interpreters understand the "announcement of judgment" in Q as a rhetorical and theological response to the rejection and persecution experienced by the Q community from their fellow Jews.[27] Thus the vituperative and reproachful critique of "this generation" is provoked by the negative response of the majority of Jews to the Q people's *basileia* preaching. The causal relationship is only implied: if they had not been rejected and persecuted, they might never have said or thought such things. Because Lührmann and others interpret "this generation" as "all of Israel"[28] and as beginning to mark a group boundary for the Q community, the responsibility for inciting the apocalyptic judgment finally lands in the lap of a collective Jewish "other" that stands outside of the identity group being constituted by the Q community.[29] Given the persistence of Christian anti-Judaism, many of these scholars are committed to naming and resisting interpretations that deny or obfuscate Jesus' Jewishness or the Jewish origins of early Christianity.[30] However, the ways in which interpretive frameworks replicate dichotomies between Jesus and Jesus' followers and a Jewish "other" must also be evaluated routinely.

It is by no means the case, however, that the opposite argument—one that equates the historical Jesus with the judgmental and apocalyptic Jesus

---

For Mack, the apocalyptic mythmaking apparent in Q[2] lands the responsibility for the content of that mythmaking in the laps of contemporary Christians: "Q's challenge to Christians is therefore an invitation to join the human race, to see ourselves with our myths on our hands and mythmaking as our task" (*Lost Gospel*, 255).

[27]For example, Arnal ("Redactional Fabrication," 176) suggests that the language of apocalyptic judgment was produced because the Q people were "embattled" and "marginal."

[28]Tuckett, Horsley, and Draper reject the interpretation of "this generation" as "all of Israel" and prefer to identify John's audience in 3:7–9, 16–17 as the "unresponsive in Israel" (Tuckett, *Q*, 115) or the Jerusalem elite (Horsley and Draper, *Whoever Hears*, 254). Both interpretations, however, maintain an insider/outsider distinction between the Q community and the targets of the judgment preaching. This approach does not leave room for judgment language used for various (even competing) rhetorical purposes. Thus, judgment language continues to function as insider/outsider language similar to its function for Kloppenborg: "While ostensibly directed at the 'out-group,' these polemical and threatening materials function in fact to strengthen the identity of the 'in-group'" (*Formation*, 168).

[29]Wendy Cotter's schematization of Q 3:7–9 illustrates the strong lines drawn between the Q community and "Israel" by this redactional model: Q 3:7bc represents "the perversity of Israel"; 3:8a represents the "sterility of Israel"; 3:8bc represents the "presumption of Israel"; 3:16, 17 represent the "coming agent of judgment"; and 3:8 also represents the "displacement of Israel" (Cotter, "Yes," 137). According to Cotter, each of these themes echoes throughout Q[2].

[30]Kloppenborg Verbin, *Excavating Q*, 435.

of Q—is immune to the tendency to transfer vituperative apocalyptic judgment language onto a collective Jewish "other." Marius Reiser argues that most of the judgment sayings attributed to Jesus in Q and the synoptics are authentic. In his conclusion, however, the responsibility for the theologically objectionable aspects of the apocalyptic tradition is transferred elsewhere:

> The depictions of judgment in early Jewish writings are quite often dictated by an unconcealed hatred and thirst for revenge: the hatred of the pious against the godless, of the righteous against the wicked, of the tortured against their torturers. . . . Nothing of this can be found in the preaching of Jesus. His words about judgment are not inspired by hatred of sinners, but solely by love for them. In fact, he has come especially to call them to the eschatological banquet. Of course, a rejection of the invitation would mean nothing other than self-imposed judgment.[31]

Not only does judgment-as-revenge belong to "early Jewish writings," but the responsibility for the judgment fire brought down on people by Jesus is transferred to Jesus' stubborn audience as well. Crossan's theological evaluation of this kind of stance as inherently anti-Jewish is important to reiterate here: "Yahweh is a God not of revenge but of justice. I reject absolutely the ancient libel that the God of the Old Testament or of Judaism is a God of anger and vengeance while the God of the New Testament or of Christianity is a God of love and mercy."[32] Are there other ways to evaluate and classify judgment language? Are origin and ownership the only things worth examining in Q's announcement of judgment? We will return to this question below.

John's Doctrine of the Future

In contrast to the redactional tendency to distance the historical Jesus or Q^1's Jesus from the judgmental thinking of John's preaching, some scholars establish continuity between Jesus and John by classifying the preaching of both figures as "eschatological" or "apocalyptic." This approach similarly results in interpreting John's speech primarily in terms of its role in introducing Q's Jesus rather than its role in centering the urgent significance of Q's communal vision.

---

[31]Reiser, *Jesus and Judgment*, 321–22.
[32]Crossan, *Birth*, 586.

"The coming wrath" (τῆς μελλούσης ὀργῆς) in Q 3:7b is Q's first reference to something that in the world of the text has not yet occurred. The
most common conclusion made from the observation of the futurity of John's
speech is to classify it as signaling a Jewish apocalyptic or eschatological
worldview. For example, Tuckett suggests that "the basic thrust of John's
preaching relates to a belief in an imminent event which may be catastrophic
for those who are unprepared. . . . Clearly one is in the thought world of Jewish eschatology, with a vivid expectation of an imminent End culminating in
some kind of judging process."[33]

Clearly this text makes sense in the thought world of Israelite tradition
and its language of God's judgment against the enemies of Israel and/or the
unrighteous of Israel. Identifying John's speech as "Jewish eschatology,"
however, serves to locate John's preaching (and often John himself[34]) on the
theological and social landscape of first-century Galilee and Judea. Implicit
in Tuckett's descriptive terms are their counterterms: John is Jewish (not
Hellenistic), eschatological (not sapiential), and believing (not secular). By
asserting Jesus' continuity with John, interpreters can assert certain things
about the identity of Jesus in Q and resist the alternative characterizations
of Jesus presented by other scholars. As with the redactional approach, we
need to be aware of what questions we are asking about the text and why
we are asking them.

Applying the doctrinal category "Jewish apocalyptic" or "Jewish eschatology" to John's speech also results in overlooking the rhetorical function of
urgent language about imminent judgment in Q. These features are too often
taken as markers of a larger theological system before they are understood
as part of the narrative exigencies and rhetorical strategies of the text itself.[35]

[33]Tuckett, *Q*, 115.

[34]Arnal rightly notes that much of Q 3:7–9, 16–17 is taken prima facie as a reminiscence of
the preaching of the historical John ("Redactional Fabrication," 166). Whether Q 3:7–9, 16–17
reflects authentic John the Baptist tradition is not a question considered in this book.

[35]George Nickelsburg points to this problem in his review of "Early Jewish Eschatology"
in the *Anchor Bible Dictionary*: "This term [eschatology] and its traditional use have been
misleading, however, because they have often been governed by theological agendas that have
attempted to extrapolate from the texts a unified and systematic doctrine about the 'end of the
world' or one's state and fate at the end of one's life. Also problematic is the implication that
all the texts designated as 'eschatological' envision a decisive end to the present order and the
beginning of a totally new order. Given the variety that contemporary scholarship has begun to
discover in the sources, it is appropriate to hear the texts, each on its own terms, and to develop
categories that reflect the differences and points of continuity. . . . This task, which awaits
doing, is substantial" (*ABD* 2 [1992] 580).

Tracing the motif of God's wrath in early Christian and Jewish literature shows that the futurity of the judgment enacted by God's wrath varies with context. For example, in 1 Thessalonians God's wrath is "to come" in 1:10 and has come (upon "the Jews") in 2:16. Whether or not the anti-Jewish polemic in 2:14–16 is an interpolation, it still illustrates that the temporal element of the motif shifts with context.[36] In Sirach the wrath of God is both a future event that is called down on Israel's adversaries[37] and the time of judgment upon Noah's generation.[38] Both temporal assertions make sense in the context of their usage.[39] The rhetorical force of the judgment motifs modulates greatly according to context. Below we will explore how John's speech uses the notion of impending judgment as an incentive for its instructions in Q. From this view, both the futurity and the imminence of that judgment are rhetorical necessities.

When examining the effects of doctrinal classification of John's speech, it is also important to note that this approach shifts the emphasis away from the ways in which the motif of judgment gives rhetorical muscle to John's teachings and toward what doctrine or worldview is indicated by such a motif. This effectively de-centers John's rhetoric and centers John's doctrine or "beliefs" as the chief interest of our interpretation. Once again, this serves the ongoing debates about Christian origins, Q, and an apocalyptic worldview or theology, in that it locates John on the theological spectrum

[36]This argument applies if Paul wrote 2:14–16, in that Paul himself shifts the timing of the "wrath" to the present in order to critique the way that the Jews in Judea treat the Jesus followers in Judea. It also works if 2:14–16 is an interpolation, in that the fall of the Temple in 70 C.E. was interpreted by the Christian interpolator as God's judgment on the Jews, thus the wrath has come.

[37]In a prayer for Israel's deliverance from its enemies, the author calls for God to "Rouse your anger and pour out your wrath; destroy the adversary and wipe out the enemy. Hasten the day, and remember the appointed time" (Sir 36:8–10).

[38]In the hymn to honor the famous men of Israel, Sirach states that "Noah was found perfect and righteous; in the time of wrath he kept the race alive; therefore a remnant was left on the earth when the flood came" (Sir 44:17).

[39]The fact that the temporal characterization of God's wrath shifts with its usage is indirectly illustrated by the *TDNT*'s distinction between the "historical" and "eschatological" wrath of God in the article on "ὀργή." Throughout the discussion of the Hebrew Bible, Septuagint, and "later Judaism," the authors make this distinction between historical and eschatological wrath, illustrating precisely that all tenses, not only future, are connected with God's wrath ("ὀργή," *TDNT* 5:382–447; see especially 404–5 and 415). Sirach provides the best example of such variation in that it speaks of God's wrath in the past (44:17) and the day of wrath in the future of the individual (i.e., death; 18:24) and creation (39:28).

of apocalyptic vs. sapiential (or judgmental vs. non-judgmental). Insofar as John's eschatological or apocalyptic worldview is compared to Jesus' worldview, such a categorization of John also serves to locate Q's Jesus in relation to those same dichotomies.[40]

Both the redactional and the doctrinal approaches to John's speech show great interest in Jesus' relationship to the judgmental language in Q. Since contemporary discourse equates Jesus' identity with Christian identity, this focus situates contemporary Christians in relation to theological thinking about judgment. In our pluralistic context, this is an important ethical question and it is natural that biblical scholarship would reflect similar interests. The question is not whether we should inquire about judgmental language in the tradition but rather what the effect is of focusing primarily on Jesus. One result is the tendency to interpret Q as similarly interested in explicating Jesus' identity in relationship to judgment. This approach results in using genre taxonomies and doctrinal categories to understand the origins of judgment language in Q. But, as we asked above, are there other ways to evaluate and classify judgment language in Q?

Although he continues to use historical stratigraphy, Crossan has proposed his own criteria for theological evaluation of judgment language:

> When Judaism imagines apocalyptic consummation, what will happen to the pagans; and when Christianity imagines apocalyptic consummation, what will happen to the Jews? If, confronted with the blinding glory of God, all convert freely *not* to Judaism or Christianity *but* to justice and righteousness, then all is well with our religious imagination.[41]

In other words, if envisioning judgment promotes the superlative value of "justice and righteousness" rather than the superlative value of one's group identity, then "all is right with our religious imaginations." This approach creates more options for reading Q and for evaluating how judgment language can function in our own theological imagination. In what follows, I attempt to classify the judgment motifs of John's opening

---

[40]This works both in terms of a proposed contrast between John's apocalyptic outlook and Jesus' wisdom outlook in Q (Crossan, *Historical Jesus* [for historical Jesus]; Kloppenborg, *Formation* [for Q]) or in terms of a continuity between John and Jesus' apocalyptic outlook (Bart Ehrman, *Jesus: Apocalyptic Prophet of the New Millennium* [Oxford: Oxford University Press, 1999] [for historical Jesus]; Tuckett, *Q* [for Q]).

[41]Crossan, *Birth*, 586 (Crossan's emphasis).

speech *not* according to origin or doctrine but according to the *work* they do in relationship to the communal vision, that is, their rhetorical function vis-à-vis the *basileia* of God. This approach sets aside our tendency to focus on the relationship between Jesus and John, and thus on the relationship between Jesus and judgmental theology. It attempts to open up new approaches to Q by focusing on the work that such language does in the ongoing struggle to envision a just world.

Invoking Q's Symbolic World: Q 3:7–9, 16–17

Despite its brevity, there are extensive intratextual connections between John's opening speech and the rest of Q.[42] The extent of these connections has led William Arnal to comment that John's words are "practically a *summary*" of Q's message.[43] John's speech evokes two traditions from Israel's epic history: the destruction of Sodom, and the figure of the prophet Elijah. Neither of these traditions is referred to directly; they can only be inferred from the vocabulary of the unit and the appearance of these traditions elsewhere in Q. The echoes of the Sodom story and the allusions to the figure of the prophet Elijah in John's opening speech correspond well with the two major functions of John's judgment speech at the beginning of Q: (1) the speech serves a parenetic function to add the threat of judgment to the community-oriented teachings of Q; and (2) the speech serves to introduce the "coming one"—later identified in Q with Jesus—who will somehow participate in God's judgment. After discussing how Q 3:7–9, 16–17 invokes these two epic traditions, we will examine these two rhetorical interests in the speech.

John Kloppenborg presents a synchronic exploration of the way that John's speech in 3:7–9, 16–17 functions at the beginning of Q to define its "narrative world."[44] Kloppenborg argues that the minor agreement between Matt 3:5 and Luke 3:3 concerning John's location in "all the region of the Jordan" ($\pi\hat{\alpha}\sigma\alpha[\nu]$ $\dot{\eta}$ $[\tau\dot{\eta}\nu]$ $\pi\epsilon\rho\acute{\iota}\chi\omega\rho o[\nu]$ $\tauo\hat{\nu}$ $\text{'Io}\rho\delta\acute{\alpha}\nuo\nu$) shows a dependence on Q for the introduction to John's speech. This phrase appears repeatedly

---

[42]See also Uro, "John," 239–43.

[43]Arnal, "Redactional Fabrication," 172 (Arnal's emphasis).

[44]Kloppenborg, "City and Wasteland," 145. Kloppenborg defines "narrative world" as the "spatial and temporal world within which the sayings are framed and heard" (146).

in the Septuagint, most notably several times in the story of Lot in Genesis.[45] Kloppenborg adds that "John's speech itself contains several images which evoke the story of Lot: the images of flight (3:7b: φευγεῖν, 'flee') and fiery destruction (Q 3:9, 16d, 17) are for obvious reasons associated with Lot (Gen 19:20, 24; Wis 10:6; 3 Macc 2:5; 1 Clem 11.1)."[46] Although the theme of flight and fiery destruction are fairly common in Israelite prophetic literature,[47] it is striking that the story of Lot and the destruction of Sodom appears explicitly in two other places in Q (10:12 and 17:28–30). A final argument in favor of the allusions to the story of Lot in 3:7–9, 16–17 is the emphasis on the claim to be children of Abraham. According to Kloppenborg, Jewish and Christian traditions have several examples of interpreters who attempt to expand the parenetic function of the story by emphasizing Lot's righteousness. But in the Genesis story, Lot seems to escape Sodom simply because he is a kinsman of Abraham. We will return to the function of these allusions to the Lot story in the next section.

The other Israelite tradition that is alluded to at the beginning of Q concerns the figure of the prophet Elijah. In Mark 9:13, when Jesus is asked by his disciples about the coming of Elijah, he answers that "Elijah must come first to restore all things. . . . But I tell you that Elijah has come, and they did to him whatever they pleased, as it is written of him." Matthew redacts Mark by adding: "Then the disciples understood that he was speaking to them of John the Baptist" (Matt 17:12–13).[48] When Matthew redacts Q 16:16 (which Matthew places in the context of Q 7:24–28), he adds the following: "And if you are willing to accept it, he is Elijah who is to come (μέλλων ἔρχεσθαι).[49] Matthew's deliberate effort to establish that John was Elijah *redivivus* stands in contrast with the Baptist's own words in the Gospel of John: "And they

---

[45]Full phrase: Gen 13:10–11 (twice) and in the retelling of the Sodom story in Jub 16.5 and 1 Clem 11.1; abbreviations (πᾶσα ἡ περίχωρος or περίοικος): Gen 19:17, 25, 28, and 29. See Kloppenborg, "City and Wasteland," 151. See also C. C. McCowan, "The Scene of John's Ministry and Its Relation to the Purpose and Outcome of his Mission," *JBL* 59 (1940) 113–31.

[46]Kloppenborg, "City and Wasteland," 151.

[47]Fleddermann, "Beginning," 158.

[48]Luke omits the Markan pericope. For a discussion of the Elijah traditions in Luke, see Robert J. Miller, "Elijah, John, and Jesus in the Gospel of Luke," *NTS* 34 (1988) 611–22. Miller suggests that Luke omits this part of Mark because while he is willing to associate John with Elijah (see 1:17; 1:76), he is unwilling to give him the role of restorer of all things spoken of in Mark 9:12. Luke saves this role for the ascended Jesus (Acts 3:21).

[49]Q has just quoted Malachi 3:1 in Q 7:27; so, Matthew is making explicit what Q only infers.

asked him, 'What then? Are you Elijah?' He said, 'I am not'" (John 1:21). These contrasting views attest to a lively debate in early Christianity over the interpretation of John in relationship to the prophet Elijah.

Although Matthew explicitly interprets John as Elijah, Q's route from John to Elijah is more circuitous. Q never directly mentions Elijah or any of the stories from his career recorded from 1 Kings 17 to 2 Kings 2, but arrives at Elijah via the book of the prophet Malachi. As discussed in chapter 2, Jesus' saying about John in Q 7:27 is an amalgamation of Mal 3:1 and Exod 23:20: "This is the one about whom it has been written: 'Look, I am sending my messenger ahead of you, who will prepare your way in front of you.'" Mal 3:21–23 LXX makes the connection between the messenger in Malachi and Elijah: "And behold, I will send to you Elijah the Tishbite before the great and terrible day of the Lord comes. He will turn the hearts of parents to their children and the hearts of children to their parents, so that I will not come and strike the land with a curse."[50] The not quoted portion of Mal 3:1–2a introduces this messenger as one who is coming before God's coming: "Behold, I send my messenger, and he will look upon the way before my face, and the Lord, whom you seek, will come suddenly into his temple. And the messenger of the covenant, whom you desire—Look, he is coming (ἔρχεται), says the Lord almighty. But who can endure the day of his entering, and who can stand when he appears?" Thus despite the question of John's disciples about whether Jesus is the "coming one," Q 7:27 implicitly defines John as one who is "coming" like Elijah before God's coming.

But it is in Q 3:16 that John first speaks of the "coming one." Indeed, when the rest of Malachi 3 is considered, several parallels to the whole of John's preaching in 3:7–9, 16–17 become apparent.[51] In Mal 3:2b–3, the messenger who is coming before the Lord comes in judgment (ἐν κρίσει; Mal 3:5) is "like a refiner's fire (πῦρ) and like a fuller's soap" that will purify the temple priests "until they present offerings to Yahweh in righteousness." Sir 48:1 refers to Elijah as "a prophet like fire (πῦρ), and his word burned like a torch." Q scholars have long pointed out that πῦρ is one of the catchwords that holds John's speech together (3:9, 16, and 17).

---

[50]These are the last verses in the Christian Old Testament canon. In the process of canonization, the minor prophets were moved to the end and thus Malachi was positioned as the last word before the beginning of the gospels.

[51]See Jeffrey A. Trumbower, "The Role of Malachi in the Career of John the Baptist," JSNTSup 104 (1994) 28–41, esp. 34–36.

The image of burning occurs again in Mal 3:19–20a, but here in reference to the fire of judgment that burns up the straw[52] after winnowing and the roots and branches of trees:

> See, the day is coming, burning like an oven, when all the arrogant and all evildoers will be stubble (καλάμη); the day that comes (ἡ ἡμέρα ἡ ἐρχομένη) shall burn them up, says the Lord of hosts, so that it will leave them neither root (ῥίζα) nor branch (κλῆμα). But for you who revere my name the sun of righteousness shall rise, with healing in its wings.

The vocabulary is not exact, but the similarity to the imagery in Q 3:9 and 3:16–17 is unmistakable.[53]

There is one further link between the Israelite Elijah tradition and Q 3:7–9, 16–17. Sirach's summary of Elijah's career partially depends upon Mal 3: 22–23 LXX. After mentioning Elijah's being taken up into heaven in 48:9, Sirach goes on to say: "At the appointed time, it is written, you are destined to calm the wrath (ὀργὴν) of God before it breaks out in fury, to turn the hearts of parents to their children, and to restore the tribes of Jacob."[54] In Q 3:7, John asks his audience, "Who warned you to flee the coming wrath (ὀργῆς)?" Both Mal 3:23 and Sir 48:10 state that Elijah's role is to avert the coming wrath, not to herald it. The same is the case for John's preaching. If the listeners heed John's warning and bear fruit worthy of repentance, then they shall be among the trees that remain standing or the wheat that is gathered into the granary. Indeed, the allusions to the Lot narrative and the figure of Elijah are instructive. Both contain language about the wrath of God bringing judgment and destruction, but both also speak of such wrath being avoided (by Lot; Gen 19:29; Wis 10:6; Q 17:28–29) or averted (by the coming Elijah; Mal 3:24; Sir 48:10). If John's speech functions as an envisioning (or warning) of judgment rather than an "apocalyptic announcement of judgment," then the rhetorical goals of the speech as urgent parenetic exhortation begin to come into view.[55]

---

[52]Reiser (*Jesus and Judgment*, 176–77) points out that the chaff blows away in the wind. It is the remaining stubble or straw that is burned by fire.

[53]Trumbower rightly points out that although similar imagery appears throughout the prophetic literature, such as in Isa 5:24 and 33:10–12, "only Malachi combines this imagery with talk of a 'Coming One' and with reference to Elijah" ("Role of Malachi," 36).

[54]This role as restorer is alluded to in Mark 9. The Elijah cycle in 1 Kings makes no mention of his role as restorer or messenger of the covenant who comes before judgment.

[55]Steve Mason also argues that interest in the comparison of John and Jesus overshadows

Bear Fruit Worthy of Repentance: Q 3:7–9

John's negative tone, futuristic claims, and fiery images often preoccupy interpreters and result in a description of John as "the gloomiest preacher of repentance within Judaism."[56] The threat of an imminent and disastrous "coming wrath" in John's opening speech, however, is neither a prediction[57] nor a condemnation, but an exhortation.[58] The first part of John's speech (3:7–9) can be mapped as a coherent unit[59] that urges the inscribed audience to "bear good fruit":

3:7b: Brood of Vipers	(Charge or Accusation)
3:7b: Who warned you to flee the coming wrath?	(Question)
3:8: Therefore,[60] bear fruit worthy of repentance	(Command)
And do not presume to say	(Command)
We have Abraham as father	(Audience's claim)
For I say to you that God can raise up Children for Abraham from these rocks	(John's counter claim)
3:9: The ax already lies at the root of the trees	(Urgency of Message)
So every tree not bearing healthy fruit is to be chopped down and thrown into the fire.	(Consequences of Not Heeding)
(Therefore, bear fruit worthy of repentance)	(Implicit conclusion)

Themes of judgment surround the extremely brief characterization of John's teaching in 3:8, which outlines the expectations for averting the fiery fate

---

John's role as a preacher with his own message ("Fire, Water and Spirit: John the Baptist and the Tyranny of Canon," *Studies in Religion* 21 [1992] 175).

[56]Cited from Becker (*Johannes der Täufer und Jesus von Nazareth* [BibS(N) 63; Neukirchen-Vluyn: 1972] 25) in Uro, "John," 231–55, at 255.

[57]"The point of the threat of what is to come is not to state what is about to happen anyway; it is to warn people of what will happen *if* they do not change their ways" (Tuckett, *Q*, 123, Tuckett's emphasis).

[58]Sato concludes that despite its prophetic forms and content, Q 3:7–9, 16–17 has an admonitory function ("Wisdom Statements in the Sphere of Prophecy," in Piper, *Gospel*, 144–45).

[59]Kirk (*Composition*, 6–7) suggests the following structure on the basis of a *Scheltwort* or scolding word: "(1) opening with an arresting, indignant, reproach-filled rhetorical question (sometimes expressed ironically or sarcastically), followed by (2) a critical description of the addressee's fault and, occasionally, (3) a description of unpleasant consequences attendant upon the bad behavior." The second element of the *Scheltwort* is represented in 3:7–9 by the double admonition of 3:8 (p. 7).

[60]This οὖν probably has an allative force. "Thus the implied answer to the question may

of 3:7 and 9. The urgency of the threat of judgment suggests that in light
of impending judgment, it is John's teachings, and not his threats, that
are rhetorically constructed as vital—so vital that ignoring them is catastrophic.[61] As Fleddermann notes, "John threatens imminent destruction.
. . . But his threat is also conditional. The ax threatens only the trees that
do not produce fruit. John develops the command of the preceding saying
[3:8] by setting an alternative before his audience—either produce fruit
or be thrown into the fire."[62]

The rhetorical force of the opening of John's speech in 3:7 depends on
both the inscribed audience of the preaching and the audience of Q understanding the shorthand the "coming wrath." Standing alone this phrase tells
us almost nothing. It begs several questions: Whose wrath? When is it coming? What will it look like? Why must one flee it? How does one flee it?
Since the inscribed audience has been warned to flee it, the "coming wrath"
is presumably undesirable. It is also avoidable. Instructions for avoiding the
"coming wrath" follow in Q 3:8a: "Therefore, bear fruit worthy of repentance
and do not presume to say to yourselves, 'We have Abraham as our father.'"
The structure of the speech—as it moves from query to instruction to warning—links the "coming wrath" to the ax that will cut down ill-producing trees
in 3:9. Thus, although the "coming wrath" does not appear again in Q,[63] its
content—at least in this context—is supplied by the metaphor of the ax that
chops down trees not bearing healthy fruit. This is the wrath to be avoided
by "bearing fruit worthy of repentance."

The reference to Abraham suggests a link to the symbolic world of Israelite
tradition.[64] In that context, the "coming wrath" is Yahweh's wrath that enacts

---

be '*I* warned you to flee; *therefore* . . . take what I say seriously and produce fruit worthy of
repentance'" (Tuckett, *Q*, 113).

[61]The dominance of the image of John as a "preacher of apocalyptic doom" to the exclusion
of his teachings is implicitly recognized by Joan Taylor (*The Immerser: John the Baptist within
Second Temple Judaism* [Grand Rapids: Eerdmans, 1997] 101–2) when she intentionally "un-
derplays" that apocalyptic image in her chapter on John's teachings in order to allow John's
ethical teachings to come into view.

[62]Fleddermann, "Beginning," 158.

[63]It does not appear anywhere else in the New Testament in this formulation. Paul speaks of
the "coming wrath" in 1 Thessalonians 1:10 as τῆς ὀργῆς τῆς ἐρχομένης. Here Paul commends
his readers who "turned to God from idols, to serve a living and true God, and to wait for his
Son from heaven, whom he raised from the dead, Jesus who delivers us from the wrath to
come" (1 Thess 1:9b–10).

[64]Another link is the imagery of harvest, which is frequently used to describe the gathering
of the righteous and the destruction of the unrighteous (Gentiles or in Israel) in the Hebrew

judgment upon humans.[65] Insofar as this wrath is "coming" (μελλούσης),[66] it is in the future of the world of the text. In the ax metaphor, that future is very, very near. The ax is already at work ("the ax already [ἤδη] lies at the root of the trees"). The text heightens this sense of urgency and crisis by using the present tense verbs ἐκκόπτεται and βάλλεται.[67] In the metaphor of the threshing floor in 3:17, the verbs shift to the future tense (διακαθαριεῖ, συνάξει, κατακαύσει), but the winnowing shovel is already *in the hand* of the "coming one" from 3:16.[68] The metaphors of John's speech heighten the threat of God's coming wrath by emphasizing its nearness. The rhetorical effect of this urgent threat is to cast the present time of the inscribed audience (and the audience of Q) as a crucial time. Now is the time to bear good fruit—or else you'll bear no fruit.

If the imminent threat of judgment serves to center John's teaching, then what is the content of that teaching? There is precious little to work with in 3:8. Two imperatives mark the commands of the speech: bear [fruit], and do not presume to say (ποιήσατε and δόξητε λέγειν). The movement from positive command to negative command logically links the two admonitions: If you bear good fruit, you will not presume to say [an excuse]; and if you say [an excuse], you will not bear good fruit. "For I tell you" (λέγω γὰρ ὑμῖν)[69]

Bible and the Pseudepigrapha. The text draws on agricultural images for its depiction of the judgment that will surely come to those who do not heed John's warning. Q 3:9 and 17 construct John's audience as trees and as winnowed wheat and straw. Q 3:7 promises that the ax at the root of the trees will only strike down for burning those trees that bear bad fruit. The winnowing shovel in 3:17 will gather in the wheat and throw the stubble into an everlasting fire. Q returns to the imagery of good and bad fruit-bearing trees in Jesus' inaugural sermon in Q 6:43–44. When Jesus sends out his disciples to go from town to town in Q 10:2–10, he speaks of them as workers at harvest time. For wheat and stubble imagery in the context of judgment, see Isa 17:13; 29:5; 33:11; 41:15; Jer 13:24; Dan 2:35; Hos 13:3; Mic 4:12; and Zeph 2:2 (Horsley and Draper, *Whoever Hears*, 253).

[65]Of course, ὀργή is not the sole property of the God of Israel. In its discussion of ὀργή in the Greek world, the *TDNT* quips that "wrathful deities are so vividly present to the consciousness of all peoples that attempts have been made to explain every cult as an effort to anticipate or soften the anger of the gods" ("ὀργή," *TDNT* 5:385).

[66]The participle of μέλλω is used in the NT as an absolute meaning "future" or "to come" (BAG, s.v. "μέλλω").

[67]Reiser, *Jesus and Judgment*, 175.

[68]The future tense of the verbs in 3:17 may correspond to the future tense of βαπτίσει in 3:16. In the symbolic world of Q, the identity of the "coming one" has yet to be revealed as Jesus (13:35) and his coming is at a time people do not know (12:40).

[69]This formulaic introduction to sayings is very common in Q, appearing at least 31 times

introduces John's refutation of the excuse and thus links the two sayings about Abraham (δόξητε λέγειν and λέγω γὰρ ὑμῖν).

The sum total of John's teachings in 3:8 usually is taken as the contrast between the claim to have Abraham as a father and John's refutation of that claim. This emphasis, however, misses the first pairing of commands: bear fruit and do not tell yourselves [an excuse]. Indeed the theme of fruit-bearing trees (in 3:8a and 3:9) brackets the exchange between those who would claim Abraham as their father and John's counterclaim that God can raise children for Abraham from the rocks. The command to bear fruit constructs the audience of the speech as the trees that will be spared or chopped down and burned by the ax in 3:9. The qualifying phrase "worthy of repentance" prescribes the kind of fruit that the trees and the audience should bear, that is, fruits that are equal in value to or fitting of repentance (or "a change of mind or heart"[70]). Although one can assume that the audience understood the range of meaning of the metaphorical instruction, the text does not explicate what precisely constitutes "good fruit" except that it should be worthy of repentance. Although the reference to claiming Abrahamic ancestry is of great interest to interpreters inquiring after the relationship between the Q community and other Jews, the structure of Q 3:8–9 suggests that exhorting a Jewish audience to bear fruit worthy of repentance is the primary rhetorical interest of the text.

Bearing Good Fruit Throughout Q

John's urgent command to bear good fruit stands at the beginning of Q as a summative and urgent call to practice the teachings that will follow in Q.[71] Indeed, Q provides a clue for interpreting John's command this way when it returns to the image of good and bad fruit at the end of Jesus' inaugural sermon in 6:43–44: "No healthy tree bears rotten fruit, nor [[on

---

(see the concordance to Q in Kloppenborg, *Q Parallels*, or Robinson, *Critical Edition*). Jesus is the speaker in all cases except 3:8.

[70]For an extensive discussion of repentance in Luke-Acts as requiring a change of heart and mind, see Guy D. Nave, Jr., *The Role and Function of Repentance within the Narrative of Luke-Acts* (Atlanta: Society of Biblical Literature, 2002). This interpretation of repentance also makes sense of its usage in Q.

[71]Kirk makes a similar argument but by means of a comparison with ancient wisdom genres and conventions. "John's speech replicates the widely attested instructional convention of the scolding, angry instructor who assumes a threatening demeanor in order to arrest the

the other hand]] does a decayed tree bear healthy fruit. For from the fruit the tree is known. Are figs picked from thorns, or grapes from thistles?"[72] The sermon concludes with a rhetorical question ("Why do you call me, 'Master, Master,' and do not do what I say?"; 6:46) and then a comparison between the fate of those who hear Jesus' words and act on them, and those who do not act on them (the house built on bedrock and the one built on sand; 6:47–49). The conclusion of the sermon calls for a correspondence between one's claims (to be good, to hear) and the product or practice of one's claims (good fruit, acting on the words). John's admonition to "bear fruit worthy of repentance" displays a similar interest in the correspondence between one's claims (to have repented) and the product or practice of one's claims (repentance-worthy fruits). In addition, both Jesus' and John's teachings are followed by a statement of the consequences of a lack of correspondence between word and deed (6:47–49; 3:9).

A similar parenetic interest in promoting the community-oriented teachings of Q appears in the sayings traditionally interpreted as being primarily concerned with announcing the impending final judgment in Q. For example, Q 12:40 warns the audience of Q to be ready because the hour of the coming of the son of humanity is not known. In the parable of the faithful and wise slave (12:42–46) that follows, however, it is the slave's treatment of his or her fellow slaves that dictates the reward or punishment when the master returns. The faithful slave gives the others their food on time, while the unfaithful slave beats the other slaves, hoards the food and wine, and consumes it all at once (with other drunkards). The faithful slave of the parable enacts the ideal of the *basileia* of God evoked elsewhere in Q: the hungry eat their fill (6:21), all have their daily bread (11:3), and no one has to worry about what he or she will eat (12:29–31). The importance of such faithful practices is underlined rhetorically by the unpredictable coming of the son of humanity, but the interests of the text do not shift to explicating the coming of the son of humanity nor does the judgment of the slaves depend on their recognition of the son of humanity.

Similarly, the criticism of the audience for not being able to interpret the times in 12:54–55 temporally intensifies the saying about settling accounts

---

attention of complacent, wayward students, disabuse them of their delusions, and motivate them to attach themselves to a wise instructor able to impart the wisdom requisite for a successful blessed life" ("Upbraiding Wisdom," *NovT* 40 [1998] 6).

[72]This saying is followed by a similar comparison between the good brought forth by good treasure and the evil brought forth by evil treasure (6:45).

with one's opponents before arriving at court. Although the short parable does not specify the problem, the image of resolving conflicts outside of court evokes the inaugural sermon, which directs the audience to love one's enemies (6:27), to renounce one's rights (6:29),[73] to lend without repayment (6:30; and 11:4), and to be merciful and forgiving (6:36; and 17:3). Likewise in the elaboration on the saying about the narrow door (13:24–29), those who stand at the door and knock claim to have been companions of the Master. They have eaten with him and heard him teach in the streets. But the Master says that he does not know them. He says, "Get away from me, [[<<you>> who]] do lawlessness!" This contrast between hearing the teachings and not practicing them evokes the end of the inaugural sermon, where Jesus warns his audience that hearing his teachings (and calling him κύριε, as do those who stand at the door in 13:25) is not enough. One must practice the teachings to avoid devastation (6:46–49) and to gain access to the banquet with the patriarchs (13:28–29). In the parable of the great banquet (14:16–26), it is the invitees who decline due to their business with daily life. The result is an elevation in status for all those "in the streets" who received the invitation instead.

Redacting the Judgment

Matthew and Luke's redaction of Q also confirms the parenetic purpose of John's speech about impending judgment. Matthew, well-known for presenting Jesus as a teacher and interpreter of the Law, imports elements of John's speech in Q into Jesus' speeches at three different points. John's warning that trees not bearing good fruit will be thrown into the fire (3:9b) is repeated verbatim by Jesus after his saying about good and bad fruit in the inaugural sermon (Q 6:43; Matt 7:18–19). John's accusation (γεννήματα ἐχιδνῶν) and rhetorical question are also repeated in Jesus' criticism of the scribes and Pharisees (Matt 23:33) and in his teaching about blasphemy against the holy spirit (Matt 12:34). All three Matthean redactions occur in the context of teachings that concern the continuity between speech and action. It is important to note, however, that all three redactions also occur in contexts where the polemic has been heightened in comparison with Q. For example, the speech about blasphemy has been moved to follow

---

[73]Matthew's version of Q 6:29b even suggests a court scene for the saying about giving your coat to the one who takes you to court to take your shirt; see Matt 5:40. The IQP prefers the Matthean reading and places it in double brackets since it is singly attested.

directly on the Beelzebul pericope making the Pharisees (Matt 12:24) who accuse Jesus of casting out demons by the power of Beelzebul guilty of the unforgivable sin of blasphemy against the holy spirit (Matt 12:32).[74] These redactions show that Matthew interprets John's speech as calling for continuity between speech and action. They also show that judgment language lends itself well to divisive polemic. In all three cases, however, Matthew has to make additional redactional moves to deploy John's speech (in the mouth of Jesus) as internecine critique.

Even as Matthew does not hesitate to attribute John's words (from Q) to Jesus, so Luke attributes teachings to John that make an explicit link between John's preaching and Jesus' inaugural sermon. Luke 3:10–14 places the following pericope directly after the threat of ill-bearing trees being thrown into the fire:

> And the crowds asked him, "What then shall we do?" And he answered them, "He who has two tunics (χιτῶνας), let him share with him who has none; and let the one who has food do likewise." Tax collectors also came to be baptized and said to him, "Teacher, what shall we do?" And he said to them, "Collect no more than you are entitled." Soldiers also asked him, "And we, what shall we do?" And he said to them, "Do not extort or falsely denounce anyone, and be content with your wages."

In Luke's narrative, John's threat of judgment results in the crowd seeking further instruction, confirming the importance of John's exhortation to "bear fruit worthy of repentance."[75] The repetition of the question "What shall we do?" strengthens the connection between John's admonition to bear good fruit and Jesus' sayings about good and bad fruit in the inaugural sermon by emphasizing the importance of right practice.[76] Luke 3:11 is

---

[74]This is accomplished by changing the "finger of God" in Q 11:20 to the "spirit of God" in Matt 12:28. In addition, Matthew's repetition of Q 3:9b in Matt 7:19 occurs in the context of a polemically intensified critique of false prophets (Matt 7:15). Matt 23:33 repeats John's name-calling and rhetorical question in the context of the polemic against the Pharisees. Matthew's sustained interest in critiquing the Pharisees is one of the arguments for taking his identification of John's addressees in Matt 3:7 ("the Pharisees and Sadducees") as redactional.

[75]If Luke 3:10–14 was in Q, the explicit connection between John's teaching about bearing good fruit and the teachings of Jesus in the inaugural sermon would confirm the parenetic function of the language of judgment in Q 3:7–9. For bibliography of those who support Luke 3:10–14 as from Q, see Kloppenborg, *Q Parallels*, 10.

[76]Q 6:46: "Why do you call me, 'Master, Master,' and not do what I say?" It is also significant that both Matthew and Luke recognize the connection between John and Jesus'

an obvious application of Q 6:29 about not withholding your coat from one who demands your shirt (χιτῶνα). As in the inaugural sermon and the householder and banquet parables in Q, all of the teachings attributed to John in Luke 3:10–14 focus on non-abusive economic exchanges, the fair distribution of food, and the willingness and ability of members of society not normally noted for their righteousness to practice what Q preaches.

Judging the Children of Abraham

Interpreting John's speech in Q as judgment imagery in the service of paraenesis for the *basileia* raises questions about the traditional identification of John's audience in Q 3:7a, which is notoriously difficult to reconstruct. Many interpreters suggest that the Q community would not have imagined John's speech—with its negative tone—being spoken against themselves. This results in a general consensus that the audience of John's speech in the text is an "outsider" audience, whether unresponsive Jews, religious leaders, or all of Israel. As I have suggested for "this generation" in Q, however, it is more likely that the rhetorical force of the judgment language is aimed at the Q audience itself. From this view, the urgency and imminence function to confirm that the Q community's own enactment of the *basileia* vision is crucial to the present and future of Israel, of which they are a part.

For the inscribed audience, the alternative to following John's command is to make an excuse. This excuse, "We have Abraham as a father," is usually interpreted as an argument whereby "Jews" argue for their acceptance by God with a claim to national election based on lineage. With this interpretation, the Q community, through the voice of John, promotes other avenues to election or salvation[77] and argues that lineage claims are irrelevant: "For I tell you that God can raise up children to Abraham from these rocks." However, 3:8b should be read in the context of 3:8a. The way to avoid a negative judgment is to bear good fruit. Saying that one is a child of Abraham

---

references to bearing good fruits, but they strengthen the connection in completely different ways. While Luke expands John's ethical teachings, Matthew intensifies Jesus' teaching by importing John's warning of fire.

[77] Carl Kazmierski, for example, concludes that "the gist of the prophet's message is that Israel itself no longer has the means to be the salvation-community" ("The Stones of Abraham: John the Baptist and the End of the Torah [Matt 3,7–10 par. Luke 3,7–9]," *Bib* 68 [1987] 33).

will not keep one from being chopped down by the ax and burned (God's wrath). In the context of the scene, everyone in earshot of John can claim to be a child of Abraham, but that will not guarantee the outcome of God's judgment. Only their righteous living will do so.[78] This focus on the urgent importance of righteous action is confirmed by the allusions to the story of Lot in Q 3:7–9, 16–17. Kloppenborg points out that the claim to have Abraham as father (3:8b) "recalls the fact that Lot was Abraham's kinsman (Gen 18:17–19; 19:29)."[79]

> Indeed, from the narrative in Genesis one might get the impression that Lot was spared merely because he was kin to Abraham. It is perhaps for this reason that later treatments of the Lot story corrected this impression by referring to Lot as "righteous Lot" (Wis 10: 6; 2 Peter 2:6–7) or by expressly stating that he was rescued because of his piety and hospitality (*1 Clem* 11.1). John's oracle follows this corrective tradition: only the "fruit of repentance" will serve as exculpatory evidence in the judgment.[80]

John's refutation of the excuse, therefore, is not based on who can and who cannot claim to be children of Abraham but rather on the fact that, with God, Abraham's children are endless—even the rocks can be raised up and made into offspring.[81] This is a reaffirmation of the threat of the "coming wrath." This wrath will, most assuredly, cut down the trees that do not bear good fruit because God can just create more trees. John's speech does not redefine what it means to be a child of Abraham; it simply

---

[78]Jacobson (*First Gospel*, 81) suggests that 3:7 "announces a fundamental theme: who are the true people of God?" Later he argues that 3:8 introduces an "entirely novel idea . . . God's election of Israel is not denied, and yet at the same time it is suggested that others might be created as children of Abraham" (p. 83). According to Jacobson, these new children are Gentiles who serve to put Israel to shame. Kloppenborg (*Formation*, 104) rightly points out, however, that the idea of the stones being made into children of Abraham is "prophetic hyperbole" and not obviously a reference to Gentiles.

[79]Kloppenborg, "City and Wasteland," 151.

[80]Ibid.

[81]This image echoes both God's creation of Adam out of the dust and God's covenant with Abraham that promised that his offspring would be as numerous as the grains of sand. This image of the infinite number of the "children of Abraham" could be in tension with an interpretation of the judgment announced by John as an eschatological or final judgment, since presumably raising up more offspring of Abraham after the judging of those who only claimed to be children of Abraham (but did not act like it) would be unnecessary if God had ended history and settled all accounts.

reiterates that God expects righteousness from the children of Abraham. Thus, it is the rhetorical combination of the urgency of the times and the call to righteous living that recur in the speeches of Jesus throughout Q and which are programmatically introduced by John's preaching in Q 3:7–9, 16–17.[82]

Introducing Jesus as the Coming One: Q 3:16–17

What immediately stands out when moving from Q 3:7–9 to 3:16–17 is that the cast of characters has expanded. In 3:7–9 the characters are John and the audience of John's message (referred to in the plural). In 3:16–17, John still speaks of himself as "I" and to the audience as "you" (plural), but he also speaks of "the coming one after me."[83] This one—according to John himself—is more powerful than John.[84] This one will baptize with spirit and fire.[85] In the progression of the speech, this one to come also wields the shovel that will deliver the wheat and the straw to their respective fates in 3:17. With the introduction of the "coming one," John's speech serves its programmatic function not only to center the communal vision of Q

---

[82]Kirk ("Upbraiding Wisdom," 7) also argues that Q 3:7–9 "constitute deliberative discourse intended to move addressees to decisive moral action." I differ from Kirk insofar as he sees the rhetorical function of such deliberative discourse as moving the audience to accept the authority of the sage and his teachings.

[83]Q 3:16 is notoriously difficult to reconstruct because of the Mark-Q overlap with Mark 1:7b–8. See Harry Fleddermann, "John and the Coming One (Matt 3:11–12//Luke 3:16–17)," *SBLSP* 23 (1984) 377–84.

[84]John says that he is not worthy to wear his sandals in the presence of the "coming one." This evokes the scenes of Moses (Exod 3:5) and Joshua (5:15) removing their shoes in the presence of the burning bush and the "commander of the army of the Lord" respectively. See Bretscher, "'Whose Sandals?'," and n. 7 above.

[85]There is a long-standing debate about the text of Q here and the meaning of the text. Jacobson (*First Gospel*, 84) takes the view that πνεύματι should be translated "wind" since the context is the baptism of judgment. Trumbower ("Role of Malachi," 37) points out that Sib. Or. 4.165 also speaks of judgment as a baptism of fire. Horsley and Draper (*Whoever Hears*, 254) understand the baptism as one of renewal and judgment and thus take πνεύματι as spirit (see Ezek 37:1–4; Joel 2:28–29; 1QS 3:6–9). Tuckett (*Q*, 122) also takes πνεύματι as spirit baptism for those who respond positively. Similarly, Webb, "Expected Figure," 109; and James D. G. Dunn, "Spirit-and-Fire Baptism," *NovT* 14 (1972) 81–92. Steve Mason points to the predominance of the river or lake of fire in Jewish apocalyptic tradition and concludes that Q 3:16 only had "fire" and thus juxtaposed John's water baptism with the apocalyptic baptism by fire ("Fire," 171). Uro ("John," 251) concludes that Q originally spoke of only water and spirit baptism.

as crucial but also to locate Jesus at a critical moment in the future of the community. What is the effect of introducing Jesus as the coming one on Q's urgent call to enact the teachings of Q? Does recognizing Jesus become the ledger in which the community's accounts will be settled?

To begin to answer these questions, we should take note of the continuities between the two parts of John's speech. Q 3:17 continues the theme from 3:7–9 of the separation of people into those who will be judged positively and those who will be judged negatively. Here the agricultural implement shifts from the ax to the winnowing shovel and the crops from good and bad fruit to wheat and straw. Just as the trees that bear good fruit presumably will be left standing, the wheat will be gathered into the granary. Like the trees that bear unhealthy fruit, so the straw will be burned up in fire. Like 3:9, this reckoning is something that will happen to the listeners in the future if they do not make sure they are wheat and not straw.[86] In addition to the continuation of the motif of judgment, the two units of the speech are tied together by the repetition of πῦρ and the references to baptism. The "coming wrath" in 3:7–9 is made vivid in the metaphor of the ax that chops the trees. In 3:16–17, the metaphors are anthropomorphic and thus the "coming one" wields a winnowing shovel to sort the wheat from the straw. The "coming one" (ὁ ἐρχόμενος), the baptism of spirit and fire, and the acts of harvest (clearing, gathering, burning) are all in the future of the world of the text. But as the ax was at the root, so the winnowing shovel is in the hand of the coming one. Thus, the two parts of the speech (3:7–9 and 16–17) attest a similar combination of future and imminence or urgency. This temporal deployment of God's judgment (or wrath) makes sense in the context of an appeal for right action that will ensure positive judgment.

In the context of Q, the "coming one" appears to be Jesus, but this connection is never unequivocally made.[87] The expression appears again in John's question to Jesus in 7:18 and in Jesus' own words (about himself) in 13:35.[88]

---

[86]Kirk (*Composition*, 369) argues that 3:16–17 "is a self-contained unit focused on characterizing the 'Coming One' and thus represents a shift in attention from repentance preaching to the announcement of the coming judge." While 3:16–17 does introduce the "coming one," it still functions in an admonitory way similar to 3:7–9.

[87]John's description of the "coming (ἐρχόμενος) one" in 3:16–17 may have originally spoken of God coming in judgment. Thus, the "coming (μελλούσης) wrath" is God's wrath, and God is the one coming with a baptism of spirit and fire and a winnowing shovel to collect the wheat and to throw the straw into the fire. The saying about John's sandals fits with this interpretation.

[88]See Robinson, "Sayings Gospel," 361–66.

But 7:18–23 only very obliquely confirms Jesus as the one predicted by John in Q 3:16. Indeed, chapter 2 suggests that in the context of 7:18–35, Jesus' answer to John's question redirects the focus away from Jesus' identity and onto the significance of what is happening among the people. The lack of continuity between Jesus' answer to John's disciples in 7:22 and the figure of 3:16–17 is obvious. In addition, Q 7:27 identifies John, not Jesus, as the Elijianic messenger from Malachi.[89]

The primary development of the theme of Jesus as the "coming one" in 3:16 is not in 7:18–35 but in the last major section of Q, commonly called the "Eschatological Discourse."[90] This discourse begins with the third occurrence of the expression ὁ ἐρχόμενος.[91] In Q 13:34–35 Jesus says:

> O Jerusalem, Jerusalem, who kills the prophets and stones those sent to her! How often have I wanted to gather your children together, as a hen gathers her nestlings under her wings, but you were not willing! Look, your house is forsaken! . . . I tell you, you will not see me until the time comes when you say: Blessed is the one who comes [ὁ ἐρχόμενος][92] in the name of the Lord.[93]

Q 13:35b is a quotation of Ps 117:26a LXX, which presents a song of thanksgiving to God for victories over the nations. In the psalm the chorus sings blessing upon the psalmist (a king) who enters the Temple. In Mark this same LXX passage is ascribed to the crowds who welcome Jesus into Jerusalem as he rides on a donkey (proleptically fulfilling Zech 9:9). In Q, the connection between Jesus and ὁ ἐρχόμενος is made indirectly by sug-

---

[89]Given the affirmation of John as a "coming one" (Elijah) in 7:27, and the shifting of the scriptural quotation to imply that John has prepared Jesus' way (rather than God's), the identification of Jesus with Elijah's successor Elisha in Q 7:18–28 is just as possible. Indeed, the summary of events in Q 7:22 subtly connects Jesus with Elisha since it is Elisha, not Elijah, that heals a leper. Many interpreters have pointed out that raising the dead and healing the lepers do not evoke Isaiah but the Elijah/Elisha cycle. Sir 48:8 notes that Elijah anointed "prophets to succeed you."

[90]See Kirk, *Composition*, 289–308.

[91]I follow Kirk (*Composition*, 312) who places Q 13:34–35 after 11:49–51 in Q (Matthean order). This results in the discourse that has the most intratextual links to John's opening speech being introduced by a saying about the "coming one."

[92]Note that the IQP does not translate ὁ ἐρχόμενος here as "the one to come," because this would make no sense in the context of a quotation of Ps 117:26 LXX. This points to the fact that the expression does not function in Q as a title but rather as an intratextual deliberation on the significance of Jesus.

[93]Translation from Robinson, *Critical Edition*, 420–23.

gesting that the rebellious and difficult Jerusalem will only see Jesus again when it lauds him as blessed. The text of Q constructs this as something that will happen in the future of the text, thus "you will not see me again until you say . . . ." Subsequent units construct that future as very near. In Q 12:40, Jesus declares, "You must also be ready, for the son of humanity[94] is coming (ἔρχεται) at an hour you do not expect."[95] In 12:49, Jesus claims to have come (ἦλθον) to cast (βαλεῖν; see Q 3:9, 12:28, 14:35) fire (πῦρ) on the earth. Precisely the opposite of Elijah in Mal 3:23 LXX and Sir 48:10, Jesus has come (ἦλθον) to divide the generations in families (Q 12: 53; 14:26). The day of the son of humanity will be like lightning streaking (ἐξέρχεται) through the sky (17:24). And finally, the master of the household in the parable of the talents instructs his slaves to "do business until I come" (ἔρχομαι; 19:13; also 19:15, 23).

Q 17:22–37b also shows intratextual links to John's "coming one" in 3:16–17.[96] There is repetition of the theme of people being divided into two groups, the common vocabulary of fire, an allusion to the Lot story, and the emphasis on urgency. The "day of the son of humanity" will be like the days when only Noah and Lot and their families escaped God's wrath. Like John's speech, Q 17:22–37b locates the inscribed audience at one of those critical moments in their epic history when people need to be in the right "place" at the right time to survive. It presses the listener to be like righteous Noah and get into the ark or to be like righteous Lot and get out of town. But neither 3:16–17 nor 17:22–37b presents Jesus as a figure who assigns judgment. In 3:17, the "coming one" delivers the winnowed grain and straw to its appropriate fates but does not separate it.[97] In 17:30, the son of humanity is revealed (ἀποκαλύπτεται) but the agent who takes and leaves the men and women doing their everyday tasks is not identified (17:34–35). Indeed, the

---

[94]Arnal points out ("Redactional Fabrication," 173) that Theodotion's version of Daniel "witnesses to a literal rendering of the Aramaic of the Son of Man text in 7:13 as *hôs huios anthrôpon erchomenos ên*, a rendering that could have also been available to the much earlier Q redactor."

[95]Both the thief (12:39) and the master (12:43, 46) in the household parables are referred to as "coming" with ἔρχομαι.

[96]Arnal also points out ("Redactional Fabrication," 171) that the "coming one" in 3:16 coheres with the son of humanity in Q 12 and 17 rather than with Jesus in 7:18–23.

[97]Webb argues ("Expected Figure," 111) that it is the response to John's repentance baptism that separates the wheat and the straw and then they await the ingathering or burning that comes with Jesus' arrival.

epic examples of the flood and the fiery destruction of Sodom suggest that it is God who enacts the separation of people depicted in Q 17:34–35.

Q links Jesus' return to a time of future judgment, but it is ambiguous as to Jesus' role in that judgment. This suggests that Q is not preoccupied with the community's understanding of Jesus. However, four Q passages may begin to turn the community's attention to Jesus' singular significance. For example, in 6:22–23 those who suffer on account of the son of humanity are blessed and their "pay is great in heaven." In Q 12:8–9, acknowledging Jesus before people is likened to being acknowledged before God. In Q 12:30, Jesus, as the son of humanity, will be the only sign given to this generation. In Q 10:16, however, the receiving of those sent out to "bring near" the *basileia* is aligned with the receiving of Jesus in addition to the receiving of God. This could suggest that the Q community equates sharing the *basileia* vision with being loyal to Jesus. If so, then suffering like, acknowledging, and recognizing Jesus in Q 6:22–23, 12:8–9, and 12:30 could similarly be related to commitment to the movement. Thus, standing with Jesus corresponds to standing for the values of the community as expressed in the vision of the *basileia*. If Q places the recognition of Jesus as the "coming one" or the "son of humanity" at the fulcrum of God's judgment, it does not do so in a way that de-centers the urgent call—delivered in the preaching of both Q's John and Q's Jesus—for Israel to enact the vision of the *basileia* of God.

Conclusion

John's opening speech in Q 3:7–9, 16–17 serves a double purpose in Q: one that emphasizes the crucial importance of the values and visions of the movement in which both John and Jesus are a part, and one that locates Jesus in the community's present and future. The judgment language functions in John's speech and throughout Q to heighten the urgency and significance of enacting the vision of the *basileia* of God in the life of the community. In this sense, it can fulfill Crossan's interest in valuing a religious imagination which places superlative value on "justice and righteousness" rather than on one's group identity. This aspect of John's preaching coheres with similar rhetorical emphases in sayings attributed to Jesus in the inaugural sermon and in the sayings about the coming of the son of humanity in Q 12. With the introduction of Jesus as the "coming one," however, John's speech also introduces Q's central figure. If there is a tension between these emphases, it does not rest in the classification of Jesus and John as conflicting or compatible. Nor does it reside in the presentation of John and Jesus over and against the opponents of Q. Rather, it lies in the tension between the ways in which the communal vision of justice and well-being is central or de-centralized in the self-understanding of the community as a whole.

CHAPTER 4

Eschatology and Christology:
The Problem of the Uniqueness of Jesus

Popular public discourse on religion links Christian identity to an understanding of Christ as unique. Thus, while the *Newsweek* article discussed in chapter 1 presents diverse views of Jesus among world religions, it is headed by a quotation from Pope John Paul II that authoritatively establishes the uniqueness of Christ for Christians. Later in the article, the author asserts that "for Christians, [Christ] is utterly unique—the only Son of God. . . . Clearly, the cross is what separates the Christ of Christianity from every other Jesus."[1] The article claims that it is the crucified and resurrected Son of God that marks the uniqueness of Christ for Christians and non-Christians alike, affirming for Christians that the uniqueness of Christ—as the Pope confirms—is essential to Christian identity. Jesus' uniqueness is constructed in two interrelated ways: (1) as the Son of God, Jesus Christ died and was resurrected as the Gospels report; and as a result, (2) he is fundamentally unlike the central figures of other religions. Thus the logic goes: it is Christians' belief in the first claim (a belief essential to their identity, according to the article) that necessitates the second claim. Since the first claim invokes ontological Truth for Christ's uniqueness, the difference between Christ and Buddha or Muhammad also receives ontological value as well.

Many theologians have pointed out the difficulty raised for interreligious relations by such claims to ontological uniqueness and its attending claims of superiority with respect to other religious traditions. Feminist theorists

---

[1] Kenneth L. Woodward, "The Other Jesus," *Newsweek* (March 27, 2000) 52.

and theologians in particular have pointed repeatedly to the anti-Jewish tendencies of christological doctrines. Since most New Testament scholarship takes for granted the centering of Jesus in Christian texts, this chapter examines certain methodological moves that reinscribe this focus on Jesus. As we will explore, contemporary historians and exegetes have pointed out the unarticulated theological tendency in much biblical scholarship to replicate this view of Jesus and the Christian *kerygma* as unique in comparison to the multifaceted religio-political environment of the Greco-Roman world. The category "eschatology" is often implicated in establishing that uniqueness. Scholars have criticized the ways that uniqueness claims have functioned to insulate Christianity from unwanted comparisons, yet they rarely articulate their own interests in the rejection of Christian uniqueness. The following discussion examines four characteristics of contemporary debates over Christian uniqueness, eschatology, and Q.

Apologetics and Christian Origins

Often underlying interests of claims for the uniqueness of Jesus and/or the early Christian proclamation are Christian apologetics and the quest for pure origins. This point has been made in many different ways in North America and Europe for the past fifty years. One example is Jonathan Z. Smith's *Drudgery Divine: On the Comparison of Early Christianities and the Religions of Late Antiquity*. Smith critiques biblical scholarship for a relentless focus on origins, which Smith locates in Protestant anti-Catholic apologetics. In a chapter titled "On Comparison," Smith also challenges biblical scholarship to dispense with the notion of uniqueness. According to Smith, uniqueness can have an "ordinary sense" whereby the taxonomist necessarily classifies one thing A as unique from another B, imparting difference to both and thereby making comparison possible. But he calls for the end of uniqueness as a term which links difference to "superlative value" and thus transforms it into an ontological rather than taxonomic category.[2]

Smith quotes Burton Mack to describe the pervasiveness of uniqueness claims (that is, difference plus superlative value) in New Testament studies—particularly with regard to the "Christ-event." Mack argues in *A Myth of Innocence*:

---

[2]Jonathan Z. Smith, *Drudgery Divine: On the Comparison of Early Christianities and the Religions of Late Antiquity* (Chicago: University of Chicago Press, 1990) 36–37.

The fundamental persuasion is that Christianity appeared unexpect-
edly in human history, that it was [is] at core a brand new vision of
human existence, and that, since this is so, only a startling moment
could account for its emergence at the beginning. The code word
serving as a sign for the novelty that appeared is the term unique.
. . . For the originary event the word is transformation (rupture,
breakthrough, inversion, reversal, *eschatological*). It is this startling
moment that seems to have mesmerized the discipline and determined
the application of its critical methods.[3]

In both Smith's and Mack's work, there is a clear convergence of the
critique of uniqueness claims and the critique of biblical scholarship's
quest for the origins as a singular and momentous person (the historical
Jesus), program (the *basileia* of God), or event (the crucifixion and/or resurrection). According to Smith, this myth of pure origins is a particularly
Protestant one: "If Christianity is 'unique' with respect to other religions,
then apostolic (or Pauline) Christianity is 'unique' with respect to other
(especially later) modes of Christianity. This is a modulation of the Protestant historiographic myth: a 'uniquely' pristine 'original' Christianity
which suffered later 'corruptions.'"[4] Smith calls for an end to such an
"enterprise undertaken in bad faith." Clearly making the link between
uniqueness claims, the quest for origins, and theological apologetics, he
continues: "The interests have rarely been cognitive, but rather almost
always apologetic. As such, no other purpose for comparison has been
entertained but that of genealogy."[5]

For at least two decades, feminist and liberationist biblical scholars have
been discussing the problem of uniqueness claims for Jesus and Christianity
in the context of Christian anti-Judaism and inter-religious conversations.[6]
Although this debate is often discussed in terms of "feminist anti-Judaism,"[7]
Elisabeth Schüssler Fiorenza has rightly pointed out that "much of what is

---

[3]Ibid., 39 (quoting Burton Mack, *A Myth of Innocence: Mark and Christian Origins*
[Philadelphia: Fortress, 1988] 4; (my emphasis).

[4]Smith, *Drudgery Divine*, 43.

[5]Ibid., 143.

[6]See *The Myth of Christian Uniqueness: Toward a Pluralistic Theology of Religions* (ed.
John Hick and Paul F. Knitter; Maryknoll, N.Y.: Orbis, 1987).

[7]For a review and analysis of this ongoing discussion, see Elisabeth Schüssler Fiorenza,
Jesus: Miriam's Child, Sophia's Prophet (New York: Continuum, 1994) 67–96; and eadem,
Politics, 115–44.

considered to be feminist anti-Judaism is simply Christian anti-Judaism internalized by wo/men."[8] The tendency in Christian feminist biblical scholarship to portray Jesus' relationship to wo/men in a positive light by placing him against a negative background of the desperate plight of Jewish wo/men is analogous to and participates in the dominant androcentric discourse of the myth of pure origins.[9] As mentioned above, scholars such as Mack and Smith have criticized the pervasive influence of this myth of origin and its attendant myth of decline, in which the radical and unique beginnings of Christianity vis-à-vis the other religions of antiquity face decline because of a return to traditional Judaism or the pollution of Greco-Roman "paganism."[10]

Eschatology Renders Jesus and Q Incomparably Unique

The category "eschatology" has played a significant role in the construction of the uniqueness of Jesus and early Christianity. In his discussion of uniqueness claims for early Christianity, Smith offers two examples from biblical studies to illustrate the transfer of ontological uniqueness to historical claims: (1) the theory that the Gospels are a unique phenomenon in the history of literature; and (2) that eschatology has become a category of "absolute (ontological) uniqueness."[11] To explicate the latter, Smith offers Dieter Georgi's critique of Bultmann's use of "eschatological" as a "magic wand":

> [Bultmann] opposes what he calls the relativism of the history-of-religions school. [In this context] I need to mention the term "eschatological." It works for Bultmann and for many New Testament scholars and systematic theologians ever since as a magic wand. Whereas for the history-of-religions school the term "eschatological" described the foreignness of Jesus and of the early church—together with Jewish apocalypticism and other comparable ancient eschatologies—for Bultmann and many contemporary New Testament scholars and Christian theologians the term "eschatological" stands for the novelty of Christianity, its incomparable superiority, the uniqueness of the victorious religion. . . . Wherever a comparison is ventured, wherever analogies lift their head, wherever challenges are heard from other religious options but the canonical ones, the invocation

---

[8]Ibid., 121.
[9]Ibid., 128.
[10]Ibid., 129.
[11]Smith, *Drudgery Divine*, 41.

of the "eschatological" is made, and the demons, the shadows have to disappear. Historical criticism thus turns into exorcism. Thus my major criticism of Bultmann's *Theology* is that it demonstrates an inability to keep criticism and construction in continuous dialectical relationship. Especially the historical dimension of Bultmann's criticism is cut short.[12]

It is important to note that Georgi does not refute Bultmann's attribution of the term "eschatological" to the outlook of Jesus or the early Christians. Georgi's critique is leveled against Bultmann's existentialist interpretation of eschatology, which demythologizes Jesus' proclamation of the *basileia* of God into a "moment of decision" for every person everywhere.

In the same collection of essays in honor of Bultmann, Helmut Koester suggests that Bultmann's emphasis on eschatology as an existential understanding of life individualizes eschatology to the exclusion of the "political and social factors which determine such experience of existence in a particular historical situation."[13] The following is an example of Bultmann's existentialist interpretation of Jesus' eschatology:

> Because Jesus sees [humanity] . . . in a crisis of decision before God, it is understandable that in his thought the Jewish Messianic hope becomes the absolute certainty that in this hour the Kingdom of God is coming. If [people] are standing in the crisis of decision, and if precisely this crisis is the essential characteristic of their humanity, then every hour is the last hour, and we can understand that for Jesus the whole contemporary mythology is pressed into the service of this conception of human existence. Thus he understood and proclaimed his hour as the last hour.[14]

Both Georgi and Koester point out the role that the categorization "eschatological" can play in removing Jesus and early Christianity from their complex historical contexts. In addition, each of them has subsequently interpreted Christian eschatology in comparison with Roman imperial

---

[12]Dieter Georgi, "Rudolf Bultmann's *Theology of the New Testament* Revisited," in *Bultmann, Retrospect and Prospect* (ed. Edward C. Hobbs; HTS 35; Philadelphia: Fortress, 1985) 82.

[13]Helmut Koester, "Early Christianity for the Perspective of the History of Religions: Rudolf Bultmann's Contribution," in *Bultmann, Retrospect and Prospect* (ed. Hobbs) 59–74, at 72.

[14]Rudolf Bultmann, *Jesus and the Word* (German original, 1926; New York: Scribner, 1934) 51–52.

political ideology.[15] Smith adopts their critique to conclude that "what is required is an end to the imposition of the extra-historical categories of uniqueness and the 'Wholly Other' upon historical data and the tasks of historical understanding."[16]

Although Smith does not articulate the connection, the category "eschatology" is also implicated in Smith's first example of uniqueness claims, that is, the tendency to view the Gospels as a unique form of literature. Drawing on the work of Robinson and Koester,[17] John Kloppenborg compares Q with wisdom collections across Jewish, Christian, and "pagan" lines, seeking to clarify Q's genre. Kloppenborg notes that the tendency to avoid comparing gospel literature with non-Christian genres originates from the work of Franz Overbeck, who argued that Christian literature was *Kleinliteratur* (or, popular literature as opposed to high literature from the circles of the cultural elite), in that it "grew up on the basis of, and for the unique inner interests of, the Christian community, before its intermixture with the surrounding world."[18] Kloppenborg credits Ehrhart Güttgemanns with showing that the notion of *Kleinliteratur* "emerged as a corollary to the thesis that the church was an eschatological community which was not oriented towards the world."[19] Kloppenborg concludes that scholars cannot "adopt too quickly the dogmatic assumption that early Christianity did not, in view of its eschatology, use the literary conventions of antiquity."[20]

[15]Dieter Georgi, "Who is the True Prophet?" in *Christians Among Jews and Gentiles: Essays in Honor of Krister Stendahl* (ed. George McRae et al.; Philadelphia: Fortress, 1986) 100–26; Helmut Koester, "Jesus the Victim," *JBL* 111 (1992) 3–15; and idem, "The Historical Jesus and the Cult of the *Kyrios Christos*," *Harvard Divinity Bulletin* 24 (1995) 13–18.

[16]Smith, *Drudgery Divine*, 42.

[17]Robinson and Koester provide the preliminary work on the question of the genre of Q. See *Trajectories through Early Christianity* (ed. James M. Robinson and Helmut Koester; Philadelphia: Fortress, 1971).

[18]Franz Overbeck, "Über die Anfänge der patristischen Literatur," *Historische Zeitschrift* n.F. 12 (1882) 417–72, at 443 (translation from Kloppenborg, *Formation*, 4). Kloppenborg (ibid., 6) also quotes Dibelius to illustrate this position: "The company of unlettered people which expected the end of the world any day had neither the capacity nor the inclination for the production of books, and we must not predicate a true literary activity in the Christian Church of the first two or three decades" (Martin Dibelius, *From Tradition to Gospel* [trans. B. L. Woolf; New York: Scribner, 1935] 9).

[19]Kloppenborg, *Formation*, 6. See Ehrhart Güttgemanns, *Candid Questions Concerning Gospel Form Criticism* (trans. W. D. Doty; Pittsburgh: Pickwick, 1979).

[20]Kloppenborg, *Formation*, 7.

Kloppenborg's comparison of Q to the Egyptian wisdom instruction genre precedes but coheres well with Jonathan Z. Smith's challenge that New Testament scholars stop taking "refuge" in Jewish comparatives in order to shield their texts from less theologically acceptable "pagan" comparatives.[21] While at home in Smith's critique of New Testament studies' Protestant anti-Catholicism, this challenge nevertheless stands in tension with the uniqueness critique proposed by Jewish and Christian feminists, wherein not locating Jesus fully within a Jewish context can unwittingly participate in Christian supersessionism and anti-Judaism. Indeed, Kloppenborg's *Formation of Q* has been criticized for its lack of attention to comparatives in the Jewish wisdom tradition.[22] In addition, the comparison of Q's earliest stratum with the philosophy and rhetoric of the Cynics has drawn the charge of anti-Judaism from many quarters despite the fact that no scholar is proposing that Jesus was not Jewish.

At this point, it should be clear that the category "eschatology" has been implicated in the construction of Christian uniqueness. It is important to point out, however, that the construction of early Christian eschatology can participate in Christian anti-Judaism not only as a concept that *insulates* Christianity from its "pagan" comparatives but also as a theological taxonomy[23] that *actively delineates* between first-century Christianity (or the historical Jesus) and Judaism. The classic example is the distinction, prevalent in New Testament scholarship since Weiss and Schweitzer, between "Jewish apocalyptic" and "Christian eschatology" by which "apocalyptic is often negatively identified with Jewish thought. While . . . [Christian] eschatology is understood with reference to things eternal and the real content of eschatology is strictly differentiated from the crude ideas and images of apocalyptic."[24]

---

[21]Smith, *Drudgery Divine*, 46. Smith makes a similar point: "Judaism has been made to play [a dual function] in discourse on early Christianity, serving both as an insulating device against 'hellenism,' and as an ancestor to be transcended" (117).

[22]In his review of scholarship on the redaction of Q, Alan Kirk notes that "the ease with which [Kloppenborg's] critics muster a corpus of Hellenistic-Jewish literature to show the thematic coherence of wisdom and apocalyptic reveals a vulnerability in Kloppenborg's proposal. His identification of the formative stratum is predicated largely upon comparison with ancient Egyptian Instructions and gives less attention to Hellenistic-Jewish wisdom compositions which on his theory one would think are Q's closest relatives" (Kirk, *Composition*, 41). Kloppenborg discusses the anti-Judaism issue with regard to the Cynic proposal in *Excavating Q*, 433–36.

[23]I have adopted this term from Kloppenborg Verbin, *Excavating Q*, 379–85.

[24]Elisabeth Schüssler Fiorenza, "The Phenomenon of Early Christian Apocalyptic," in

Christology and the Uniqueness of Jesus

The disputed doctrinal territory in the debates about uniqueness and/or eschatology is often Christology. In the debates among feminist biblical interpreters over the problem of a construction of Jesus as unique, there is an explicit recognition that christological issues are at stake. In her challenge to Christian feminists to recognize their own complicity with anti-Judaism, Judith Plaskow says:

> I find it especially disturbing, therefore, that the tendency to define Jesus as unique over and against Judaism remains even in feminists who do not make use of the Jesus-was-a-feminist argument, who are quite aware of Christian anti-Judaism, who are freely critical of Christian sources, who have gone very far in deconstructing notions of Jesus' divinity. . . . It seems as if the feminist struggle with patriarchal christologies leads back to the trap of anti-Judaism. If Jesus is not the Messiah and the incarnate Son of God on any traditional interpretation of these terms, then how does one articulate his uniqueness in a way that makes sense out of remaining a Christian . . . ? Can Christians value Jesus if he was just a Jew who chose to emphasize certain ideas and values in the Jewish tradition but did not invent or have a monopoly on them? If claims about Jesus' specialness are intrinsic to Christianity, then is there a way to make these claims that does not end up rejecting or disparaging Judaism?[25]

Plaskow partially locates feminist anti-Judaism in the struggle with patriarchal Christologies. Does rejecting uniqueness claims mean "deconstructing Jesus' divinity" and accepting that he was "just a Jew who chose to emphasize certain ideas?" There is a stark contrast between the christological position associated here with Jesus-as-not-unique and the Jesus-as-unique Christology presumed by the *Newsweek* article and outlined above. Therefore, the debates over Jesus' uniqueness (human or ontological) take place in the larger field of christological reflection and its relationship to Christian identity and self-understanding.

It is this same public debate about christological claims that produces much of the controversy around recent historical-Jesus and select Q research,

---

Apocalypticism in the Mediterranean World and the Near East (ed. David Hellholm; Tübingen: Mohr/Siebeck, 1983) 304.

[25]Judith Plaskow, "Feminist Anti-Judaism and the Christian God," *JFSR* 7 (1991) 106–7.

both in the wider public discourse and among academics. For example, the varied responses to the comparison of Q with Cynic philosophy show well the underlying interest in Christology that often drives the debate. In an extended analysis of the scholarly response to the "Cynic hypothesis," Kloppenborg identifies Christology and its putative continuity with the historical Jesus as one of the theological interests that underpin the out-of-hand rejection of Cynic parallels to Q.[26]

This interest in the christological implications of the Cynic-Q comparison is intertwined with a reconstruction of Jesus' eschatology. Kloppenborg observes that "a cynic Q with a cynic-like Jesus *without a strong eschatological outlook* and message is not so amenable to christological discourse as the 'eschatological prophet' with a message of a partially imminent, partly realized, but wholly definitive intervention by God."[27] Says Kloppenborg, " 'Eschatology' stands as a cipher for finality and ultimacy. Only if Jesus made ultimate and final claims about the reign of God, and only if there is some connection, however implicit, between these claims and the person of Jesus himself, can christological claims be sustained."[28] Here, once again, "eschatological" and "non-eschatological" emerge as terms in the debate that point to larger issues, in this case discourse about Christology and the continuity between the early Christian *kerygma* and the teaching of the historical Jesus.[29]

[26]See Kloppenborg Verbin (*Excavating Q*, 420–44) for discussion and bibliography. While I cannot review his entire treatment of the Cynic comparison here, I want to note that Kloppenborg does not defend the Cynic hypothesis outright, but rather analyzes other scholars' rejection of the hypothesis. He argues (with extensive analysis) that there is a lack of parity between the rigorous burden of proof placed upon the Cynic hypothesis and that placed on other hypotheses comparing Q to other ancient materials. Kloppenborg attributes this disparity to the unarticulated theological stakes of the debate and the perceived threat to those interests from the Cynic hypothesis.

[27]Kloppenborg Verbin, *Excavating Q*, 440 (my emphasis).

[28]Ibid., 439. Kloppenborg quotes Seán Freyne's straightforward assessment of the stakes: "[My insistence on the eschatological nature of Jesus' career] arises from my concern regarding the claims of ultimacy that Christian faith makes in terms of Jesus. . . . In the absence of an eschatological dimension to Jesus' utterances it would be impossible to see how any christological claims could be grounded in his earthly life, which is precisely the issue that gave rise to the quest for the historical Jesus in the first place as both an ecclesial and academic exercise" (Seán Freyne, "Galilean Questions to Crossan's Mediterranean Jesus," in *Whose Historical Jesus?* [ed. William Arnal and Michel Desjardins; Waterloo, Ontario: Wilfrid Laurier University Press, 1997] 90).

[29]Dieter Georgi's analysis of Bultmann's *Theology of the New Testmament* identifies the prominence in Bultmann's thinking of this link between eschatology, Christology, and Jesus'

Dispensing with Apologetics?

The methodological critique of uniqueness claims often constructs a divide between theological apologetics and respectable and disciplined historical scholarship. Smith calls for an end to the theological apologetics inherent in such categories as "uniqueness" and "eschatology." He concludes that "the Protestant hegemony over the enterprise of compari[son] has been an affair of mythic conception and ritual practice from the outset. It has yet to become an affair of the academy."[30] This constructs a sharp break between the theologically/ethically/politically-engaged scholar as religious practitioner and the interested-only-in-knowledge scholar as legitimate academician.[31] It is noteworthy, in light of the next chapter on the Beelzebul controversy, that Georgi, Smith, and Kloppenborg all use the imagery of exorcism to describe the effect of theological presuppositions in historical arguments.[32] It seems the charge of magic—no longer in terms of collusion with Satan, but rather in terms of collusion with Christianity—is still a tool for marking lines of legitimate and illegitimate interpretive practices.

One of the reasons such a divide emerges is that scholars are not in the habit of articulating their own theological and/or ideological interests. For example, while Kloppenborg effectively lays out the christological ground being defended by the negative response to the Cynic comparison, he does not analyze the arguments of the Cynic hypothesis itself on the same disputed

---

message: "The eschatological experience of the early church Bultmann sees described most of all in christological terms centered in the experience of the presence of Jesus as eschatological functionary communicated by the kerygma" (79).

[30]Smith, *Drudgery Divine*, 143. This marginalization of the engaged scholar is backed up by some unfortunate infantalizing language in which Smith calls the field of biblical studies to "come of age," that is, to grow up and join the academy (ibid., 52). In addition, although Kloppenborg directly acknowledges that neutral historiography is "neither possible or desirable" (*Excavating Q*, 433), his consistent description of theological (and anti-theological) interests that "lurk beneath the surface" (ibid., 422, 443) creates a similarly unfortunate characterization of the engaged scholar as harboring a monstrosity.

[31]Elisabeth Schüssler Fiorenza (*Rhetoric and Ethic*, 69) points out how the scientific character of the study of religion ends up categorizing *both* theologically-engaged and politically-engaged scholars as corrupting the purity of the discipline.

[32]Georgi, "Rudolf Bultmann's *Theology*," 82 (quoted above); Smith: "This is exorcism or purgation, not scholarship" (*Drudgery Divine*, 143); and Kloppenborg Verbin: "When critical assessment of the cynic hypothesis comes close to exorcism, we must ask why" (*Excavating Q*, 433).

christological territory. Similarly, Jonathan Z. Smith draws extensively on Burton Mack's historical work,[33] but does not discuss the way in which Mack's work is also part of a larger discourse about the uniqueness and origin of Christianity.[34] Although Smith affirms that the "'political' implications of re-visioning our data must be faced,"[35] he does not point out that Mack's reconstruction of a Cynic, noneschatological Jesus of Q has a social and political life beyond the academy.[36] Although few use the language of disinterestedness for scholarship anymore,[37] the impression created by these methodological critiques is that the flip side of theological interest is a value-free interest in knowledge for its own sake.

Of course, knowledge is never produced for its own sake. Indeed, this divide has long been deconstructed in theory and in practice by feminist, liberationist, and postmodern critics in and of the discipline.[38] Insofar as scholars use historical arguments to "re-make the Jesus-sign"[39] for their contemporary

---

[33]The concatenation of topics in Smith's analysis—origins, the "Christ-event," gospel genres, and eschatology—is no coincidence. In a later chapter, Smith turns to Mack's interpretation of Q to show that "there is a set of Jesus-traditions which either do not focus on his death, or conceive of his death without attributing either saving significance to the death or linking it to a resurrection" (*Drudgery Divine*, 138).

[34]This stands in contrast, again, with Georgi's criticism of Bultmann ("Rudolf Bultmann's *Theology*"). Georgi suggests that Bultmann cuts short the historical aspect of the dialectic between "criticism and construction." Georgi writes: "This does not merely apply to the historical context of the New Testament and of its documents, it applies also to the historical context of the theologian Rudolf Bultmann" (82).

[35]Smith, *Drudgery Divine*, 52.

[36]Mack (for example, *Lost Gospel*, 254–57) goes farther to locate his work in the context of current ideological and political issues.

[37]Kloppenborg's conclusion to his analysis of reactions to the Cynic hypothesis attests to the awareness that scholars are participating in larger spheres of meaning making: "A similar analysis of many of the historiographic endeavors in the field of Christian origins will show, I think, that ideological (theological as well as antitheological) subtexts lurk beneath the often pretended objectivity of criticism. That is not a defect of criticism. It is what makes historical criticism of interest in the first place" (Kloppenborg Verbin, *Excavating Q*, 443).

[38]See, for example, Fernando F. Segovia, "'And They Began to Speak in Other Tongues': Competing Modes of Discourse in Contemporary Biblical Criticism," in *Reading from This Place: Social Location and Biblical Interpretation in the United States* (ed. idem and Mary Ann Tolbert; Minneapolis: Fortress, 1995) 1–34.

[39]I adopt this phrase from William Arnal's insightful analysis of the epistemological contours of recent historical Jesus debates (William E. Arnal, "Making and Re-Making the Jesus Sign: Contemporary Markings on the Body of Christ," in *Whose Historical Jesus?* [ed. Arnal and Desjardins] 308–19).

readers, they are participating in the larger public discourse about Christian identity in a pluralistic world.[40] Insofar as they cloak their own interests with historical scientism, they reinscribe the dominant discourse in such a way that historical-scientistic methodology functions as "the reverse side of the fundamentalist literalist coin":

> In and through a literalist dogmatic reading, fundamentalist christolo-gies seek to "fix" the pluriform expressions of Christian scriptures and traditions, and to consolidate the variegated texts and ambiguous metaphors of Jesus Christ into a single, definite discourse of mean-ing. In response to such reifying fundamentalist theological read-ings, Historical-Jesus scholarship insists on the scientific character of its production of knowledge as factual and historical, stressing its objectivity and detachment from all theological interests. Just like fundamentalist readings, Historical-Jesus books are concerned with authority. However, they assert not theological revelatory positivism but historical positivism in order to shore up the scholarly authority and scientific truth of their research portrayals of Jesus.[41]

The epistemological nature of this dichotomy is apparent in Luke Timothy Johnson's characterization of the current state of biblical scholarship as a contest between two orientations to Christianity: (1) "Christianity is regarded as a way of life rooted in and organized around a genuine experi-ence of ultimate reality mediated by the crucified and raised Messiah," as opposed to (2) "the other perspective [that] sees Christianity as another among the world's religions, that is, fundamentally a cultural reality rooted in the human construction of symbolic worlds."[42]

---

[40]Arnal notes that "history is really about ourselves: it is a rhetorical game, played by certain rules, commenting elliptically on the world as it is by casting current categories and basic understandings into the past. This serves the universalizing function of ideology: to make particular and contingent world-views appear to be ubiquitous" ("Making and Re-Making," 317).

[41]Schüssler Fiorenza, *Politics*, 5. While not using the language of fundamentalism, Arnal similarly registers the conservative tendencies of the claim to disinterestedness: "The ultimate value that undergirds the desire to avoid epistemic bias—hence the most basic and hidden epistemic bias of all—is the desire to conserve the world roughly as it is" ("Making and Re-making," 317).

[42]Luke Timothy Johnson, *The Real Jesus: The Misguided Quest for the Historical Jesus and the Truth of the Traditional Gospels* (San Francisco: HarperSanFrancisco, 1996) 57.

In the context of such an epistemological divide, historians are expected to continue to avoid the articulation of their own interests. Smith does confirm at several points in his book that it is (often unstated) scholarly interests that govern the procedure of comparison. He points out that the comparative phrase "*x* resembles *y* . . . is never dyadic, but always triadic; there is always an implicit 'more than,' and there is always a 'with respect to.'"[43] Thus the phrase is more accurately construed as "*x* resembles *y* more than *z* with respect to . . ." "In the case of academic comparison," Smith continues, "the 'with respect to' is most frequently the scholar's interest, be this expressed in a question, a theory, or a model."[44] Thus:

> Comparison does not necessarily tell us how things 'are' (the far from latent presupposition that lies behind the notion of the 'genealogical' with its quest for 'real' historical connections); like models and metaphors, comparison tells us how things might be conceived. . . . Comparison provides the means by which *we* 're-vision' phenomena as *our* data in order to solve *our* theoretical problems.[45]

In his conclusion, Smith suggests that an end to the Protestant hegemony over comparisons in the academy "will bring about a radical reformulation of the generative questions and a thorough revaluation of the purposes of comparison."[46] While it is clear that Smith links both an interest in pure origins and the tendency to render early Christianity incomparable with theological apologetics, it is not clear what interests and questions should replace these predominant notions in the study of early Christianity.

This non-statement of competing interests becomes more obvious in the case of the Cynic comparison. William Arnal notes that the scholars producing analyses comparing the Cynics with Q's Jesus locate their work within the framework of Smith's methodological suggestions and, therefore, repeatedly assert that their interests are not "identity so much as comparability," that is, not genealogy but analogy.[47] However, Arnal identifies three ways in which the Cynic comparisons do not consistently follow through with this methodological framework. First, some of the works actually do make genetic

---

[43]Smith, *Drudgery Divine*, 51.

[44]Ibid.

[45]Ibid., 52 (Smith's emphasis).

[46]Ibid., 143.

[47]William E. Arnal, *Jesus and the Village Scribes* (Minneapolis: Fortress, 2001) 54.

claims for the relationship between the Q people and Cynics.[48] Second, the emphasis on the comparability of Q^1 to the Cynics and the implication that Q^2 represents "later, and less interesting corruptions of the original impulse," implies that "disclaimers to the contrary, proponents of the Cynic comparison are no more historiographically sophisticated than the theologically minded commentators they seek to discredit."[49] According to Arnal, there is a persistence of a "conception of origins as normative, pristine, enviable—and of later developments as rigidifying an initially supple 'experiment.'"[50] Third, Arnal suggests that the questions and interests that produce the comparison (according to Smith's method[51]) are not articulated in the case of the Cynic comparison. "If comparison is indeed a disciplined exaggeration for our own (ideally, stated) theoretical and practical purposes, what are these purposes? What are the set of grounds, the fixed questions that the comparison is imagined to address?"[52] Arnal concludes that "we are left with an identity equation (the Q people were Cynics) with all its attendant problems, as well as its methodological naïveté, or with the assertion that the people behind Q were merely, in some unspecified way, comparable to the Cynics, which raises the questions, So what? What have we learned?"[53]

Conclusion

According to Smith, "the 'unique' is a thoroughly modern notion. . . . One no earlier than those same nineteenth-century German Protestant discussions which yielded, in reaction to comparative religious data, such diverse

---

[48]Arnal, *Village Scribes*, 53. In addition, the fact that those making the Cynic comparison answer their critics with proof that there were indeed Cynics in Galilee also indirectly shows the way that issues of identity and genealogy still frame the question (ibid., 57).

[49]Ibid., 54.

[50]Ibid.

[51]According to Smith, "[A]ll comparisons are properly analogical. . . . In the case of the study of religion, as in any disciplined inquiry, comparison, in its strongest form, brings differences together within the space of the scholar's mind for the scholar's own intellectual reasons. It is the scholar who makes their cohabitation—their 'sameness'—possible, not 'natural' affinities of processes of history. Taken in this sense, 'genealogy' disguises and obscures the scholar's interests and activities allowing the illusion of passive observation (what Nietzsche has termed [*Zarathustra* 2.15], the 'myth of the immaculate perception')" (*Drudgery Divine*, 51).

[52]Arnal, *Village Scribes*, 57.

[53]Ibid.

innovations as the notion of 'universal Christianity' . . . and the study of religion as an academic pursuit."[54] But Christian claims of "difference plus superlative value"—particularly with regard to interpretations of Jesus—are as old as the Gospels (and the *kerygma*) themselves. Indeed, the doctrines often at stake in discussions of eschatology and uniqueness claims are christological doctrines, which both the *Newsweek* article and the query from Judith Plaskow associate with the basic building blocks of Christian identity.

The methodological critique of claims of uniqueness plays a role in the ongoing discourse over Christology, Christian identity, and Christian anti-Judaism. Thus, rather than attempting to set aside our own interests in the contemporary discussion, we need to locate our interpretations within this ongoing debate. Given the persistence of prejudice and anti-Judaism, how do we interpret and evaluate Christologies (or difference plus superlative value claims) in early Christianity? For some, the historical claim that "there was a time when Christology was not" gives us something to work with to promote justice and liberation for all people. But this misses the fact that the Christian and Jewish traditions have *always* been characterized by competing emphases—by traditions and interpretations that dominate and divide, and traditions and interpretations that envision justice and promote human equality.

In order to develop criteria for evaluating discourses of Christian uniqueness, therefore, one must begin not with "disinterested" methodology, but rather with the contemporary situation. Indeed, the starting place of feminist biblical interpretation and theology is the contemporary situation of wo/men's struggle for equality. Thus, in her investigation of the issue of "feminist anti-Judaism," Elisabeth Schüssler Fiorenza begins with the following statement:

> Such an investigation is important particularly because of the frightening increase of neo-Nazism, racism, and antiforeign sentiments in the United States and Europe. The worldwide increase of the practice of hate and the language of oppression in the name of religion underscores the need for interreligious dialogues, especially between the so-called Abrahamic religions, Judaism, Islam, and Christianity. Such interreligious dialogues are, however, of interest not only to religious people. Since religion often plays a divisive role in nationalistic and

---

[54]Smith, *Drudgery Divine*, 38.

antidemocratic struggles, interreligious dialogue must fashion an ethos
and ethics that can contribute to the solution of hostilities rather than
continuing to fuel national and international conflicts.[55]

The following re-readings of the Beelzebul and Sign of Jonah units in Q,
chapters 5 and 6, respectively, take seriously the contemporary Christian
feminist rejection of Christian anti-Judaism and attempt to contribute to
the ongoing effort to foster a common vision of equality and its manifestations and challenges in particular traditions. As with the John materials
in Q, taking a different approach to these texts also results in interpretations that can make sense of certain aspects of the texts that have troubled
previous interpreters.

---

[55]Schüssler Fiorenza, *Jesus*, 67.

CHAPTER 5

Eschatology and the *Basileia*:
The Uniqueness of Jesus in Q 11:14–26

> The early Christian story about Jesus' collusion with Beelzebul, the
> ruler of the demons, marks one of the most significant and talked
> about texts in the history of New Testament scholarship. It is signifi-
> cant because it contains a most remarkable saying about the kingdom
> of God: "If I cast out demons by the finger [Spirit] of God, then
> the kingdom *has come* upon you." The saying maintains a central
> position in the discussion of Christian origins and the meaning of
> the kingdom of God, especially as it bears upon the longstanding
> debate about some nascent eschatological [future] kingdom vis à vis
> a present kingdom.[1]

As this inscription attests, the interpretation of the Beelzebul controversy
in Matt 12:22–30, 43–45, Mark 3:22–26, and Luke 11:14–26 figures
prominently in the larger scholarly discussions of Christian origins and
early Christian eschatology. This chapter examines and interprets the reconstructed Q Beelzebul text at the crossroads of contemporary discourses
on the uniqueness of Jesus, the interpretation of the *basileia* of God, and
the singular and superlative value of Jesus in the traditions of Q.

The re-reading of Q 11:14–26 presented in this chapter builds on the
methodological assumption deployed in chapters 2 and 3 whereby alternative
interpretations become possible when a different framework or set of interests
is brought to bear on a text. The assumption of many modern interpreters
that Jesus was/is unique or at least the sole focus of group identity formation

---

[1]Michael L. Humphries, *Christian Origins and the Language of the Kingdom of God*
(Carbondale: Southern Illinois University Press, 1999) 11 (Humphries's emphasis).

reduces the possibility that "gospel" texts might have had rhetorical goals other than explicating Jesus' unique identity and significance. My interpretation of the Beelzebul pericope is not based upon a new piece of data or on a new comparison that makes the meaning of the text transparent, but rather upon taking a different approach to certain aspects of the text that scholars have long debated. For example, most interpreters see a tension between the claims of Q 11:19 and Q 11:20:

> And if I cast out demons by Beelzebul, by whom do your sons cast them out? Therefore they shall be your judges. (Q 11:19)

> But if by the finger of God I cast out demons, then upon you has come the *basileia* of God. (Q 11:20)

The argument of 11:19 depends upon an affirmation of exorcisms performed by the "sons" of the opponents, while 11:20 identifies Jesus' exorcisms as indicative of the coming of the *basileia* of God. As we will see, scholars resolve this tension by relativizing the weight of 11:19—or redirecting its meaning—in light of the seeming claims of uniqueness for Jesus' exorcisms in Q 11:20. However, this tension disappears if we interpret Q 11:14–26 as an extended argument for solidarity among those who share the communal vision of the *basileia* of God. Before presenting this interpretation of the text, we will first review the reconstruction of the text and examine the way that Q 11:20 has figured prominently in shaping the interpretation of the unit as a whole.

Establishing the Text

There is a great deal of overlap between Luke 11:14–26 and Matt 12:22–30, 43–45 and thus the reconstruction of the Q text is relatively undisputed. The major disagreements have to do with the placement of Q 11:16 and 11:24–26, and whether the parable of the strong man's house was present in Q. Except where noted, the Greek reconstruction[2] follows the IQP:

Q 11:14: καὶ ἐ⟦⟨ξέ⟩⟧βαλ⟦⟨εν⟩⟧ δαιμόνιον κωφόν· καὶ ἐκβληθέντος τοῦ δαιμονίου ἐλάλησεν ὁ κωφὸς καὶ ἐθαύμασαν οἱ ὄχλοι	And he cast out a mute demon. And once the demon was cast out, the mute person spoke and the crowds were amazed.

[2]Robinson, *Critical Edition*, 222–42.

Q 11:15: τινὲς δὲ εἶπον· ἐν βεελζεβοὺλ τῷ ἄρχοντι τῶν δαιμονίων ἐκβάλλει τὰ δαιμόνια.

But some said, "He casts out demons by Beelzebul, the ruler of demons!"

Q 11:16:[3] ἕτεροι ⟦δέ⟧ ἐζήτουν παρ' αὐτοῦ σημεῖον.

And others were seeking a sign from him.

Q 11:17: εἰδὼς δὲ τὰ διανοήματα αὐτῶν εἶπεν αὐτοῖς· πᾶσα βασιλεία μερισθεῖσα ⟦καθ'⟧ ἑαυτῆ⟦ς⟧ ἐρημοῦται καί πᾶσα οἰκία μερισθεῖσα καθ' ἑαυτῆς οὐ σταθήσεται.

But knowing their thoughts, he said to them, "Every *basileia* divided against itself is laid waste, and every house divided against itself will not stand.

Q 11:18a: καὶ εἰ ὁ σατανᾶς ἐφ' ἑαυτὸν ἐμερίσθη, πῶς σταθήσεται ἡ βασιλεία αὐτοῦ;[4]

And if Satan is divided against himself, how will his *basileia* stand?

Q 11:19: καὶ εἰ ἐγὼ ἐν βεελζεβοὺλ ἐκβάλλω τὰ δαιμόνια, οἱ υἱοὶ ὑμῶν ἐν τίνι ἐκβάλλουσιν; διὰ τοῦτο αὐτοὶ κριταὶ ἔσονται ὑμῶν.

And if I by Beelzebul cast out demons, by whom do your sons cast [them] out? Therefore, they shall be your judges.

Q 11:20: εἰ δὲ ἐν δακτύλῳ[5] θεοῦ ἐγὼ ἐκβάλλω τὰ δαιμόνια, ἄρα ἔφθασεν ἐφ' ὑμᾶς ἡ βασιλεία τοῦ θεοῦ.

But if it is by the finger of God that I cast out demons, then the *basileia* of God has come upon you.

[3]I follow Kloppenborg and the IQP in 1991 (see Robinson, *Critical Edition*, 246) in placing Q 11:16 after 11:15 (Luke's order) rather than after Q 11:32 (Matthew's order). For further discussion, see ch. 6 below, pp. 172–74. Similar to Kirk (*Composition*, 184–85 n. 135), I discuss 11:16 in the context of the Sign of Jonah pericope. Placing Q 11:16 after 11:15 signals that "the collocation of themes in 11:14–16 is one of the several means the Q editor uses to signal that the two controversy instructions are to be read together" (ibid.).

[4]Most scholars consider v. 18b ("For you say that I exorcise demons by Beelzebul") a Lukan insertion that is influenced by Mark 3:30 (for bibliography, see Kloppenborg, *Q Parallels*, 92).

[5]There is an ongoing debate over whether Q had Luke's "finger" or Matthew's "spirit." Several interpreters argue that "finger" is from Luke: Robert G. Hamerton-Kelly, "A Note on Matthew XII.28 Par. Luke XI.20," *NTS* 11 (1964–1965) 167–69; A. George, "Note sur quelques traits lucaniens de l'expression «Par le doigt de Dieu» (Luc XI.20)," *Sciences Ecclésiastiques* 18 (1966) 461–66; C. S. Rodd, "Spirit or Finger," *ExpTim* 72 (1960–1961) 157–58; J. M. Van Cangh, " 'Par l'esprit de Dieu—par le doigt de Dieu' Mt 12,28 par. Lc 11,20," in *Logia. Les paroles de Jésus* (ed. Joël Delobel; Leuven: Leuven University Press, 1982) 337–42. The IQP follows Kümmel and argues that "finger" is from Q. See Kloppenborg, "Q 11:14–20: Work Sheets for Reconstruction," *SBLSP* 24 (1985) 147.

Q 11:21:[6] [[«ὅταν ὁ ἰσχυρὸς
καθωπλισμένος φυλάσσῃ τὴν
ἑαυτοῦ αὐλήν, ἐν εἰρήνῃ ἐστὶν τὰ
ὑπάρχοντα αὐτοῦ·»]]

[When the strong man, fully
armed, guards his own palace, his
possessions are in peace.]

Q 11:22: [[«ἐπὰν δὲ ἰσχυρότερος
αὐτοῦ [ ] ἐπελθὼν νικήσῃ αὐτόν,
τὴν πανοπλίαν αὐτοῦ αἴρει ἐφ᾽
ᾗ ἐπεποίθει καὶ τὰ σκῦλα αὐτοῦ
διαδίδωσιν»]].

[But when one stronger than he
... conquers him, he takes away
his armor in which he trusted, and
divides his spoil.]

Q 11:23: ὁ μὴ ὢν μετ᾽ ἐμοῦ κατ᾽ ἐμοῦ
ἐστιν, καὶ ὁ μὴ συνάγων μετ᾽ ἐμοῦ
σκορπίζει.

The one who is not with me is against
me, and the one who does not gather
with me scatters.

Q 11:24: ὅταν τὸ ἀκάθαρτον
πνεῦμα ἐξέλθῃ ἀπὸ τοῦ ἀνθρώπου,
διέρχεται δι᾽ ἀνύδρων τόπων ζητοῦν
ἀνάπαυσιν καὶ οὐχ εὑρίσκει. [[τότε]]
λέγει· εἰς τὸν οἶκόν μου ἐπιστρέψω
ὅθεν ἐξῆλθον·

When an unclean spirit has gone
out of a person, it passes through
waterless places seeking rest and
finds none. Then it says, I will return
to my house from which I came.

Q 11:25: καὶ ἐλθὸν εὑρίσκει
σεσαρωμένον καὶ κεκοσμημένον.

And on coming it finds it swept and
put in order.

Q 11:26: τότε πορεύεται καὶ
παραλαμβάνει μεθ᾽ ἑαυτοῦ ἑπτὰ
ἕτερα πνεύματα πονηρότερα ἑαυτοῦ
καὶ εἰσελθόντα κατοικεῖ ἐκεῖ· καὶ
γίνεται τὰ ἔσχατα τοῦ ἀνθρώπου
ἐκείνου χείρονα τῶν πρώτων.

Then it goes and brings with it seven
other spirits more evil than itself,
and they enter and dwell there; and
the last state of that person becomes
worse than the first."

---

[6]Because of the Markan parallel, it is possible that the saying about the strong man's house
(Matt 12:29//Luke 11:21–22//Mark 3:27) was not in Q. The IQP places square brackets around
the English translation indicating that they ascribe the whole verse to Q but do not attempt
to reconstruct the Greek text. Kloppenborg lists the several authors who take 11:21–22 as
part of Q and notes that the "main argument for the inclusion of the parable in Q is that the
agreement of Matthew and Luke in independently placing the parable of the strong man
between Q 11:20 and 11:23 cannot be coincidental, but indicates that the parable also stood
in Q at this point" (*Q Parallels*, 92). The opposing view argues that the agreements are too
slim to posit a Q text and in this case Matthew follows Mark and Luke rewrites Mark (see
ibid.). The Greek reconstruction is from the IQP's version of Q published in *JBL* (109–14
[1990–95] passim).

The pericope consists of a very condensed narrative in 11:14, where Jesus casts out a demon and heals the formerly possessed man of the muteness caused by the demon. The man speaks, and the crowds display amazement. The scene provides the occasion for the accusation in 11:15 that Jesus casts out demons by Beelzebul, the ruler of demons. Verses 17–20 contain four sayings of Jesus in response to this accusation, culminating in the intriguing but intractable saying: "But if by the finger of God I cast out demons, then upon you has come the *basileia* of God." This saying is followed by the parable of the strong man, a saying on scattering and gathering in 11:23, and another parable about the activity of an unclean spirit in 11:24–26.[7]

This unit shows signs of coherence as a composition. The sharp thematic breaks between the preceding unit on prayer (Q 11:2–4 and 9–13) and the subsequent request for a sign (Q 11:29–32) mark Q 11:14–26 as one rhetorical unit. Keywords such as δαιμόνιον,[8] βασιλεία,[9] and ἐκβάλλω[10] occur throughout 11:14–20. But even without such strong keyword connections, the two parables (11:21–22 and 24–26) and the saying on gathering (11:23) continue the themes of 11:14–20: the image of the household (οἰκία/οἶκος [11:17, 24], αὐλήν [11:21]), the semantic fields of warfare and division (11:17–18; 11:22; 11:23), and the theme of demonic possession (11:14–20 and 11:24–26) tie the discourse together.

All of these verbal and thematic connections, however, are often viewed as thin threads holding together a disjointed and—in the case of 11:19 and 11:20—discordant set of sayings. As a result, most approaches to the text

[7]There is some disagreement whether this parable belongs after Q 11:14–23 (as in Luke), or after Q 11:29–32 (as in Matthew). The majority of scholars follow the Lukan order (see Kloppenborg, *Q Parallels*, 94). Vassiliadis ("The Original Order of Q: Some Residual Cases," in *Logia* [Delobel] 379–87) argues that Matthew breaks up a ring structure in Q, in which 11:24–26 is the center of 11:14–32. Others argue that 11:24–26 summarized the controversy sections in both Q and Matthew. This depends partially on whether Luke 11:16 was after Luke 11:15 in Q. If the units were already woven together, then either argument is plausible. Since Q tends to group sayings thematically and by catchwords, it is more likely that Q 11:24–26 followed Q 11:23. Matthew's own efforts to use Q 11:24–26 as a summation of the unit may be apparent in the addition of Matt 12:45c, which links 11:24–26 to the end of the Sign of Jonah pericope.

[8]Of the seven occurrences of δαιμόνιον indexed by the IQP (Robinson, *Critical Edition*, 563–81), six of them are in Q 11:14–20. The other appears in the charge of demon possession against John in Q 7:33.

[9]The term βασιλεία occurs in Q 11:17, 18, and 20.

[10]Of the thirteen cases of ἐκβάλλω indexed by the IQP (ibid.), six of them are in Q 11:14–20. The remaining seven (Q 6:42–45 [5 times]; Q 10:2; and Q 13:28) do not refer to exorcism.

of Q 11:14–26 center around redaction-historical questions. From an early point, the issue of the relationship between 11:19 and 11:20 played a role in the development of compositional theories for the unit. Bultmann classifies 11:14–18a as the original apophthegm, which was expanded by two independent sayings (vv. 19 and 20) that "have nothing to do with each other originally."[11] A review of Kloppenborg's summary of the three main proposals for the process by which 11:19 and 11:20 came to be juxtaposed in Q illustrates that the incompatibility of the two sayings is instrumental to each proposal. The first proposal is that Q 11:14, 15, and 19 are original, and that Q 11:20 was added as a commentary on Q 11:19 in order to obviate potential misunderstanding "that Jewish exorcisms have something to do with the kingdom."[12] In the second proposal, Q 11:14, 15, 17, and (18a?) are original and secondarily expanded by vv. 19–20. Whether Q 11:19 and 20 were added together or separately is disputed.[13] Kloppenborg rules out one option by suggesting that "Q 11:19 can hardly be a redactional clasp since it actually undermines 11:20 by inviting inference that the kingdom is also manifest in the work of Jewish exorcists."[14] Thus he disagrees with the third option, which takes Q 11:14, 17a, 20 as original and v. 19 as a redactional clasp created when 11:17b–18b was later added.[15] Kloppenborg argues that the most economical solution is that "the basic tradition was 11:(14), 15, 17–18a, and that this was elaborated successively by vv. 19 and 20."[16]

Two recent treatments of this text focus at length on the literary composition of the Beelzebul accusation as a rhetorically cohesive discourse.[17] Setting

---

[11]Bultmann, *History*, 162.

[12]In this proposal, Q 11:17 and 18a are also secondary expansions. This is the view of E. Schweizer, Wanke, Marshall, and Zeller. See Kloppenborg, *Formation*, 123.

[13]Although Polag, Schulz, and Lührmann agree on this approach, each has a different solution to what they view as the problematic juxtaposition of 11:19 and 11:20. Polag (*Die Christologie der Logienquelle* [WMANT 45; Neukirchen-Vluyn: Neukirchener Verlag, 1977] 40) proposes that the two were formed together and can be understood as successive argumentative steps: v. 19 rejects that Jesus exorcises by Beelzebul and then v. 20 confirms that Jesus exorcises by God. Schulz (*Spruchquelle*, 206) suggests that vv. 18, 19, and 20 were added in succession. Lührmann (*Redaktion*, 33) takes Q 11:20 as an authentic saying of Jesus that was attached to Q 11:14–18 by the creation of 11:19.

[14]Kloppenborg, *Formation*, 123.

[15]Heinz Schürmann, "Der Zeugnis der Redequelle für die Basileia-Verkündigung Jesu," in *Logia* (ed. Delobel) 155–56. For a literary-critical assessment of Schürmann's proposal, see Kirk, *Composition*, 183–84.

[16]Kloppenborg, *Formation*, 124.

[17]Humphries, *Christian Origins*; and Kirk, *Composition*, 183–92 and 309–36. See also

aside the persistent interest in Q 11:20 as an indicator of Jesus' eschatology, Michael Humphries suggests that the *basileia* saying in Q 11:20 should be examined in the context of the text's rhetorical organization. Similarly, Alan Kirk suggests that "the nature of Q's text as carrying out a communicative, rhetorical strategy must be recovered and foregrounded in analysis."[18] "Far from being haphazard arrangements," he says, "relations between constituent units and the structures which implement them (for example, sequencing) are manifestations of a communicative strategy."[19] Kirk and Humphries nonetheless differ in their rhetorical classification of the sayings in the Beelzebul pericope. Humphries identifies Q 11:14–26 as an elaborated *chreia* and gives a sustained reading of the text in that framework. Kirk concurs that Q 11:15, 17 is a double *chreia*, but classifies 11:18–23 according to compositional patterns he has identified elsewhere in Q and in other ancient instructional genres.[20]

Q 11:20 and the Interpretation of Q 11:14–26

Two general approaches to Q 11:20 have had a substantial impact on the interpretation of Q 11:14–26 as a whole. The first views 11:20 as a window on the eschatology of Jesus. Thus the saying figures prominently in the discussion about the eschatology of the historical Jesus,[21] centering on the

---

Tuckett, *Q*, 289–91. Although Horsley and Draper (*Whoever Hears*) similarly take an approach to Q texts that focuses on the coherence of Q discourses, they do not treat the Beelzebul pericope at any length.

[18]Kirk, *Composition*, 68.

[19]Ibid.

[20]Kirk (ibid., 184–89) identifies Q 11:18 and 19 as rhetorical questions that refute the initial charge, 11:20 as the central aphorism, 11:21–22 as an example of the central aphorism, and 11:23 as a maxim that serves as an inclusio with the programmatic maxim of 11:17. Although recognizing its elaborative connection to the Beelzebul controversy, Kirk leaves the parable of the return of the unclean spirit (11:24–26) to serve as a discrete coordinating unit between 11:14–23 and 11:29–35 (see ibid., 330–32).

[21]Q 11:20 is "one of the very few sayings in the tradition, the authenticity of which has not been seriously questioned in more than a half century of intensive discussion of Jesus' eschatological teaching" (Norman Perrin, *Rediscovering the Teaching of Jesus* [London: SCM, 1967] 64). See, however, Mack, *Lost Gospel*, 90 and 140; and Heikki Räisänen, "Exorcisms and the Kingdom: Is Q 11:20 a Saying of the Historical Jesus?" in *Symbols and Strata: Essays on the Sayings Gospel Q* (ed. Risto Uro; Helsinki: Finnish Exegetical Society; Göttingen: Vandenhoeck & Ruprecht, 1996) 119–42.

question, "What does this passage say about Jesus' own eschatology and self-understanding?"[22] C. H. Dodd[23] greatly influenced this line of inquiry by suggesting that Q 11:20 is evidence that Jesus originally preached that the *basileia* had arrived in his own ministry. Dodd's work has received strong critique and modification but also has had substantial influence on the discussion of this passage.[24] Focusing on Q 11:20 as providing direct access to Jesus' teachings on the *basileia* of God places the identity and purpose of the historical Jesus at the center of inquiry and requires that the entire unit participate in the process of revealing Jesus' identity in the crescendo of 11:20. In effect, this approach interprets Q 11:20 apart from its context and then requires the context to conform to that interpretation. As we will see, this has the effect of silencing both the argument from common ground in 11:19 and the argument against divisiveness in the face of a common enemy in the unit as a whole.

The second approach to Q 11:14–26 suggests that 11:20 reflects the Q community's attempt to account for itself, that is, assert its own identity vis-à-vis outsiders. Although interest in Christian origins and the historical Jesus still permeates the methods and central questions with which scholars approach Q, recent monographs on Q ostensibly set aside tradition-historical questions in favor of interpreting Q as a gospel in its own right.[25] Within

---

[22]The relationship between authenticity, eschatology, and Christology is apparent in the view of Edward Meadors: "If 11:20//12:28 is, indeed, an authentic saying of Jesus as most modern critics have agreed, there appears no way of getting around the fact that Jesus himself had an awareness of his own personal role in transmitting God's saving power to people. To that extent 11:20//12:28 is motivated by the soteriological and christological understandings of Jesus not a Q community" (*Jesus the Messianic Herald of Salvation* [Tübingen: Mohr/Siebeck, 1995] 194–95).

[23]C. H. Dodd, *The Parables of the Kingdom* (rev. ed.; New York: Scribner, 1961).

[24]For example, the proper translation of the aorist verb ἔφθασεν became a central research question for the interpretation of Q 11:20. Matthew Black, "The Kingdom Has Come," *ExpTim* 63 (1951–1952) 289–90; J. Y. Campbell, "The Kingdom of God Has Come," *ExpTim* 48 (1936–1937) 91–94; Robert F. Berkey, "ΕΓΓΙΖΕΙΝ, ΦΘΑΝΕΙΝ, and Realized Eschatology," *JBL* 82 (1963) 177–87. Dodd's classification of Jesus' *basileia* preaching as "realized eschatology" also received a good deal of evaluation and critique. Clarence T. Craig, "Realized Eschatology," *JBL* 56 (1937) 17–26; Kenneth W. Clark, "Realized Eschatology," *JBL* 59 (1940) 367–83; Clayton Sullivan, *Rethinking Realized Eschatology* (Macon, Ga.: Mercer University Press, 1988); and Jean Carmignac, *Le mirage de l'eschatologie* (Paris: Letouzey et Ané, 1979).

[25]Kloppenborg, *Formation*; Tuckett, *Q*; Kirk, *Composition*; Horsley and Draper, *Whoever Hears*; Hoffmann, *Studien*; Jacobson, *First Gospel*; and Mack, *Lost Gospel*, etc. A large number of the most recent scholarly articles on specific Q texts take a similar approach.

this approach, the text acts as a mirror of early Christian identity formation by presenting the community's interpretation of the traditions of Jesus in light of their own experiences and worldview. The Q "data," then, primarily give us a view of the Q community's self-understanding and their use of the Jesus traditions to make sense of themselves and their world. In this context, Q 11:20 is examined not for what it says about Jesus' understanding of the *basileia* of God and his relationship to it, but rather for what it says about the Q community's self-understanding and for how it plays a role in group identity formation.

It is important to consider how texts function to construct the audience's self-understanding. However, in the prevailing interpretation, Q 11:14–26 is a controversy story that reflects the community's struggle to defend itself and define itself in response to the experience of hostility from other Jews. The text, in this interpretation, is a tool of community identity formation over and against outsiders. This dictates that 11:19 *cannot* be an unqualified affirmation of Jesus' accusers. It also requires that 11:20, as the climax of Jesus' argument in 11:14–20, presents a program of counter-stigmatization whereby the community's "insider" status is re-established through a reversal of the status of the accusers in the text. This approach creates the expectation that the "controversy" is over issues of identity and difference in relationship to other Jews, and that the community's claims about the singular significance of Jesus must be a central issue being negotiated by the text. This results in assuming a substantial distance between the identity of Jesus and his accusers. For example, despite the fact that everyone affirms that Jesus is a Jewish exorcist in the text, the label "Jewish exorcists" is used routinely for "your sons" in Q 11:19 but not for Jesus in 11:20.

Claiming the Common Ground

Interest in Jesus' self-understanding or the community's claims to his uniqueness shapes how we interpret Q 11:14–26. What if we approach the text with new questions? The following interpretation illustrates how the text can have different meanings, if we approach it with different questions. By placing the communal vision of the *basileia* of God at the center of our inquiry, we can interpret Q 11:14–26 as an extended argument for common ground and thus common cause between Jesus and his accusers. This reading becomes possible by setting aside the common assumption that Q 11:20 implicitly makes unique and christological claims for Jesus by linking him uniquely to the *basileia* of God. Once this reading is considered, it can also be judged for how well it explains the rest of the pericope.

Against the Disasters of Divisiveness: Q 11:15–18

A compact miracle story (Q 11:14) serves as the occasion for the accusation in 11:15: "But some[26] said, 'He casts out demons by Beelzebul, the ruler of demons!'" The accusation grants that Jesus casts out demons (ἐκβάλλει τὰ δαιμόνια), but claims that he performs them with the power of Beelzebul, the ruler of demons (ἐν βεελζεβοὺλ τῷ ἄρξχοντι τῶν δαιμονίων). Thus the opponents call Jesus' exorcisms into question on the grounds that he draws on or manifests demonic power. Where Mark 3:22 includes a charge of demon possession, Q 11:15 focuses on Jesus' collusion with Beelzebul. Scholars have long sought to identify "Beelzebul" and to explain his appellation "the ruler of demons" and the resulting link with Satan in 11:18a. Because the name is connected to "Baal," the ancient Canaanite enemy of the God of Israel,[27] the charge explicitly links Jesus' exorcisms with a foreign or non-Israelite deity.[28] The accusation is "an effort to label Jesus as an outsider,"[29] that is, as in league with the enemies of Israel's God.

[26]All three gospels attribute the accusation to someone different: Matthew to the Pharisees (two times in Matt 9:34 and 12:24), Mark to the "scribes who came down from Jerusalem" (in Mark 3:22), and Luke to "some of them" (possibly referring to some members of the crowds who were amazed). Since Matthew tends to identify the opponents of Jesus as Pharisees, Luke's "some of them" is usually taken as the Q text. While this is certainly possible, it is important to note that the Pharisees do appear in Q (at minimum at 11:39 and 11:43). Thus it is also possible that Luke edits out the Pharisees at this point. See Kloppenborg, *Formation*, 121 n. 93. It is clear, therefore, that someone accuses Jesus of casting out demons by Beelzebul, but it is not clear precisely who that someone is in Q.

[27]*Beel* in this case is the Greek transliteration of the Hebrew *Baal*, which means "owner," "lord," or "prince." Humphries reviews the proposals for interpreting Beelzebul as "Baal, ruler of heaven," or "Baal, ruler of the diseased," or "prince Baal, lord of the earth." Humphries prefers the last proposal that "Beelzebul" is a "provincial manifestation of Yahweh's traditional chief rival, namely, 'prince Baal, lord of the earth' (*zbl Bʿl ʾrṣ*), whose name here has been shortened to the simple form of 'Prince Baal' (*Bʿl zbl*, i.e., Beelzeboul). . . . Naturally, 'prince Baal,' a chief among foreign deities and traditional rival of Yahweh, is designated 'ruler of demons'" (*Christian Origins*, 30).

[28]Lloyd Gaston ("Beelzebul," *TZ* 18 [1962] 247–55) offers the intriguing suggestion that Beelzebul is another way of speaking of *Baalshamaim* ("lord of heaven") who is equivalent to Zeus Olympios (see the Syrian translation of Zeus Olympios in 2 Macc 6:2). See also W. E. M. Aitken, "Beelzebul," *JBL* 31 (1912) 34–53.

[29]Humphries, *Christian Origins*, 29.

The rhetoric of the accusation establishes the unit's interest in issues of difference. Humphries rightly applies Jonathan Z. Smith's observations about the charge of devil worship to this accusation of demon collusion: " 'Devil Worship,' properly understood, is not a substantive category. It does not refer (save in rare and usually artificial cases) to people worshiping devils or demons. Rather it is a measure of distance, a *taxon*, a label applied to distinguish 'us' from 'them.' "[30] Humphries draws on the broad identification of Beelzebul as a foreign deity to conclude:

> Beelzebul is regarded as demonic precisely because he is foreign, and therefore the charge of Jesus' collusion with him is at the same time a charge of deviance: "This man operates under the auspices of that foreign deity Beelzebul; he is not one of us; he is an outsider, a deviant." The accusation is thus "locative," serving to locate Jesus (or more precisely the Q community) outside of the traditional Israelite scheme of things as perceived by the opponents.[31]

In the world of the text the accusation of Jesus' collusion, therefore, constructs Jesus as a deviant in comparison to his accusers.

Q 11:17 presents Jesus' initial response to the accusation of deviance.[32] In the scene created by the apophthegm, Jesus answers the charge of collusion with Beelzebul (11:15) with a double saying about a divided *basileia* and house (11:17): "But knowing their thoughts,[33] he said to them, 'Every

[30]Ibid., quoting Smith.

[31]Ibid., 30.

[32]Kirk (*Composition*, 328) and Humphries identify Q 11:15, 17 as a double *chreia*: "two sayings by different characters, with the second often given in the form of a retort against the first" (Humphries, *Christian Origins*, 29). Both provide an example of the form from Quintilian's *Institutio Oratoria* (6.3.63): "There was a Roman knight drinking in the seats of the theater, to whom Augustus sent word, saying: 'If I wish to have lunch, I go home.' The knight said: 'Certainly, for you are not afraid that you will lose your place!'" Vernon Robbins ("Rhetorical Composition & the Beelzebul Controversy," in *Patterns of Persuasion in the Gospels* [ed. idem and Burton L. Mack; Sonoma, Calif.: Polebridge, 1989] 162–63) does not take up the framework of the double *chreia* but does identify v. 17 as the first response to the charge in 11:15.

[33]The agreement between Matthew and Luke on Jesus knowing the others' thoughts is one of the arguments for there being a Q text of this unit at all (given the Mark-Q overlap). In Mark, Jesus summons the scribes and speaks to them "in parables" (Mark 3:23). In Q, Jesus knows the thoughts of the accusers. Kloppenborg describes the Q text as "stating that the response was provoked by a supernatural knowledge of the thoughts of the opponents" (*Formation*, 121–22). For a discussion of the text in light of divine man traditions, see Schulz, *Q*, 208. The

basileia divided against itself is laid waste, and every house divided against itself will not stand.'"[34] This is a general aphorism about division, that is, a "proverbial form of everyday wisdom about the disastrous results of dissension."[35] It is actually a pair of figurative sayings, a form that is common to Q.[36] Although the precise metaphor of a divided *basileia* does not appear in other extant ancient literature, the double saying draws on the pervasive socio-political language of *basileia* and household and invokes images of civil war and internal strife.[37] This image of civil war is echoed in Q 11:20 and in the parable of the strong man in Q 11:21–22.

The saying in v. 17 is general and open-ended. Kirk classifies it as the "programmatic general maxim" from which "the argumentative maneuvers which follow take their thematic and key word references."[38] Indeed, only in v. 18a is the logic of the double saying applied to the question at hand: "And if Satan[39] is divided against himself, how will his *basileia* stand?" Thus

---

text, however, does not say that the knowledge is supernatural; it does not explain the source or kind of knowledge. Humphries (*Christian Origins*, 30) suggests that the claim to knowledge expresses Jesus' "ability to discern the stratagems of his opponents, an ability suitable to one who is about to outwit his detractors with a clever rejoinder." He also points out that εἰδὼς δὲ τὰ δαινοήματα can mean simply that Jesus could perceive their plan and knew how best to respond (ibid., 73 n. 8). Jacobson's observation (*First Gospel*, 161 n. 26) that "Jesus hardly needs to discern their thoughts, since they have just openly expressed them" lends support to Humphries's interpretation.

[34]The reconstruction of the second part of the saying is difficult. Luke 11:17 has only οἶκος ἐπὶ οἶκον πίπτει ("house collapses upon house" or "house that is against house collapses" [Kloppenbborg, *Q Parallels*, 91]). Matthew retains most of the vocabulary of the first part of the Q saying but adapts Mark for the second half.

[35]Humphries, *Christian Origins*, 30.

[36]There are eleven occurrences of this form in Q: 6:43–44a; 6:44b; 6:45; 7:32; 9:58; 11: 9–13; 11:17; 12:24–28; 12:33; 13:24; and 17:34–35. See Jacobson, *First Gospel*, 64; and Michael G. Steinhauser, *Doppelbildworte in den synoptischen Evangelien. Eine form- und traditionskritische Studie* (FB 44; Würzburg: Echter-Verlag, 1981).

[37]The verb ἐρημόω (BAG: "to lay waste," "to depopulate a city") derives from the semantic field of warfare. See also Jacobson, *First Gospel*, 161; and Kloppenborg, *Formation*, 125.

[38]Kirk, *Composition*, 186.

[39]The shift from Beelzebul to Satan has prompted some scholars to see v. 18a as a redaction of an original apophthegm (11:15, 17). See Schulz, *Q*, 206; and Steinhauser, *Doppelbildworte*, 141. Kloppenborg argues that "if 11:18a was not original, it must have been an early addition since it appears also in the Marcan version (3:26)" (*Formation*, 122). Some explain the move from Beelzebul to Satan in the context of Jesus' saying insofar as it challenges the assumption of the accusation that the demonic world is pluralistic with a monistic understanding of the demonic world ruled by Satan. See Jacobson, *First Gospel*, 161 and 164; and Humphries, *Christian Origins*, 31.

the argument progresses "from a general principle to an increasingly specific application."[40]

The initial response to the accusation in Q 11:17 does not appear to answer the charge of deviance directly. It rather draws on common knowledge to expose the absurdity of the opponents' claim: "The charge of demon collusion is absurd, for everyone knows that a divided kingdom will fall."[41] It has gone unnoticed, however, that the double saying in v. 17 does directly counter the *divisive rhetoric* of the accusation by reminding the accusers of what they already know, that is, that such in-fighting is the downfall of *basileiai* and households alike. The charge of deviance in 11:15 constructs a radical divide between the accusers and Jesus:

> But some said, "He casts out demons by Beelzebul, ruler of demons!" (Q 11:15)

Jesus' initial response does not counter the charge of deviance but rather points to the *disastrous effects of divisiveness itself*:

> But knowing their thoughts, he said to them, "Every *basileia* divided against itself is laid waste, and every house divided against itself will not stand." (Q 11:17)

This saying can function, therefore, both as an illustration of the absurdity of the charge and as a critique of the accusers' divisiveness. The critique of divisiveness is possible only if we assume that the audience recognizes common ground between the accusers and the protagonist that has been divided by the accusation. The metaphors of a shared *basileia* or a shared house have force as a critique of the divisiveness of the deviance charge only if the audience knows that the accusers and Jesus somehow—even figuratively—share a *basileia* or a house. Indeed they do. Q's Jesus will use this same common ground to his rhetorical advantage in Q 11:19 when he asks: "And if I by Beelzebul cast out demons, by whom do your sons

[40]Piper, *Wisdom*, 122. Mark provides an interpretation of the saying about division as the initial response to the charge. Thus the question "How can Satan exorcise Satan?" (Mark 3: 23b) precedes the sayings about division in Mark 3:24–25. In contrast, Q offers the sayings themselves as the first response and then applies them to the situation with v. 18. Piper (*Wisdom*, 121–22) identifies this same type of progression in Q 11:9–13; 12:22–31; 6:37–42; 6:43–45; and 12:2–9.

[41]Humphries, *Christian Origins*, 30.

cast [them] out?" The rhetorical force of the charge of deviance itself lies in the text's assumption that Q's audience shares the symbolic world of both the accusers and Jesus. In other words, Beelzebul functions in the accusation as a foreign deity specifically from *within* the symbolic world of ancient Judaism. Apparently neither Jesus' identity in relation to Judaism nor the audience's relationship to Judaism is a rhetorical interest of this text. Rather, the text assumes the common Jewish identity of Jesus and his accusers and attempts to persuade the audience to solidarity in the face of a common enemy.

The Sons of the Accusers and the Basileia *of God: Q 11:19–20*

Verse 19, like v. 18a,[42] begins with a rhetorical question: "And if I cast out demons by Beelzebul, by whom do your sons cast [them] out?" The protasis in v. 19 supplies a restatement of the accusation. The apodosis links the evaluation of Jesus' exorcisms to those of the accusers' "sons." If he casts out by Beelzebul, so do they; if they do not, then neither does he. The success of the argument rests squarely on the position that the accusers' sons and Jesus have a "quality in common"[43]—that is, that they both stand against Satan in their exorcisms. Jacobson rightly insists that "Q 11:19–20 implies that the other Jewish exorcists do indeed cast out demons by the power of God; this must be so, otherwise Jesus' answer to his opponents is not valid. Jesus and they stand, therefore, on much the same level."[44] Humphries argues similarly:

> In light of the logic of the preceding *chreia*, this sentiment is not only fair but also necessary. What the accusers grant to their own sons *cannot* be refused for Jesus. Indeed, the rule of the divided kingdom still stands: Satan cannot cast out Satan. Hence the practice of exorcism itself precludes demon collusion and demonstrates the power of God, and none other, is at work. It is not the person performing the act but the success of the act itself (here undisputed) that proves decisive. The fact that the accusers' own sons cast out demons by the power of God discloses the absurdity of the charge

---

[42]Kirk (*Composition*, 187) notes that the paired rhetorical questions in vv. 18a and 19 reflect Q's "preferred stylistic technique." A similar pattern appears in Q 6:41–42; 6:44; 11: 5–8, 11–12. These rhetorical questions supply "concretizing illustrations" of Q 11:17.

[43]Humphries, *Christian Origins*, 32.

[44]Jacobson, *First Gospel*, 163; see also Piper, *Wisdom*, 123.

and thereby also serves as judgment against them. As the argument unfolds, the implication is that *Jesus occupies the same space as that of his detractors.*[45]

If the accusers grant this "quality in common," they must accept the proposition that follows in Q 11:20: that Jesus' exorcisms—like the sons' exorcisms—reflect the power of God.

For all of the attention that it has received, Q 11:20 functions quite predictably as a third conditional construction that clinches the refutation of the accusation:

> Q 11:20: But if [εἰ] it is by the finger of God that I cast out demons, then [ἄρα] the *basileia* of God has come upon you.

Q 11:20 echoes but reverses the accusation of 11:15 by replacing ἐν βεελζεβοὺλ with ἐν δακτύλῳ θεοῦ in the protasis. The apodosis then reverses the language about Satan's basileia (ἡ βασιλεία αὐτοῦ) in 11:17–18 to identify Jesus' actions with God's *basileia* (ἡ βασιλεία τοῦ θεοῦ).

The most common interpretation of Q 11:20, however, is that Jesus has just made an extraordinary claim. Alan Kirk's description of the verse is a good example:

> In 11:20 Jesus first audaciously announces the unsurpassable, astonishing significance of himself and his actions [ἐγώ] in connection with a corresponding announcement of the arrival of the Kingdom of God, and thus startlingly answers the question of identity posed by the accusation leveled in the opening chreia.[46]

But how can v. 19 make a claim for a "quality in common" between Jesus' exorcisms and those of the "sons" of the accusers and then clinch the argument with a claim of unique significance for Jesus alone with regard to the coming *basileia*? Nothing in the saying itself marks Jesus as "unsurpassable," "astonishing," or even "audacious," but the assumption is that this is what 11:20 must mean.

---

[45]Humphries, *Christian Origins*, 32 (my emphasis).

[46]Kirk, *Composition*, 189. Kirk adds that a similar compositional strategy can be seen in 7:18–23; 7:24–28; and 7:31–35. However, the concluding statements of these units say more about the community than the identity of Jesus. The use of ἐγώ coheres with Jesus' self-defensive posture in both 11:19 and 20.

What then does v. 19 mean? Scholars have puzzled over this question for some time. Solutions to the problem fall into three types: (1) vv. 19 and 20 were not created at the same time; (2) v. 19 does not in fact mean what it seems to mean; or (3) v. 20 does not make uniqueness claims for Jesus and thus does not conflict with v. 19. Only a few take the third position. I discuss each option in turn in the following sections.

1. THE REDACTIONAL SOLUTION TO THE PERCEIVED INCOMPATIBILITY

In this approach the expectation that 11:20 must make christological, eschatological, and/or uniqueness claims for Jesus requires that 11:19 and 11:20 are incompatible. For example, Käsemann is very clear about the theological problem raised by taking the two verses as compatible: "The logical results conceal the theological dubiousness of the argument. The eschatological uniqueness of Jesus is not preserved if one compares him to Jewish exorcists."[47] Similarly, in his discussion of the interpretation of Loisy, B. S. Easton notes that the compatibility of 11:19 and 11:20 is unthinkable:

> Loisy argues further that 19 and 20 do not belong together, as in one case Christ's exorcisms are paralleled with those of the Jews while in the other their uniqueness is insisted on,—as the two verses stand at present the Jewish exorcisms could be taken as proofs of the advent of the Kingdom. But such a complete equation of the Jews' exorcisms with Christ's was scarcely to be apprehended.[48]

[47]Ernst Käsemann, "Lukas 11:14–28," in *Exegetische Versuche und Besinnungen, 1. Band* (Göttingen: Vandenhoeck & Ruprecht, 1960) 244 [author's translation]. Bultmann also argues that the two are basically incompatible: "The two sayings placed together in Q have nothing to do with each other originally. The former looks very much like Church polemic, though without supplying the basis for anything to be said confidently about it. But the latter can, in my view, claim the highest degree of authenticity which we can make for any saying of Jesus: it is full of that feeling of eschatological power which must have characterized the activity of Jesus" (Bultmann, *History*, 162).

[48]B. S. Easton, "The Beelzebul Sections," *JBL* 32 (1913) 64. I have removed Easton's parenthetical citations of concurring views from Jülicher, Wellhausen, Klostermann, Holtzmann, and B. Weiss. In his discussion of Matt 12:27–28, F. W. Beare comments on the lack of logic in the juxtaposition: "But if the work of the Jewish exorcist is valid, and gives rise to neither conjectures that the exorcist is the Messiah nor to the accusation that he is an agent empowered by the prince of demons, why should the exorcisms of Jesus lead to either conclusion about him? On the other hand, if Jesus' exorcisms are worked 'by the Spirit of God,' and this is an indication that the Kingdom of God has already arrived in power, why should not the successful exorcisms of the Jewish exorcists be equally good evidence of the arrival of the Kingdom? In sum, the

Dale Allison appeals to Q's overall eschatological and christological claims about Jesus to support his view of incompatibility:

> Certainly one cannot believe that the compiler of or community behind Q deemed the exorcisms of Jesus and others to be of equal religious significance. Among other things, Q 7:18–23, although it admittedly does not mention exorcisms, nonetheless construes Jesus' ministry of miracles as the unique, eschatological fulfillment of passages in Isaiah.[49]

Indeed, the assessment of Räisänen seems to hold true: "Indeed, those scholars who interpret v. 11:20 as a forceful statement by Jesus on the presence of God's kingdom *only* in his own activities (and not in that of other Jewish exorcists as well) are forced to *separate the verse from its context* and to regard it as an isolated saying."[50]

As noted above, several redaction-critical proposals have been made in light of the perceived incompatability between vv. 19 and 20. However, as Jacobson and Humphries have noted, the tension between 11:19 and 11:20 is overstated. The "quality in common" of v. 19 is central to the effectiveness of the argument of the unit. In addition, there are at least three details that further support the view that vv. 19 and 20 are compatible with each other in Q. First, the compositional structure of two rhetorical questions followed by a declarative saying is attested elsewhere in Q.[51] Second, both verses draw on the vocabulary and exigency of the accusation in Q 11:15. And third, neither Matthew nor Luke shows any signs of needing to control the meaning or modify v. 19 or 20. In fact, of the entire Beelzebul unit, only these two verses and the scattering/gathering saying in 11:23 are attested in nearly verbatim agreement by Matthew and Luke.[52]

2. THE HERMENEUTICAL SOLUTION TO THE PERCEIVED INCOMPATIBILITY

The second solution to the perceived tension between vv. 19 and 20 is to conclude that v. 19 does not in fact mean what it seems to mean. The

---

argument of these verses is wholly lacking in logic" (*The Gospel According to Matthew* [Oxford: Blackwell, 1981] 207).

[49]Allison, *Jesus Tradition*, 126; see also Perrin, *Rediscovering*, 63–64.

[50]Räisänen, "Exorcisms and the Kingdom," 127 (Räisänen's emphasis).

[51]Kirk, *Composition*, 188. Polag (*Christologie*, 40–41) points out that the εἰ δέ of v. 20 presupposes a preceding conditional clause.

[52]Matthew and Luke disagree only on πνεύματι (Matthew) and δακτύλῳ (Luke).

argument of Q 11:19 depends upon a claim of common ground between Jesus and the "sons" of the accusers:

> And if I cast out demons by Beelzebul, by whom do your sons cast [them] out? Therefore they shall be your judges. (Q 11:19)

The sameness that v. 19 uses rhetorically, however, is already beside the point if one assumes distance and incomparability between Jesus and his opponents. Such assumptions necessitate alternative meanings for v. 19; otherwise, vv. 19 and 20 seem incompatible. There are two primary ways that the argument from a "quality in common" in v. 19 is rejected or redirected by interpreters in light of 11:20. The first approach realigns the meaning of "your sons." The second approach interprets vv. 19 and 20 within the overall context of polemic and controversy. Both approaches presuppose a sharp dichotomy between Jesus and his opponents in the text and a corresponding dichotomy between the Q community and other Jews.

The first approach, which realigns the meaning of "your sons," has been around for some time. Several early Christian authors interpreted "your sons" as Jesus' disciples, thereby identifying the common ground as between Jesus and his followers rather than between Jesus and his accusers. In his homily on Matt 12:25, John Chrysostom says:

> See here too His gentleness. For He said not, "my disciples," nor, "the apostles," but "your sons;" to the end that if indeed they were minded to return to the same nobleness with them, they might derive hence a powerful spring that way; but if they were uncandid, and continued in the same course, they might not thenceforth be able to allege any plea, though ever so shameless. But what He saith is like this, "By whom do the apostles cast them out?" For in fact they were doing so already, because they had received authority from Him, and these men brought no charge against them; their quarrel not being with the acts, but with the person only. As then it was His will to show that their sayings arose only from their envy against Him, He brings forward the apostles; thus: If I so cast them out, much more those, who have received their authority from me.[53]

Chrysostom's interpretation recognizes that Jesus' claim rests on the common ground shared by Jesus, the accusers, and the sons, but equates the sons with the disciples that have just returned from a mission of exorcism

---

[53]John Chrysostom, *Homily* 41 on Matt 12:25–26 (trans. *NPNF*[1], vol. 10)

and healing. Chrystostom maintains a distance between Jesus and his accusers not only by identifying "your sons" as Jesus' disciples but also by interpreting the saying as a testimony to Jesus' gentleness in contrast to the enviousness of the accusers.

A modern attempt to revive Chrysostom's interpretation illustrates more directly how the assumption of distance between Jesus and his accusers often outweighs the argument for sameness in 11:19. In 1992 Robert Shirock surveyed fifty modern works to conclude that most interpreters understand "your sons" in Matt 12:27//Luke 11:19 to refer to "Jewish exorcists who were in some way associated with the Pharisees."[54] Shirock shares the general view that vv. 19 and 20 are incompatible christologically, but rejects redaction-critical solutions that suggest "editorial naiveté" or "textual and logical confusion."[55] He proposes a revival of the view that Jesus refers to his own disciples when he speaks of "your sons." This interpretation, he argues, makes the logical problems of the compatibility of 11:19 and 11:20 disappear.[56]

What is interesting about Shirock's description of the logical problem is what he wants to avoid by turning to Chrysostom's interpretation. He asks: "What are the implications of putting into the mouth of Jesus words with which he vindicates his own person and work by means of a comparison with contemporary Jewish exorcists?" The answer is: "To put it simply, he would have been endorsing and comparing his own Spirit-led work to the work of Jewish magicians." Citing the comments of Bruce and Barclay that the work of Jewish exorcists "operated in a conventional fashion by use of herbs and magical formulae"[57] and resembled "witch-doctoring,"[58] Shirock asks, "Are we then to conclude that Jesus made some endorsement, however slight, of 'witch-doctoring'?" This problem disappears, according to Shirock, if Jesus speaks of his own disciples in v. 19: "Their Spirit-empowered work signals the same thing as his does: the inbreaking of the kingdom of God. . . . In short, the united work of this group of Jewish exorcists (Jesus and his disciples) testifies convincingly to their own fellow countrymen that the kingdom of God has arrived."[59]

---

[54]Robert Shirock, "Whose Exorcists Are They?" *JSNT* 46 (1992) 41.

[55]Ibid., 43.

[56]Ibid., 44 and 47.

[57]Ibid., 46 n. 1 (citation from A. B. Bruce, "Matthew," in *Expositor's Greek Testament* [ed. W. R. Nicoll; 5 vols.; Grand Rapids, Mich.: Eerdmans, 1979] 1:187).

[58]Shirock, "Whose Exorcists," 46 n. 1 (citation from Barclay, *The Gospel of Matthew* [Philadelphia: Westminster, 1975] 2:38).

[59]Shirock, "Whose Exorcists," 51.

In this case, it is not the uniqueness of Jesus' exorcisms that is at stake; in fact, both Chrysostom and Shirock rightly recognize that the synoptic gospel traditions do not claim that Jesus' exorcisms alone are valid (see Q 10:9; Mark 9:36–40). For Shirock, however, a qualitiative difference is at stake—a difference between the Spirit-led exorcisms of Jesus and his followers, and the "magical" exorcisms of other exorcists. Shirock affirms that both groups are Jewish, and yet there is a strong distinction between religion (Jesus and the Jewish exorcists on his side) and magic (other Jewish exorcists) that informs his interpretation. In some sense, the exigencies that press Shirock to redirect the meaning of "your sons" replicate the accusation of deviance made against Jesus in Q 11:15. As Dale Allison has pointed out: "When faced with explaining the exorcisms of their opponents, Christians have ironically often responded just like those whom Jesus rebukes in Mt 12:24 par., that is, by saying that exorcists outside their circle must be in league with demons."[60]

The second approach to realigning the meaning of v. 19 is to interpret Q 11:19–20 in the larger context of Q 11:14–32. Taken as part of a controversy speech in a larger polemical discourse against the Pharisees, Q 11:19–20 is interpreted not as an explicit confirmation of the common ground between Jesus and his accusers but as an implicit threat of judgment against the opponents of Jesus, and more importantly, the opponents of the Q community.

Reading Q 11:19–20 within a larger polemical context redirects the meaning of v. 19. For example, Kloppenborg's evaluation of the various redaction-critical approaches to the Beelzebul controversy partially depends on the recognition that 11:19 invites "the inference that the kingdom is also manifest in the works of Jewish exorcists."[61] In his explanation of the eventual juxtaposition of vv. 19 and 20, however, Kloppenborg redirects the interpretation of 11:19 that has heretofore been central to his redaction-critical analysis:

> In view of the exclusivity of the statement made in 11:23, it is hardly likely that Q intended to include Jewish exorcists as evidence of the kingdom (*pace* Jacobson). Q 11:19 in fact does not draw this conclusion: the force of the rhetorical question is to reveal the absurdity of the Beelzebul accusation. However, the question is followed by the assertion "Therefore they will be your judges." The logic of the argument is strikingly similar to that of Q 11:31–32:

[60]Allison, *Jesus Tradition*, 126.
[61]Kloppenborg, *Formation*, 123.

like 11:31–32, which imputes a forensic function to the Queen of the South and the Ninevites, Q 11:19 confers this function on the Jewish exorcists.[62] Neither the double saying nor 11:19b states that the kingdom is manifest in the activity of these persons, but both imply that divine activity should be recognized as such, and that failure to do so brings the threat of judgment. Q 11:20 then functions in the same way as the phrase "and behold, something greater than Solomon (Jonah) is here." It takes the argument one final step: if it is a serious matter—provoking divine judgment—to mistake the workings of God in lesser phenomena (Jewish exorcisms), how much more is it to misapprehend the manifestation of the presence of the kingdom in Jesus' activity! Therefore the Q composition begins by exposing the absurdity of the Beelzebul accusation by appeal to the double metaphor of the divided kingdom and household, and by use of the *reductio ad absurdum* of 11:19a. But then it changes its rhetorical posture and shifts to the offensive, declaring that Israel's heedlessness of divine activity will lead to her eschatological condemnation.[63]

By assigning a forensic role to the "sons" of the accusers, Kloppenborg shapes his interpretation of Q 11:19 in such a way that separates Jesus from them. The common ground between the "sons" and Jesus is recognized but the exorcisms are placed in a hierarchy of value in which theirs are "lesser" and Jesus' are "greater." In addition, the common ground between the "sons" and Jesus is "divine activity" but not a manifestation of the kingdom of God. Thus the *basileia* of God is reserved for Jesus' exorcisms alone. Jesus' affirmation of the divine activity of the "sons" functions rhetorically to draw sharp lines of distinction between Jesus' followers and a heedless Israel. Thus for Kloppenborg Q 11:19 serves to create a separation between Jesus and his accusers despite its dependence upon an argument that "Jesus occupies the same space as his detractors."[64]

This interpretation is part of the overall view discussed above in which Q 11:14–32 functions rhetorically for the Q community in the process of

---

[62]While the logic may be similar, the comparison is not parallel. The Queen of the South and the men of Nineveh will stand up at the judgment and witness against "this generation." Neither will be doing any judging at all. "The sons," however, will be "your judges." Being a judge in the context of 11:14–26, therefore, may simply refer to being the ones to decide who is right.

[63]Kloppenborg, *Formation*, 124–25 (my emphasis). I will discuss the exclusivity of 11:23 in the next section of this chapter.

[64]Humphries, *Christian Origins*, 32.

group identity formation, particularly vis-à-vis "Israel." For example, Michael Humphries suggests that Q's Beelzebul "discourse is not about distinguishing between valid and invalid exorcisms but about being for Beelzebul or for Yahweh . . . an outsider or an insider. Clearly the Q people understand themselves as insiders."[65] According to Humphries, however, in the process of the discourse, the accusers are rendered as outsiders:

> It is also quite clear, however, that Jesus' response turns the tables on his accusers. Insofar as they refuse to recognize the power of the kingdom in his exorcisms, they find themselves in danger of standing outside the kingdom. No one belonging to the kingdom of God could identify Jesus' exorcisms, or any exorcism for that matter, as satanic. If the accusers do not accept the "quality in common" expressed in verses 19 and 20, if they do not grant to Jesus what they grant to their own sons, then it is precisely this failure of recognition that renders the accusers themselves as deviant. And so a sharp distinction is indeed established. The exchange between Jesus and his accusers constitutes a battle over who represents the legitimate expression of Israel.[66]

The view that the community's identity as a "legitimate expression of Israel" is at stake in the text necessitates that the accusation of collusion is answered not only by a defense of Jesus' collusion with God, but also by a process of counter-stigmatization in which the tables are turned and the accusers are rendered outsiders.[67] Because this approach expects that this text must be a polemic against outsiders, it must find polemical counter-accusations in the text regardless of the fact that the logic of the text depends upon an affirmation of the "sons" of the accusers.

3. DISSOLVING THE INCOMPATIBILITY

The third approach to the tension between vv. 19 and 20 is to entertain the possibility that there is no tension at all. We see a very early and interesting example of this approach in Tertullian. In his treatise *Against Marcion*, Tertullian uses the Beelzebul controversy in Luke to argue that Jesus' God was the Creator God of the Jews:

---

[65]Ibid., 33–34.
[66]Ibid., 33.
[67]Kirk (*Composition*, 328–30) takes a similar approach.

When He cast out the "demon which was dumb" (and by a cure of this sort verified Isaiah), and having been charged with casting out demons by Beelzebub, He said, "If I by Beelzebub cast out demons, by whom do your sons cast them out?" By such a question what does He otherwise mean, than that He ejects the spirits by the same power by which their sons also did—that is, by the power of the Creator? For if you suppose the meaning to be, "If I by Beelzebub, etc., by whom your sons?"—as if He would reproach them with having the power of Beelzebub—you are met at once by the preceding sentence, that "Satan cannot be divided against himself." So that it was not by Beelzebub that even they were casting out demons, but (as we have said) by the power of the Creator; and that He might make this understood, He adds: "But if I with the finger of God cast out demons, is not the kingdom of God come near unto you?" For the magicians who stood before Pharaoh and resisted Moses called the power of the Creator *"the finger of God."*[68]

Tertullian not only accepts that Jesus claims similarity with the "sons" in 11:19, but also argues that 11:18 requires this meaning since "Satan cannot be divided against himself." Luke 11:20 clinches the argument for Tertullian but also gives further proof of his point, since "the finger of God" is an allusion to Exod 8:19 and thus to the Creator God of the Jews. Essentially, Tertullian accepts the logic of the argument from sameness because he needs to minimize the distance between Jesus and the Jewish tradition in order to counter Marcion's de-Judaized view of ideal Christianity. Apparently Tertullian's christological views can co-exist with his interpretation of the Beelzebul controversy because the identity of Jesus is not the issue being debated here. What is being debated are the connections between the Christians and the Jewish tradition, and hence the distance between Jesus and his accusers is less important for Tertullian than their common ground.

This approach leads some modern interpreters to suggest that the Beelzebul controversy makes the most sense if it neither makes superlative claims for Jesus nor functions to establish group identity over and against Israel. Piper makes this observation about Q as a whole: "Unlike Mark, which lacks these sayings [11:19–20], the distinctive feature of the double-tradition version of argument is that *unique* claims for Jesus are subordinate to more general persuasive reasons for accepting his *genuineness* as one who

---

[68]Tertullian *Adv. Marc.* 4.26.10 (trans. *ANF*, vol. 3).

represents God's *basileia*. It is more important to show that Jesus' authority is valid than to show that it is unique."[69] Arland Jacobson similarly notes that "without question the juxtaposition of Q 11:19 and 11:20 jeopardizes the eschatological uniqueness of Jesus. But we have seen elsewhere in Q that this was apparently no problem. No christological screen apparently existed to filter out statements which jeopardize Jesus' uniqueness. In this instance, exorcism, whether by Jesus or other exorcists, is construed as evidence of the presence of the kingdom and of God's spirit."[70]

If this interpretation is plausible, then it is not only the uniqueness of Jesus that is de-centered in this text, but also the sole proprietorship of the Jesus tradition over the manifestations of the *basileia* of God. I explore the implications of this interpretation in the last section of this chapter. Before that, however, it is necessary to show that this interpretation of vv. 19–20 can cohere with the rest of the unit. As we will see, vv. 21–26 continue the argument that Jesus does not cast out demons by Beelzebul by asserting that there are only two possible sides in the battle and that victory depends upon the strength and unity of the winning side.

Common Ground and Exclusion: Q 11:21–26

The expectation of a fundamental divide between Jesus and his accusers presses the argument for common ground in 11:19 into the shadows, while the expectation that the text's interests lie in establishing the uniqueness of Jesus—or the social identity of the Q people—pulls his own claim to manifest the *basileia* of God (11:20) into the central spotlight. Interpretations of the sayings in Q 11:21–22, 23, and 24–26 usually follow suit by serving to reinforce the view that 11:14–20 makes superlative claims for Jesus over and against his accusers. All three sayings, however, depend not upon a divide between Jesus and his accusers, but rather on a sharp divide between the *basileia* of Satan and the *basileia* of God. This emphasis fits well with the overall issue of the unit, that is, the effort to locate Jesus' exorcisms either on the side of Satan or the side of God. The entire unit clusters thematically around the clash of *basileiai* and exorcism in much the same way as other units in Q show thematic groupings. In this section, therefore, I show how an interpretation that centers the argument of v. 19 from common ground can also make sense of the sayings in 11:21–26.

[69]Piper, *Wisdom*, 123.

[70]Jacobson, *First Gospel*, 163. Jacobson ("Literary Unity," *JBL* 101 [1982] 365–89) also suggests that "the coming of the kingdom is the presupposition for all exorcisms."

Indeed, throughout these seemingly disparate and perennially puzzling sayings, there is an overall argument against internal division.

The reconstruction of Q 11:21–22 presents significant problems. *The Critical Edition of Q* (IQP) does not print a Greek reconstruction of this text, given the substantial Markan parallel to Matthew. The four extant versions of the saying are as follows:

> But no one can enter a strong man's house and plunder his goods, unless he first binds the strong man; then indeed he may plunder his house. (Mark 3:27)

> Or how can one enter a strong man's house and plunder his property, unless he first binds the strong man? And then he may plunder his house. (Matt 12:29)

> When a strong man, fully armed, guards his own palace, his possessions are in peace. But when one stronger than he conquers him, he takes away his armor in which he trusted, and divides his spoil. (Luke 11:21–22)

> Jesus says: It is not possible for someone to enter the house of a strong [person and] take it by force unless he binds his hands. Then he will plunder his house. (*Gos. Thom.* 35)

All versions of the saying share the image of a two-sided struggle. Kloppenborg notes that the parable in Luke draws on the imagery of war and "a battle between armed soldiers and the seizure and distribution of the spoils of war."[71] He points out that "this coheres better with Q 11:17–18a, which evokes the spectre of a civil war, and with Q 11:17–18, 20, which implies two warring sides, than does the Markan and Matthean version of the parable."[72] I agree with Kloppenborg's assessment that the Lukan version more closely approximates Q. In the absence of significant overlap with Matthew, however, the IQP's decision that the wording of this saying cannot be reconstructed with any confidence seems wise.

Nevertheless, we can say that all versions of the saying involve the struggle between two parties and thus that the saying in Q probably participated in the larger rhetoric of two *basileiai*: the *basileia* of Satan vs. the *basileia* of God.

---

[71]Kloppenborg, *Formation*, 125. This is different from Mark's version, which focuses on a dichotomy between a householder and a thief.

[72]Ibid.

The accusation in 11:15 is locative and places Jesus on the side of Beelzebul. Jesus retorts that *basileiai* do not divide against themselves without disastrous results; therefore, successful exorcisms must point to two *basileiai*. If Jesus casts demons out, then he must stand—along with the "sons" of the accusers—on the side of God's *basileia*, rather than Satan's/Beelzebul's. The imagery of the strong man parable replicates this dichotomy. All versions of the parable also distinguish between a strong man and a stronger man, that is, one who binds or conquers the first man. Humphries identifies Q 11:21–22 as an argument from analogy, "drawn from the world of experience; it is a reminder of how things operate both in the natural order and in the social order. . . . The analogy also affirms a universal principle: The stronger man will prevail. Everyone knows this to be true."[73]

If the Q version resembles the Lukan version, then the stronger *basileia* will prevail. Typically, interpreters associate the "stronger man" with Jesus, who conquers Satan through exorcism.[74] However, this interpretation misses the basic dichotomy of the saying and its relationship to the rhetoric of the unit as a whole. Although there are multiple exorcists (11:19), there are only two sides. If the accusers grant that Jesus exorcizes by (the finger of) God, then "Satan's kingdom has been assailed by another more powerful kingdom."[75] Thus the clash is between God and Satan. The exorcisms represent "the conquest of Beelzebul by God."[76] Jesus exorcizes on the side of God's *basileia*.

Nothing in this saying, however, denies the "sons" of the accusers a place on the same side.[77] I disagree with Alan Kirk who, building on the view that 11:20 makes christological claims for Jesus, argues that Q 11:20 "marks

---

[73]Humphries, *Christian Origins*, 34–35.

[74]The association of Jesus with the "stronger man" raises problems for interpretations of this text as a window onto Jesus' eschatology. How can Jesus claim that Satan's *basileia* is not divided because it is not fallen in vv. 17–18 and also proclaim that Satan has been conquered in 11:21–22? Joel Marcus explains the tension as the juxtaposition of Jesus' own early eschatology when he understood himself as one of many Jewish exorcists in battle with Satan and Jesus' later, more apocalyptic view that, indeed, the end of Satan was being accomplished in his ministry alone ("The Beelzebul Controversy and the Eschatologies of Jesus," *New Testament Tools and Studies* 28 [1999] 247–77). This tension between vv. 17–18 and vv. 21–22 only exists if one assumes that Jesus is "the stronger man." Given the overall discussion of two warring sides, it seems more likely that the "stronger man" is God.

[75]Humphries, *Christian Origins*, 35.

[76]Killagen, "Return," 50. Killagen argues that vv. 17–18, 19, and 21–22 are three different proofs of the same point: Jesus is of God.

[77]*Pace* Kloppenborg, Piper, Kirk, and Jacobson.

the end of the refutation of the opponents' accusation. On the other hand it negotiates a shift from a defensive to an offensive posture assumed in the second half of the cluster (11:21–22, 23)."[78] According to Kirk, this offensive posture rejects neutrality and demands an "immediate determination of allegiances."[79] Kirk's own interpretation of the parable, however, does not necessitate such an offensive posture. He notes that the parable "rebuts the opening accusation by asserting Jesus' exorcisms to be an assault on Satan's kingdom" by God.[80] The parable continues the defensive posture of the entire unit. Since a *basileia* cannot be divided against itself, Jesus' effective exorcisms must be part of the only other *basileia*, God's.

The proverbial saying in Q 11:23 coheres well with this contentious struggle between two sides:

> The one who is not with me is against me, and the one who does not gather with me scatters. (Q 11:23)

The first part of the saying is a general aphorism concerning allegiances. The second part of the saying duplicates the first part but uses imagery of a gathered and scattered flock.[81] According to the saying, there are only two choices: either with "me" or against "me." Kloppenborg notes that Q 11:23 "continues the motif of the parable of the warring soldiers, declaring that one is either on the side of the conquering Stronger One or on the side of the vanquished and despoiled."[82]

As already mentioned, several interpreters view Q 11:23 as part of Jesus' offensive counter-move against his opponents. "It faces the questioners with a decision. . . . It puts them in a position in which even neutrality is excluded. This is an important extension of the earlier defensive argument."[83] Kloppenborg

---

[78]Kirk, *Composition*, 190; see also Kloppenborg, *Formation*, 127.

[79]Kirk, *Composition*, 190.

[80]Ibid., 191. Humphries and Kloppenborg also point out that the primary purpose of Q 11: 21–22 is to locate Jesus on God's side and not on the side of Beelzebul.

[81]The imagery of scattering (σκορπίζω) and gathering (συνάγω) a herd or flock appears frequently in Jewish tradition to refer to the effects of war on Israel. See 2 Sam 22:17; Ps 17:15 and 143:6; Wis 17:3; Zech 13:7–9; Sir 48:15; Tob 13:5; and *Did.* 9.4. The word "gather" also evokes the harvest gathering of 3:17 and 10:2. Joined with "scattering" in 11:23, however, the imagery of the flock comes to the fore.

[82]Kloppenborg, *Formation*, 125–26.

[83]Piper, *Wisdom*, 122; see also Schulz, *Q*, 212.

similarly argues that with Q 11:23, "Neutrality is impossible. Those who fail to recognize God's activity in Jesus (by accusing him of partisanship with Beelzebul) are God's opponents."[84] Indeed, this reading of 11:23 as demanding exclusive allegiance to Jesus as representative of the *basileia* of God plays a role in the rejection of 11:19 as claiming that the "sons" of the accusers also represent the *basileia* of God. For example, both Räisänen and Kloppenborg reject Jacobson's interpretation of 11:19 as including the other exorcisms in the work of the *basileia* of God on the grounds that this reading "collides with Q 11:23."[85]

Although it is common to reject a reading of 11:19 based on 11:23, one could allow a reading of 11:19 to shape an interpretation of 11:23. The rhetoric of the entire unit sets up a dichotomy between Satan and God. Since Satan cannot be divided against himself and exorcisms are clearly against Satan, then it is absurd to say that Jesus is on the side of Satan. "One cannot be against Satan . . . and for Satan at the same time."[86] By arguing for a quality in common with the "sons" of the accusers, Jesus locates himself on the same side of the struggle as the accusers, that is, on God's side. Q 11:23 presents an argument from the authority of popular wisdom[87] to confirm that there can be only two sides in this war-like struggle. Indeed, this saying has a non-Christian parallel in a military context. Cicero states: "Let the maxim stand which won your victory hold good today. For we have often heard you assert that, while we held all men to be our opponents save those on our side, you counted all men your adherents who were not against you."[88] Q 11:23 continues the self-defense of Jesus' exorcisms by asserting that Jesus can be on only one side in this battle. "Every exorcism constitutes an attack against Satan and

---

[84]Kloppenborg, *Formation*, 126. Kirk similarly says: "The aphorism demands a decision about allegiance to [Jesus] in light of the conflict of kingdoms depicted throughout the cluster" (*Composition*, 191).

[85]Räisänen, "Exorcisms and the Kingdom," 125 n. 36; Kloppenborg, *Formation*, 124: "In view of the exclusivity of the statement made in 11:23, it is hardly likely that Q intended to include Jewish exorcisms as evidence of the manifestation of the kingdom (*pace* Jacobson)." Jacobson (*First Gospel*, 164) argues that Q 11:23 does reject neutrality toward Jesus, but also confirms that others can "gather" with Jesus, meaning that others can do the work of the *basileia*.

[86]Humphries, *Christian Origins*, 36.

[87]As early as 1912, Anton Fridrichsen made the proposal that the saying in Luke 11:23//Matt 12:30 derives from popular wisdom ("Wer nicht mit mir ist, ist wider mich," *ZWT* 13 [1912] 273–80). See also Bultmann, *History*, 98.

[88]Cicero, *Pro Q. Ligario Orat.* 33.

his kingdom. The maxim reaffirms what the position of the accused has been all along: His activity has to do with the kingdom of God."[89]

This interpretation depends upon an assumption that Jesus is not the antecedent of ἐμοῦ. Since Jesus is the speaker in the apophthegm, most interpreters understand the "me" in 11:23 to refer to Jesus himself. Thus, in Q 11:23 Jesus demands that his audience declare their allegiance either to Satan or to Jesus. As noted above, this interpretation leads to a distinction between Jesus' defensive and inclusive posture in 11:17–19 and his offensive and exclusive posture in 11:20–26. As already explained, however, Satan and God lead the warring sides, and the location of Jesus on one side or the other is the central question of the unit. If 11:23 participates in the rhetoric of the larger unit, then ἐμοῦ refers to Satan or God but not Jesus. As the one who is either for or against, and the one who either gathers or scatters, Jesus is the subject of ὁ ὤν, ὁ συνάγων, and σκορπίζει.

Humphries argues that ἐμοῦ refers to Satan. He cites Klaus Berger, who provides a helpful explication of 11:23 when read in this way:

> Obviously this expression does not here refer to Jesus, but serves as a general rule of illustration for what has preceded. As the sentence says, there are two possibilities: If we are for someone, then we make a common cause with that person through gathering. If we are against someone, then we scatter in opposition to that person. With Jesus one can see that he scatters in opposition to Satan—hence, Jesus is not for Satan (in the context this is the apologetic meaning of the sentence). Accordingly, the sentence does not concern gathering with Jesus. The "I" of the sentence is not Jesus but Satan![90]

This approach makes sense of the second half of the saying insofar as it links Jesus' exorcisms with scattering Satan's *basileia*. If ἐμοῦ refers to Jesus, then his successful exorcisms constitute gathering God's *basileia*. There is a stronger conceptual link, however, between exorcism and scattering than between exorcism and gathering.

Kirk rejects a link between the "I" of the saying and Satan because (1) the progression of pronouns in the unit establishes Jesus as the referent of ἐμοῦ; (2) the editor of Q could have substituted "Satan" for ἐμοῦ; (3) it

---

[89]Humphries, *Christian Origins*, 36.

[90]Klaus Berger, *Formgeschichte des Neuen Testaments* (Heidelberg: Quelle & Meyer, 1984) 108; reference and translation from Humphries, *Christian Origins*, 36.

is unlikely that Jesus would act as Satan's mouthpiece when he has been trying to avoid the association throughout the unit; and (4) the equation of ἐμοῦ with Satan depends upon the assumption that Jesus makes no special claims for himself in Q 11:20.[91] Kirk is correct that one's reading of 11:23 depends partially on one's reading of 11:20. However, this does not disprove Humphries's argument, since Kirk's assumption that 11:20 does in fact make christological claims for Jesus likewise determines Kirk's interpretation of 11:23 as a demand for allegiance to Jesus. A different reading of 11:20 can result in a re-reading of 11:23.

Although the progression of first-person pronouns in 11:19 and 11:20 does point to Jesus, he is not the central character of either 11:21–22 or 11:24–26, which stand on either side of 11:23. The parable of the strong man speaks of two warring rulers and the parable of the unclean spirit focuses exclusively on the exploits of a wandering demon and his cohorts. The specificity of the pronouns in 11:19–20 reflects their relationship to the scene of the apophthegm in 11:14–15. Thus, it is just as possible that all of the sayings in 11:21–26 reflect the same interest in the two diametrically opposed sides (led by Satan and God) as the sayings in 11:17–18.

Of course, the editor of Q could have substituted Satan for ἐμοῦ to ensure that meaning for the saying. As Kirk points out, v. 18 makes this move by applying the general saying in v. 17 to the situation at hand. If the editor did something similar in 11:23, however, it would not have been by substitution but by appending a specific application of the general saying in 11:23 in the same way that v. 18 is appended to v. 17. By actively substituting Satan for "me," the editor would have undermined the authority of 11:23 as an argument from popular wisdom. However, as the citation from Cicero attests, the popular wisdom applies generically to allegiances on opposing sides, and it is the authority of this universal maxim that 11:23 invokes.

In the overall scene, however, Jesus is the speaker and thus 11:23 could make him into a mouthpiece for Satan. Kirk's third challenge does press the plausibility of Berger's and Humphries's interpretation. The enormous majority of interpreters who take 11:23 as a saying of Jesus about himself attests to the force of this problem. The solution may lie in the function of the saying as a general maxim. Humphries cites Anton Fridrichsen:

> It appears we have a proverb here . . . of such a type that we must not stress the *emou* overmuch, as if this pronoun must necessarily

---

[91]Kirk, *Composition*, 191–92 n. 161.

refer to Jesus himself. Rather, its meaning is this: If the maxim "either/or" is the rule in the kingdom of Satan, how then can there be talk of the one fighting the other?[92]

Thus, in Q 11:23 Jesus presents a general "either/or" rule that could apply to any *basileia*. In this sense, Jesus is neither the mouthpiece for Satan nor God but rather provides a general maxim that one can only be with one or the other.

In summary, Q 11:23 does not necessarily represent a counteroffensive in which Jesus demands allegiance to himself as the sole representative of the *basileia* of God. As with 11:21–22, v. 23 continues the argument of 11:14–20, which attempts to locate Jesus' exorcisms on the side of God and not Satan. The saying does not *exclude* the exorcisms of the "sons" of the accusers, but rather attempts to *include* Jesus' exorcisms on the side of the *basileia* of God. This interpretation of Q 11:23 coheres well with a parallel version of the saying in Mark.

> John said to him, "Teacher, we saw someone casting out demons in your name, and we tried to stop him, because he was not following us." But Jesus said, "Do not stop him; for no one who does a deed of power in my name will be able soon afterward to speak evil of me. Whoever is not against us is for us [ὅς γὰρ οὐκ ἔστιν καθ᾽ ἡμῶν, ὑπὲρ ἡμῶν ἐστιν]." (Mark 9:38–40)

Both versions of the saying occur in the context of stories about the validity of certain exorcisms. In Q, it is Jesus' exorcisms that are successful but suspect. In Mark, John questions the successful exorcisms of an anonymous person who casts out demons in the name of Jesus. The general maxim in Mark backs up Jesus' instruction to accept the exorcisms of the unnamed person and, therefore, functions to *include* other exorcisms on the side of Jesus and the disciples. Jesus states that the unknown exorcist should not be considered an opponent, because that exorcist is a potential ally.[93]

---

[92]Anton Fridrichsen, *The Problem of Miracle in Primitive Christianity* (trans. Roy A. Harrisville and John S. Hanson; Minneapolis: Augsburg, 1972); reference and quotation from Humphries, *Christian Origins*, 36.

[93]Although the reconstruction is highly conjectural, this notion of emerging allegiance may also appear in the *P. Oxy* 1224 version of this saying: "[A]nd p[r]ay for your [ene]mies. For the one who is not [against y]ou is on your side. [The one who today i]s at a distance, tomorrow will [b]e [near you,] and in [...] of the advers[ary]" (6:1–2); reconstruction and translation from Robert J. Miller, *The Complete Gospels* (San Francisco: HarperSanFrancisco, 1994) 424.

If the exorcist uses the name of Jesus successfully, then the exorcist will soon be unable to speak against Jesus, presumably because the exorcist will recognize the power of Jesus' name.

Many interpret Q 11:23 as an exclusive version of the inclusive Mark 9:40. However, the Markan saying depends on precisely the same dichotomy as Q 11:23, only formulated in reverse.[94] As in Q, Mark's version presents only two choices: either against us or with us. The general maxim is formulated in opposite versions—both of which appear in Cicero—because of the rhetorical context of each saying. In Mark, the saying functions to include an exorcist within the sphere of Jesus and the disciples. In Q, the saying functions to exclude the possibility that Jesus exorcizes on the side of Satan and thus includes his exorcisms on the side of God.

The last unit of Q 11:14–26 is the parable of the unclean spirit in 11:24–26. Traditional interpretations of this parable depend upon reading 11:23 as a demand for allegiance to Jesus and a rejection of neutrality vis-à-vis Jesus.

> When an unclean spirit has gone out of a person, it passes through waterless places seeking rest and finds none. Then it says, I will return to my house from which I came. And on coming it finds it swept and put in order. Then it goes and brings with it seven other spirits more evil than itself, and they enter and dwell there; and the last state of that person becomes worse than the first. (Q 11:24–26)

The most common interpretation of the story is that "a person will likely suffer a second possession by a demon if he does not replace the former possessing demon with faith in Jesus (God)."[95] A different but compatible interpretation views 11:24–26 as a critique of the Jewish exorcists in 11:19 insofar as their exorcisms make the sufferer worse than before. In light of the assumption that 11:20 makes unique and decisive claims for

---

[94]Jacobson, *First Gospel*, 164.

[95]John Killagen, "The Return of the Unclean Spirit (Luke 11,24–26)," *Bib* 74 (1993) 45–59, at 45; and bibliography at ibid., 45 n. 1. Allison (*Jesus Tradition*, 122–24) and Laufen (*Die Doppelüberlieferungen der Logienquelle und des Markusevangeliums* [Bonn: Hanstein, 1980] 140–47) provide extensive reviews of the various interpretations of this text.

Jesus' exorcisms, the failed exorcism in 11:24–26 must be a critique of the relapsed exorcized person[96] or of inept Jewish exorcists.[97]

As John Killagen has shown, however, the verbal patterns of the parable point to the demon as the central character and to a complete lack of interest in either the exorcized person or the exorcist.[98] For Killagen, Q 11:24–26 participates in the larger rhetoric of the unit by presenting yet another argument against "associating Jesus with Beelzebul."[99]

> The possession by the demon and seven others worse than it is not described as the fault of the man; rather, this enormous destruction is caused by the demon's evil desire to destroy what had been made clean and put in order. It is here . . . that one senses the point of Jesus' small story. Not only is there no compatibility between Jesus' work and the demon's work; the demon hastens to destroy what Jesus has achieved—and seems willing to call this destruction its rest.[100]

This interpretation situates 11:24–26 squarely within the overall rhetoric of the Beelzebul controversy. This alone makes Killagen's interpretation plausible.

[96]See for example, Piper (*Wisdom*, 124): "A unified perspective can be detected in the conjunction of these sayings [11:21–26]. Any form of half-hearted response, any wavering or relapse of apostasy, is attacked through these sayings. It presents a challenge not just to outsiders, but also to lukewarm insiders."

[97]See for example, Allison (*Jesus Tradition*, 127): "Following Q 11:14–22 and especially the qualification of Q 11:19a in Q 11:23, the meaning is that Jesus' exorcisms alone are truly efficacious. When others cast out demons, those demons typically return, and with a vengeance. If one does not fill the space left by a demon with faith in Jesus, then no lasting good is done. The last state will be worse than the first. In other words, non-Christian exorcists are not truly effective."

[98]Killagen, "Return," 50–57: (1) eight out of ten verbs have the unclean spirit as their subject; (2) four of the six participles have the unclean spirit as their subject; (3) the unclean spirit dominates the action of the parable to the point that it only needs to be named once at the beginning; (4) "Whereas the unclean spirit is dynamic in the story, the *anthropos* is passive and unmoving" (p. 51); (5) the story's tragic conclusion is not caused by the victim's being cleaned and swept but by an entire series of actions by the demon; (6) the dominance of the present tense suggests that the story tells what unclean spirits routinely do; (7) the compact nature of the story, with no interruption from an audience, suggests that the audience recognizes this as a predictable progression of demonic behavior.

[99]Ibid., 50. Killagen also suggests that this is the goal of 11:17–18, 19–20, and 21–22, although each accomplishes this goal in a different way.

[100]Ibid., 56.

Humphries takes a similar approach but adds a further observation about the gathering together of demons to repossess the victim. Humphries draws on scholars who identify Q 11:24–26 as an ancient demonology and identifies these verses as an argument from analogy, "drawn from the world of discourse on demonic behavior."[101] Thus, the story relates something about demons, that is, that they "do not contend with one another but often establish alliances for the purpose of resisting an opposing power more effectively. . . . Demons assist demons. . . . Demons do not cast out demons."[102] This interpretation links 11:24–26, 11:17–18, and 11:23. It confirms 11:17–18 by showing that demons prosper in alliance and not against each other. It echoes 11:23 insofar as those on the side of Satan "do not 'scatter one another,' they 'gather.'"[103]

If we do not assume that 11:24–26 must somehow confirm Jesus' exorcisms as unique or unequivocally effective, then an interpretation comes into view that makes sense of the parable in its context. On this (re-)reading, the story proves that demons ally with demons to the destruction of people, but that exorcisms scatter the demons and heal the victim. Thus, Jesus and his fellow exorcists must stand not on the side of Satan and his demons but on the side of God.

In this way, all three sayings in 11:21–26 may be understood in the context of Jesus' argument from common ground between himself and the "sons" of his accusers (vv. 19–20). The persistent argument in vv. 21–26 is not that Jesus' exorcisms alone represent the *basileia* of God, but that Jesus stands with other successful exorcists on the side of God. He cannot stand with Satan because there are only two *basileiai*, and a successful *basileia* will not divide against itself. Rather it will gather its forces together to conquer and divide the spoils of its foe.

---

[101]Humphries, *Christian Origins*, 38.

[102]Ibid., 38.

[103]Ibid. Killagen ("Return," 58–59 n. 29) does not treat 11:23 in the article's text, but does mention it in a note at the end of the article. He suggests that his unconventional reading of 11:24–26 prompts an unconventional reading of 11:23: "Under the influence of vv. 24–26 and, more generally, of the inclination to keep all members of Jesus' speech focused on his goal of self-defense against the charge that he functions for Beelzebul, it seems right to say that the 'one who is not with me' is the demon, the 'unclean spirit;' he proves to be 'against me.' Likewise, that 'not to gather with me' is to do the contradictory opposite ('to scatter') suggests that it is the demon . . . [who] scatters." My suggestion that the proverb functions as a general rule can make more sense of the connection to 11:24–26 because the demon gathers other demons while Jesus scatters through his exorcisms.

It is possible to discern one more thread of argument in the Beelzebul controversy. The sayings in Q 11:14–26 linger around issues of divisiveness and alliance. Thus the text uses a story about a challenge to the legitimacy of Jesus' exorcisms to make a plea for solidarity among the members of the *basileia*/household of God.[104] There is an implicit critique of divisiveness in 11:17–18 as well as in the sayings in 11:21–26. For example, although there is no indication in 11:21–22 as to what makes the stronger man stronger, in 11:24–26 it is the gathering together of demons that makes the victory over the victim both complete and devastating. In 11:23, those who are with the speaker "gather," while those who are against the speaker "scatter." When the stronger man does conquer the man in his home, the victor divides the possessions of his foe, that is, he scatters the other *basileia*. Q 11:19 appeals directly to the common ground between Jesus and his accusers, and thus implicitly rejects the divisiveness of the accusation itself. In this context, 11:20 identifies the *basileia* of God as the common ground between Jesus and his accusers, and thus participates in the larger effort to assert that *every basileia* divided against itself will be laid waste by its opponents.

Conclusion

There are two hermeneutical tendencies that preclude the interpretation of 11:14–26 as a sustained argument for solidarity and against divisiveness: (1) the presupposition that the bone of contention in gospel controversy stories is the singular significance or authority of Jesus; and (2) the presupposition that gospel controversy stories have their *Sitz im Leben* in the process of early Christian identity formation vis-à-vis Judaism. Both assumptions require that the distance between Jesus and his accusers constructed by the text be replicated in the eschatological, christological, or uniqueness claims made for Jesus by the text. For example, Kirk rejects Humphries's claim that 11:19–20 includes the sons' exorcisms as manifestations of the *basileia* of God, on the grounds that the difference between Jesus and the accusers is what generates the controversy in the first place:

---

[104]Kirk (*Composition*, 192) suggests that 11:23 "forms an inverse inclusio with the programmatic maxim. Verse 17 refers to a divided kingdom and house; v. 23 to undivided allegiance to Jesus; the opening image of division and fracture is replaced by a concluding call for solidarity." I agree with the call for solidarity but I argue that it centers around the *basileia* of God, not the person of Jesus.

Given the very fact of the normative occurrence of other Jewish
exorcisms, Jesus' exorcisms and healings could not have provoked
the kind of deadly hostility giving rise to the witchcraft accusation of
11:14–17 had they not had attached to them a symbolic significance
offensive enough to give rise to this bitter controversy.[105]

Thus, the raison d'être for this kind of controversy story is a defense of
Jesus' singular significance in response to rejections of Jesus' singular
significance.

Humphries, however, despite his own argument that Q 11:14–26 does not
make claims of Jesus' eschatological or christological uniqueness, maintains
that what is at stake in the text is "the issue of social positioning and the de-
marcation of boundaries."[106] Thus, the text makes claims for the superlative
value of the Q community over and against its opponents:

No one belonging to the kingdom of God could identify Jesus'
exorcisms, or any exorcism for that matter, as satanic. If the accusers do not accept the "quality in common" expressed in verses 19
and 20, if they do not grant to Jesus what they grant to their own
sons, then it is precisely this failure of recognition that renders the
accusers themselves as deviant.[107]

As we have seen, both of these approaches—Kirk's and Humphries's—
must erase or de-emphasize the way that the argument rests on a claim
of common ground between Jesus and his accusers and thus attempts to
persuade the audience to solidarity rather than divisiveness in the face of
common opposition.

In *The First Gospel*, Arland Jacobson suggests that the study of Q "requires of us some exegetical imagination to interpret it as a 'Jewish' rather
than as a 'Christian' document, granted, of course, that 'Jewish' has no
single meaning."[108] I have applied this notion of "exegetical imagination"
to Q 11:14–26 by de-centering the identity of Jesus as the central rhetorical

---

[105]Kirk, *Composition*, 189 n. 154. Kirk is drawing on the work of Paul Hollenbach ("Jesus,
Demoniacs, and Public Authorities: A Socio-Historical Study," *JAAR* 49 [1981] 567–88).
Unlike either Kirk or Humphries, Hollenbach takes Q 11:20 as an authentic saying of Jesus
that provides direct access to Jesus' self-understanding as an exorcist.

[106]Humphries, *Christian Origins*, 39.

[107]Ibid., 34.

[108]Jacobson, *The First Gospel*, 2.

interest of the text. While Jesus is certainly the main character of the text, this does not necessitate that asserting his unique identity is the rhetorical goal of the text. I have also attempted to imagine the possibility that while "Jewish" never means one thing, its meaning is not always the central issue that is being disputed in texts that occupy the borderlands between our own categories of "Jewish" and "Christian." These texts make as much if not more sense as internal struggles over the values and vision of the *basileia* of God.

In Q 11:14–26, the *basileia* of God is the common ground on which the text calls all Jews to stand against the *basileia* of Satan. The text appeals to the audience to avoid the divisiveness inherent in the claim that Jesus is not on the right side. This suggests that the Q community told this controversy story not to assert the singularity of Jesus or the superiority of their Jewishness but rather to make the case for the communal vision of the *basileia* of God over and against the *basileia* of Satan.

The mythopoeic language of clashing *basileiai* and the call to choose sides may point to the social and historical experience of Jews under the dehumanizing and divisive effects of foreign rule.[109] The solidarity of God's people is envisioned by the text as necessary to the victory of God's *basileia*. A *basileia* divided against itself cannot stand. In Q 11:14–26, Q's Jesus makes a case for common cause among those who attempt to expel the demonic forces that ravage the people. That common cause is the healing and liberating work of the *basileia*. It is significant, therefore, that when Q's Jesus does turn to delineating difference between people, it is precisely the values of the *basileia* of God that are at the center of the dispute. In Q 11:42–52, Jesus criticizes the Pharisees for what Kirk convincingly calls "ostentatious displays of prestige and rank."[110] Thus for Q, the Pharisees' notion of the *basileia* of God or the "way things should be" too closely resembles the *basileiai* of the world (Q 4:5–6). According to Q, those valued the most in the basileia of God are the poor (6:20), the sick (7:22; 10:9), the least (7:28), and the weak (10:23).

---

[109]I explore this possibility further in "Communities Resisting Fragmentation: Q and the Work of James C. Scott," *Semeia* (forthcoming).

[110]Alan Kirk, "Breaching the Frontier: Going Public with the Hidden Transcript in Q 11" (paper presented at the annual meeting of the Society of Biblical Literature, Denver, Colo., 2001) 4.

The previous chapter explored the way that interests in eschatology, Christology, and Christian uniqueness intertwine in the interpretation of Q and Christian origins. A common remedy for the problem is to insist that *proper* scholarship is interested only in (unbiased, scientific) knowledge. But this masks the ideological nature of all scholarly interpretation and its participation in larger spheres of discourse on Christian identity in a pluralistic world. In light of the persistence of Christian anti-Judaism and religious intolerance, I have tried to explore alternative interpretations of the text that resist or undermine the interest in the uniqueness of Jesus so central to current scholarly interpretations. In this regard, the re-reading of the Beelzebul text presented in this chapter is both rhetorically plausible and, from my view, ethically valuable.

CHAPTER 6

Eschatology and Apocalyptic:
The Son of Humanity in Q 11:16, 29–32

Traditional approaches to the Beelzebul pericope in Q 11:14–26 focus on Jesus' unique relationship to the *basileia* of God. With the Sign of Jonah, which follows in Q 11:16, 29–32, the interpretive focus shifts from Jesus and the *basileia* to Jesus as the son of humanity. Debates over the appellation "son of humanity" in Q 11:30 focus on whether the text speaks of a present or future son of humanity and whether it makes superlative claims about an exalted or resurrected Jesus. In several ways, however, the Sign of Jonah unit continues the emphasis of the Beelzebul unit on the communal vision of the *basileia* of God.

More than any of the other passages examined in this book, the Sign of Jonah tradition (Matt 12:38–42//Matt 16:1–4//Mark 8:11–13//Luke 11:29–32) presents interpreters with a series of vexing puzzles, the solutions to which have yet to garner any lasting consensus. A. K. M. Adam reviews the variety of interpretations of these texts among pre-critical and historical-critical readers, and rightly concludes that "scholarly erudition has not led to critical convergence."[1] These puzzles include such questions as: What kind of a sign do these people demand? Why does Jesus refuse any sign in Mark 8:11–13 but grant the sign of Jonah in the double tradition? What exactly is the "sign of Jonah"? What is the *tertium comparationis* between Jonah and the son of humanity? What exactly does the phrase "the son of humanity" mean in this context? How does that meaning relate to other Q and synoptic uses of "the son of humanity"? How do the sayings about the Queen of the South and the men of Nineveh relate to the request for a sign? In short, what

[1]A. K. M. Adam, "The Sign of Jonah: A Fish-Eye View," *Semeia* 51 (1990) 185.

did this passage communicate to the audience of Q? We cannot explore all of these questions about the Sign of Jonah in this chapter, but we will discuss the methodological and thematic issues pertinent to those raised in earlier chapters. In the context of this study, the Sign of Jonah unit provides an opportunity to consider what happens when Q turns to one of the "last things," that is, the final judgment. What role does the uniqueness of Jesus play in the motif of the final reckoning in Q, and how does recognition of Jesus relate to Q's communal vision of the *basileia* of God?

This chapter first establishes the text of Q and highlights central questions concerning the interpretation of the Sign of Jonah unit in Q. While the judgment theme creates a heightened sense of urgency in the Sign of Jonah pericope, many of the observations that Q scholars have made about the unit support an interpretation that continues to center the communal vision of the *basileia* of God rather than the singular significance of Jesus. There *are* certain aspects of this text, however, that mitigate this reading and which may shift the text toward centering the unique significance of Jesus.

Establishing the Text

As with the Beelzebul unit, Matthew and Luke show a great deal of agreement on certain parts of the Sign of Jonah unit, and thus the reconstruction[2] is relatively undisputed. The primary disagreements have to do with the placement of Q 11:16 and 11:32, and the wording of 11:29–30:

Q 11:16: ἕτεροι ⟦δὲ⟧ ἐζήτουν παρ' αὐτοῦ σημεῖον	But others were seeking from him a sign [from heaven].[3]
Q 11:29: ⟦ὁ⟧ δὲ. . .⟦εἶπεν⟧. . .ἡ γενεὰ αὕτη γενεὰ πονηρά. . .ἐστιν σημεῖον ζητεῖ, καὶ σημεῖον οὐ δοθήσεται αὐτῇ εἰ μὴ τὸ σημεῖον Ἰωνᾶ.	And he said, "This generation is an evil generation.[4] It seeks a sign, and a sign will not be given to it except the sign of Jonah.

---

[2]Robinson, *Critical Edition*, 246–55. I follow Kloppenborg and the IQP in 1991 (ibid., 246) and Kirk (*Composition*, 184–85 n. 135) in placing 11:16 after 11:15 in Q.

[3]It is not possible to determine whether Luke's "from heaven" (ἐξ οὐρανοῦ) derives from Q or from Mark 8:11b's "from heaven" (ἀπὸ τοῦ οὐρανοῦ).

[4]Or Matthew: "An evil and adulterous generation seeks for a sign." This reading may be preferable since Matthew attests this wording twice. In Matt 16:4, Matthew assimilates the wording of Mark 8:12 to Q.

Q 11:30:⁵ ⟦καθ⟧ὼς γὰρ ἐγένετο
Ἰωνᾶς τοῖς Νινευίταις σημεῖον,
οὕτως ἔσται ⟦καὶ⟧ ὁ υἱὸς τοῦ ἀνθρώπου τῇ γενεᾷ ταύτῃ.

For as Jonah became a sign to the
Ninevites, so also the son of humanity will be to this generation.

Q 11:32:⁶ ἄνδρες Νινευῖται ἀν-
αστήσονται ἐν τῇ κρίσει μετὰ τῆς
γενεᾶς ταύτης καὶ κατακρινοῦσιν
αὐτήν, ὅτι μετενόησαν εἰς τὸ
κήρυγμα Ἰωνᾶ, καὶ ἰδοὺ πλεῖον
Ἰωνᾶ ὧδε.

The men of Nineveh will rise up at
the judgment with this generation
and condemn it, for they repented at
the proclamation of Jonah, and look,
something more than Jonah is here.

Q 11:31: βασίλισσα νότου ἐγερθή-
σεται ἐν τῇ κρίσει μετὰ τῆς γενεᾶς
ταύτης καὶ κατακρινεῖ αὐτήν, ὅτι
ἦλθεν ἐκ τῶν περάτων τῆς γῆς
ἀκοῦσαι τὴν σοφίαν Σολομῶνος,
καὶ ἰδοὺ πλεῖον Σολομῶνος ὧδε.

The Queen of the South will be
raised up at the judgment with this
generation and condemn it, for she
came from the ends of the earth to
hear the wisdom of Solomon, and
look, something more than Solomon
is here.

The unit consists of a very brief introductory scene (11:16) in which
"others" request a sign from Jesus. He denies that "this generation" will
receive a sign, except the sign of Jonah (v. 29). Verse 30 explains the
enigmatic "sign of Jonah" with an analogy: as Jonah was to the Ninevites, so the son of humanity will be to this generation. A double saying
follows in which two figures from Israel's history—the men of Nineveh
and the Queen of the South—will rise up at the judgment and condemn
this generation for its rejection of the "something more" (πλεῖον) than
Jonah's preaching and Solomon's wisdom that is "here" (ὧδε).

⁵The IQP reconstruction of Q 11:30 replicates Luke 11:30. This is primarily because
Matthew's version elucidates the comparison of Jonah and Jesus with a reference to three
days in the whale/earth: "For as Jonah was three days and three nights in the belly of the sea
monster, so will the son of humanity be three days and three nights in the heart of the earth."
Matthew quotes the LXX version of Jonah 2:1b: "And Jonah was three days and three nights in
the belly of the sea monster." See Kloppenborg, *Formation*, 128 n. 120.

⁶I follow Matthew's order of the Solomon and Jonah sayings (12:41–42). Luke's order
is the opposite. Most interpreters argue that Luke's order is original. For bibliography and
discussion, see Kloppenborg, *Q Parallels*, 100. While the arguments on each side of the debate
are fairly balanced, I think the scales are tipped by the argument of William Arnal ("Gendered
Couplets in Q and Legal Formulations: From Rhetoric to Social History," *JBL* 116 [1997]
75–94) that Q 11:31–32 is a gendered couplet that is common to Q's style. All of the other
gendered couplets in Q follow the order of male then female.

Q 11:16, 29–32 effects a thematic shift away from the Beelzebul pericope. The issue of exorcism recedes from the scene and the issue of signs replaces it. In addition, the Sign of Jonah unit shares little vocabulary with the Beelzebul controversy that precedes it.[7] As with the Beelzebul unit and many of the units in Q, however, the Sign of Jonah sayings themselves cohere with each other both thematically and by catchword. The request for a "sign" (σημεῖον; 11:16, 29, 30) and the focus on "this generation" (ἡ γενεὰ αὕτη; 11:29, 30, 31, 32) tie the sayings together. Additional catchwords such as "of Jonah" (Ἰωνᾶ; 11:29, 30, 32) and "to the Ninevites" (τοῖς Νινευίταις; 11:30, 32) create a thematic unity.

Despite divergent themes, the introduction in 11:16 suggests that the Sign of Jonah unit functions rhetorically in conjunction with the Beelzebul controversy. Q 11:16 creates a link between the two units by continuing the scene in which Jesus interacts with a crowd. The connection between the two units is also created (1) through the placement of Q 11:16 after 11:15 (as in Luke), and (2) in the "some/others" structure of Q 11:16 (again, following Luke).

In terms of placement, Q 11:16 links the Sign of Jonah pericope to the Beelzebul controversy introduced by Q 11:14–15 by foreshadowing the coming focus on signs. As Kirk points out, "The collocation of themes in 11:14–16 is one of the several means the Q editor uses to signal that the two controversy instructions are to be read together."[8] Placing Q 11:16 after Q 11:15 is preferable to Matthew's placement because it is unclear why Luke would move Q 11:16 to follow Q 11:15 if it was not already there in Q. If we assume that Luke does so in order to create a narrative link between the Beelzebul and Sign of Jonah units, then why would he also create a larger crowd to receive the sign teaching in Luke 11:29? That verse begins: "When the crowds were increasing, he began to say . . . ." If Luke's source had a suitable introduction like Q 11:16 preceding Q 11:29, why would Luke move it and create a completely different introduction? Indeed if we remove Luke 11:16 from Luke altogether, nothing has been lost since the increasing crowd provides the context for the sayings about "this generation" seeking a sign.

---

[7]The description of this generation as πονηρά may echo the description of the seven spirits that inhabit the victim in 11:26 and make his or her condition worse than the first. Matthew makes this link explicit when he moves Q 11:24–26 to follow the Sign of Jonah unit and appends a summative comment: "So it shall also be with this evil (πονηρᾷ) generation."

[8]Kirk, *Composition*, 185 n. 135. For the compositional unity of Q 11:14–32, see ibid., 309–11, and the literature cited there.

Thus, Luke 11:16 reflects the location of Q 11:16. In addition, if Q 11:16 did follow Q 11:15, Matthew's omission of the introduction makes sense. Matthew distances the Beelzebul and Jonah units by inserting two blocks of material between them. He moves the saying about blasphemy from Q 12:10[9] and the sayings about good and bad fruit from Q 6:43–45 to the end of the Beelzebul controversy (Matt 12:31–37).[10] In addition, Matthew gives both sets of sayings more concrete narrative contexts by identifying the Pharisees (12:24) and the scribes and Pharisees (12:38) as Jesus' interlocutors. Thus Q 11:16 would have served little use for Matthew's composition of Matt 12:22–45.

The wording of Q 11:16 also points to an integration of the two units in Q. The scene of Jesus healing a demoniac and the crowds showing amazement (Q 11:14) leads to two challenges: one from "some" (τινὲς δὲ; 11:15) and one from "others" (ἕτεροι δὲ; 11:16).[11] The some/others structure appears to be a deliberate construction. Indeed, this structure and its placement after 11:15 may be all that one can say about Q 11:16. The lack of verbal agreement between Matt 12:38 and Luke 11:16 (besides σημεῖον) and the significant overlap in vocabulary between Luke 11:16 and Mark 8:11b raise the question of whether much of the wording of Luke 11:16 derives from Mark rather than Q:

Mark 8:11: [And the Pharisees came and began to argue with him,] seeking from him a sign from heaven, to test him [ζητοῦντες παρ' αὐτοῦ σημεῖον ἀπὸ τοῦ οὐρανοῦ, πειράζοντες αὐτόν].	Luke 11:16: And others, to test him, were seeking from him a sign from heaven [ἕτεροι δὲ πειράζοντες σημεῖον ἐξ οὐρανοῦ ἐζήτουν παρ' αὐτοῦ].

Mark 8:11 introduces Mark's version of the request for a sign. Matthew replicates this version in Matt 16:1–2a, 4 and assimilates it to Q by adding the clause "except for the sign of Jonah" to the end of Jesus' refusal to produce a sign in Mark 8:12. Matthew also moves the sayings about interpreting the signs of the times in Q 12:54–56 into the middle of the Markan unit. This suggests that Matthew was aware of the two versions

---

[9]Matthew also conflates Q 12:10 with Mark 3:28–30 (Kloppenborg, *Q Parallels*, 124).

[10]Matthew may have made these moves because both emphasize "evil speech," which Matthew criticizes in 12:36–37 (ibid., 44).

[11]Q 9:57–60 links individual sayings together with a τις / ἕτερος sequence (Robinson, *Critical Edition*, 150–54).

and sought to coordinate them. The same may have been true for Luke. But this does not explain the seemingly unnecessary location of Luke 11: 16 and the some/others structure of Q 11:15–16. Indeed, Mark 8:11 would have provided a perfectly suitable introduction immediately preceding the sayings about a request for a sign (as it does in Mark), but Luke does not place Luke 11:16 there. Despite the Markan versions of both the Beelzebul controversy (3:22–27) and the request for a sign (8:11–12), Luke shows little evidence of preferring Mark in Luke 11:14–32.[12] Luke 11:16 points to a Q version of Luke 11:16, located after Q 11:15, and possibly having significant overlap in wording with Mark 8:11. By intertwining the introductions to the two units in Q 11:14–16, therefore, Q creates an expanded apophthegm[13] that presents two challenges to Jesus' legitimacy from the crowds, each of which is followed by a response from Jesus.

Q 11:30 and the Interpretation of Q 11:16, 29–32

As with the Beelzebul controversy and its relation to Q 11:20, interest in Q 11:30 has had a substantial impact on the interpretation of the Sign of Jonah unit. Asserting the authenticity of 11:30, many interpreters attempt to peer through the text in order to catch a glimpse of the self-understanding and worldview of the historical Jesus. The interpretation of Q 11:30 has always had a place in the ongoing debate about the meaning of the expression "son of humanity" and its origins as a designation for Jesus.[14] In 1963, H. E. Tödt argued that Q 11:30 is an authentic saying of Jesus that uses the coming of a son of humanity figure as a threat against those

---

[12]Matthew, on the other hand, does tend to follow Mark. For example, Mark places sayings about blasphemy after the Beelzebul controversy as well (3:28–30).

[13]Lührmann, *Redaktion*, 36; and Schulz, *Q*, 250–53.

[14]The volume of literature on the son of humanity is staggering. For Q, see Heinz Eduard Tödt, *The Son of Man in the Synoptic Tradition* (German originals, 1959 and 1963; trans. Dorothea Barton; Philadelphia: Westminster, 1965); Hoffmann, *Studien*; Adela Yarbro Collins, "The Son of Man Sayings in the Sayings Source," in *To Touch the Text: Biblical and Related Studies in Honor of Joseph A. Fitzmyer, S.J.* (ed. Maurya P. Horgan and Paul Kobelski; New York: Crossroad, 1989) 369–89; Leif Vaage, "The Son of Man Sayings in Q: Stratigraphical Location and Significance," *Semeia* 55 (1991) 103–29. In general and recently, see Frederick Borsch, *The Son of Man in Myth and History* (Philadelphia: Westminster, 1967); Chrys C. Caragounis, *The Son of Man: Vision and Interpretation* (Tübingen: Mohr/Siebeck, 1986); Douglas R. A. Hare, *The Son of Man Tradition* (Minneapolis: Fortress, 1990); and Walter Wink, *The Human Being: Jesus and the Enigma of the Son of the Man* (Minneapolis: Fortress, 2002).

who do not respond to Jesus' preaching.[15] In contrast, Philipp Vielhauer argued that all of the son of humanity sayings originate in the early Christian response to the death of Jesus and not in the preaching of Jesus.[16] Adela Yarbro Collins rightly locates these exegetical arguments in the larger context of a theological evaluation of "apocalyptic" symbols and their relationship to the preaching of the historical Jesus. Where Bultmann and Tödt followed Johannes Weiss in identifying Jesus as an "apocalypticist," scholars such as Vielhauer and Norman Perrin "distinguish between Jesus as an eschatological teacher and prophet and the oldest Christian community in Jerusalem as an apocalyptic movement."[17] As Leif Vaage points out, "Because the term occurs in Daniel, taken as the fountainhead of the biblical apocalyptic tradition, and then is placed on the lips of Jesus especially in the synoptic gospels, attention to the 'son of man' has seemed vital to solving the modern debate about Jesus and apocalypticism."[18]

As we saw with the interpretation of John's opening speech in Q, some scholars enter this debate about Jesus' relation to apocalyptic thinking less by means of authenticity arguments and more with redaction-critical arguments. From this view, Q's son of humanity Christology is a product of early Christian reflection, and thus the tradition-history of units that invoke the son of humanity can provide a mirror reflection of this christologization of the tradition. Not surprisingly, "tradition-history accounts of the formation of this cluster proliferate."[19] Kirk has shown how the difference between Schürmann

---

[15]Tödt, *Son of Man*, 52–54. This is also the position of Bultmann, *History*, 118 and 151–52. Ragnar Leivestad questioned the existence of a coherent expectation of a figure called the "son of humanity" in contemporary Jewish tradition ("Exit the Apocalyptic Son of Man," *NTS* 18 [1972] 243–67). See also Barnabas Lindars, "Re-enter the Apocalyptic Son of Man," *NTS* 22 (1975) 52–72.

[16]Philipp Vielhauer, "Gottesreich und Menschensohn in der Verkündigung Jesu," in idem, *Aufsätze zum Neuen Testament* (TB 31; Munich: Kaiser Verlag, 1965) 55–91. See also Norman Perrin, *Rediscovering the Teaching of Jesus* (London: SCM Press, 1967) 154–206.

[17]Adela Yarbro Collins, "The Origins of the Designation of Jesus as 'Son of Man,'" *HTR* 80 (1987) 391–407, at 393.

[18]Vaage, "Son of Man Sayings," 103–4.

[19]Kirk, *Composition*, 194. See also Kloppenborg, *Formation*, 128–34; Heinz Schürmann, "QLk 11:14–36," in *The Four Gospels 1992: Festschrift for Frans Neirynck* (ed. Van Segbroeck et al.; 3 vols.; BETL 100; Louvain: Leuven University Press, 1992) 576–78; Hoffmann, *Studien*, 181; Lührmann, *Redaktion*, 41–42; Anton Vögtle, "Der Spruch vom Jonaszeichen," in idem, *Das Evangelium und die Evangelien* (Düsseldorf: Patmos, 1971) 132–33; Richard A. Edwards, *The Sign of Jonah: In the Theology of the Evangelists and Q* (Naperville, Ill.: Allenson; London: SCM, 1971) 49–58; Jacobson, *First Gospel*, 164–66.

and Lührmann's proposals, for example, depends on their assumptions about the very process they seek to describe.[20] For Schürmann, Q 11:30 presents a symbolic allusion to the resurrected Jesus that entered the tradition earlier than the themes of judgment against Israel for rejecting the Christian message.[21] For Lührmann, Q 11:29c and 11:30 are the final redaction of the unit, which strengthens the announcement of judgment against "this generation" by invoking the son of humanity coming in judgment.[22] Running through these proposals is an interest in explaining how, when, and why the apocalyptic "son of humanity" designation for Jesus entered the tradition.

In contrast to those who focus on the authenticity of Q 11:30, therefore, tradition- and redaction-critical approaches correlate the growth of the unit with the process of "christological cognition" in the Q community. Leif Vaage summarizes this approach as follows:

> If [Jesus] did not speak of himself as the son of man, the term belongs to the process of "christological cognition" whereby Jesus as a founder figure was elevated in the imagination of early Christianity to the highest conceivable status. In order to describe as accurately as possible the mechanisms of this cultural process, it is important to understand especially the first shifts in perspective "from the proclaimer to the proclaimed," one of which would be the use of "son of man" as a title for Jesus.[23]

Richard Edwards's interpretation of the redactional growth of Q 11:29–32 typifies this correlation between redactional growth and christological cognition:

---

[20]Kirk, *Composition*, 193–95. Schürmann ("QLk 11:14–36," 576–78) typifies an aggregative tradition-critical approach and suggests that 11:30 was added to 11:29 as a commentary and the pair was added to 11:33–35 before the final addition of vv. 31–32. In contrast, Lührmann (*Redaktion*, 41–42) takes a redaction-critical approach and identifies the exceptive clause in Q 11:29c and interpretation in Q 11:30 as a redactional clasp between Q 11:29a–b and 31–32. Lührmann thus places the entry of 11:30 into the unit at the overall redactional stage of Q rather than at the initial stages of the unit's development, as does Schürmann. Lührmann's view is also taken by Hoffmann, *Studien*, 181; and Edwards, *Sign of Jonah*, 85–86. Schürmann's view is also taken by Kloppenborg, *Formation*, 128–30; and Jacobson, *First Gospel*, 71. Tuckett (*Q*, 257–60) gives a useful review of the various proposals. Both Tuckett and Kirk prefer to read the unit as a whole regardless of its tradition-history.

[21]Schürmann, "QLk 11:14–36," 576–78.

[22]Lührmann, *Redaktion*, 41.

[23]Vaage, "Son of Man Sayings," 104.

Thus I suggest that the origin of the Sign of Jonah saying, "no sign will be given to this evil generation except the sign of Jonah," lies in the application of the Q community's theological outlook to the problem of a sign which is refused by Jesus and yet which Jesus himself is. The impact of Easter and the continuity of the fellowship which began during Jesus' earthly ministry have resulted in an elaboration of the judgment theme. Just as Jesus himself takes on a new meaning for the Q community (the christological cognition), so the sayings of Jesus must be understood anew from the same perspective.[24]

For Edwards, the "impact of Easter" produces a process of interpretation of the Jesus tradition in light of the growing christological conviction that the earthly Jesus is also the coming son of humanity.

For interpreters like Vaage and Mack, however, the interest in the development of the Q tradition rests not in tracing the "impact of Easter," but rather on the "cultural processes" that produced christological claims for Jesus. Thus, the combination of the son of humanity and the themes of judgment and destruction in several Q units (11:29–32; 12:8–9; 12:40; and 17:24–30) point to a process of "mythification" that betrays "an apocalyptic sensibility grappling with its social world's (imagined) downfall and hoping not to fail with it."[25] According to Mack, this apocalyptic imagination served "only one purpose for the people of Q, and that was to guarantee that threat of judgment that they wanted to bring down upon people who had frustrated their mission."[26] Thus, it is not the "impact of Easter" but the rejection of the Q community's message that produces christological claims couched in apocalyptic motifs such as future judgment and imminent destruction.

Whether scholars approach Q 11:16, 29–32 as a window onto the apocalyptic Jesus or as a mirror of early Christian myth-making, there is always a group of opponents called "the Jews" or "other Jews," who call forth this invective from Jesus or the community. As with the Beelzebul controversy, the presupposition is that these controversy stories function in the Q community to work out the identity of Jesus or of the Q people over and against others who reject them. The central marker for delineating the community's identity is the significance of Jesus himself. Here once again, the controversy stories in Q are understood to serve no purpose but to assert the singular significance of Jesus over and against opponents. However, as with the John

---

[24]Edwards, *Sign of Jonah*, 84–85.
[25]Vaage, "Son of Man Sayings," 122–23.
[26]Mack, *Lost Gospel*, 134.

material in Q, we should ask whether the language of judgment can serve other rhetorical purposes in Q. Indeed, in several respects, this text can be interpreted in a way that places the communal vision of the *basileia* of God at a crucial moment in the history of Israel. In order to explore this possibility, we will consider the following three questions: What is requested of Jesus in the unit? How does the text characterize "this generation"? Does Jesus respond to the request for a sign?

Others Request a Sign

In Q 11:15, "some" members of the crowd accuse Jesus of exorcizing by the power of Satan; and in Q 11:16, "other" members of the crowd ask Jesus to prove his claim that he is of God by providing a sign. Recent Q interpreters tend to slide by the question of what, precisely, is being requested of Jesus in the apophthegm to a consideration of what the "sign of Jonah" might mean in its Q context.[27] If we consider that requesting signs is a common literary motif in Jewish and Christian literature, it may be useful to consider the contours of such requests in comparison to Q.

Jewish tradition attests myriad examples of a request for a sign as a request for verifiable proof of a claim.[28] The classic example is Isa 7:10–25. Here the prophet says that in "sixty-five years Ephraim will be shattered, no longer a people" (7:8). Following this, the prophet has a conversation with Ahaz:

> Again the LORD spoke to Ahaz, saying, Ask a sign [Heb: אוֹת; LXX: σημεῖον] of the LORD your God; let it be deep as Sheol or high as heaven. But Ahaz said, I will not ask, and I will not put the LORD to the test. Then Isaiah said: "Hear then, O house of David! Is it too little for you to weary mortals, that you weary my God also? Therefore the Lord himself will give you a sign [Heb: אוֹת; LXX: σημεῖον]: Look, the young woman is with child and shall bear a son, and shall name him Immanuel. . . . For before the child knows how to refuse the evil and choose the good, the land before whose two kings you are in dread will be deserted (Isa 7:10–16, NRSV).

[27]Kloppenborg (*Formation*, 131–32) identifies the sign as a "legitimation sign" but does not define it; Tuckett (*Q*, 256–66) provides no definition; and Jacobson (*First Gospel*, 165) identifies the sign in Q as a "sign of the end" and not a "sign to legitimate Jesus," but does not say why or what either might mean.

[28]For much of the following discussion, I am indebted to K. H. Rengstorf, "σημεῖον," *TDNT* 7:200–61, esp. 234–36; Olof Linton, "The Demand for a Sign from Heaven," *Studia Theologica* 19 (1965) 112–29; and Jeffrey Gibson, "Jesus' Refusal to Produce a 'Sign' (Mk 8.11–13)," *JSNT* 38 (1990) 37–66.

Isaiah offers Ahaz a chance to verify the prophecy just given by requesting a sign from God. Ahaz attempts to decline, recognizing that the request of a sign is a test and thus not something requested lightly from God. Isaiah seems to take Ahaz's refusal as an implicit request and delivers the sign anyway. A young pregnant woman standing among them will have a son and will call him Immanuel. Before the son comes of age, the Syro-Ephraimite war will be over. This is a mundane sign[29] that can be verified in the near future by Ahaz's own observation.[30]

Another example of the sign motif is from the Babylonian Talmud:

> The disciples of R. Jose b. Kisma asked him [R. Joshua b. Levi], "When will the Messiah come?" He answered, "I fear lest you demand a sign from me." They assured him, "We will demand no sign of you." So he answered them, "When this gate falls down, is rebuilt, falls again, and is rebuilt again, and then falls a third time. Before it can be rebuilt the Son of David will come." They said to him, "Master, give us a sign." [He protests, but accedes to the request.] "If so, let the waters of the grotto of Paneas turn into blood." And they turned into blood.[31]

In order to verify R. Joshua Levi's prophecy[32] about the coming of the Messiah, the interlocutors request a sign. This sign is a second prophecy that is immediately confirmed by the waters of the grotto of Paneas turning to blood.[33] Luke attests a similar sequence of a prophecy that is confirmed by an additional word, one which can be verified by observation. In Luke

---

[29]Olof Linton ("Demand," 112–29) usefully reviews and refutes the common view that all of the gospel requests for a sign reflect a Pharisaic demand for "miracle of a higher order" that would verify Jesus' messianic claim.

[30]Many other Hebrew Bible texts confirm this notion of a sign as a verifiable word that guarantees the trustworthiness of the speaker's other prophecies, teachings, or promises: Exod 3:9–12; 4:1–9; Num 14:11–12, 22; Deut 13:1–12; Judg 6:14–18; 1 Sam 2:27–36; 10:1–8; 14:8–10; 1 Kgs 13:1–5; 2 Kgs 19:28–31 (Isa 37:29–32); 2 Kgs 20:1–11 (2 Chr 32:24; Isa 38:7–8, 22); Neh 9:6–10; Ps 78:42–43; 105:26–27; 135:8–9. All of the Psalms references and several of the others are to signs that God performs in Egypt. Several of these signs also serve to confirm that the person addressed has received the initial word from the Lord.

[31]b. Sanh. 98a.

[32]The Rabbinic material shows that both prophecy and teaching can be confirmed by a sign. In b. B. Mes. 59b, R. Eliezer gives several signs (all rejected by R. Joshua as irrelevant) to guarantee that the halakhah agrees with his teaching.

[33]The "sign" provided often echoes one of the acts of God performed by Moses to prove to Pharaoh that he was from God. The expression "signs and wonders" becomes a technical term for God's acts of power in the Exodus narrative.

2:11–12, the angels deliver the good news: "To you is born this day in the city of David a Savior, who is the Messiah, the Lord" (v. 11). To confirm the message, the angels offer a sign: "And this will be a sign [σημεῖον] to you: you will find a child wrapped in bands of cloth and lying in a manger" (v. 12). The shepherds know the truth of the sign—and thus the legitimacy of the message—only four verses later when they find the baby in the manger (v. 16). But the audience gets immediate gratification at v. 12 because already in 2:7 they have been told that when Mary gave birth "she wrapped him in bands of cloth, and laid him in a manger."

Throughout his extensive treatment of Greek, Jewish, and Christian examples of the motif of the sign, Karl Rengstorf identifies two persistent elements in the meaning of "sign": sense perception and confirmation. "The word simply denotes something which may be perceived and from which those who observe it may draw assured conclusions."[34] In addition to the scriptural and rabbinic support for this understanding of a sign, examples from Qumran,[35] the Pseudepigrapha,[36] the New Testament,[37] and Josephus[38] fill in the period surrounding Q. Jeffrey Gibson suggests the following five features of narratives involving signs:[39]

(1) a sign is verified publicly; it is meant to be "seen or perceived"
(2) a successful sign happens on demand; it is sought and given
(3) a sign should either "certify the truth" of a claim or establish that a person making a claim is "of God"
(4) a successful sign has occurred when there is a coincidence between a prophecy and a subsequent event
(5) it is less important whether the sign is miraculous or ordinary than that it recognizably corresponds' to the subsequent event

[34]Rengstorf, "σημεῖον," 232.

[35]1 Q 27 Fr. 1 col. 1, 5.

[36]4 Ezra 4.51; 6.11, 20; 7.26; and 8.63–9.2. Here the signs are verifiable predictions that back up God's prophecy of the end of the age.

[37]Mark 13:4; 13:22; 16:17, 20; Matt 24:3; Luke 21:7; John 2:18–22; 6:28–34; Acts 4: 13–16, 22; 8:12–13; 14:3; 1 Cor 1:22; 2 Thess 2:9; Rev 13:13–14.

[38]J.W. 2.258–259, 261–263; 6.258, 288; Ant. 8.347; 10.28; 20.97–99, 167–168, 188.

[39]Gibson, "Jesus' Refusal," 38–40. This list paraphrases Gibson's schema, but the basic framework is his. Gibson labels his list "Characteristics of the 'Sign' Phenomenon" (ibid., 38). Since all of the data is textual, however, these are aspects of a literary motif rather than a "phenomenon."

The request for a sign, therefore, at minimum suggests a request for public and visible proof of Jesus' claims.

Located in a crowd scene, the request for a sign in Q 11:16 is public and on demand. Jesus has just made claims about being on the side of God and not on the side of Satan, and about the *basileia* of God having come upon the audience in the successful exorcisms of Jesus and the "sons" (11:19–20). Jesus heals a mute demoniac and the crowds are amazed (11:14). This sets the scene for two challenges to Jesus' legitimacy as one who claims to be on the side of God. The first challenge locates Jesus on the side of Beelzebul. The second challenge locates Jesus on the side of a false prophet or teacher. If Jesus cannot produce a verifiable sign to guarantee his own claims that he exorcises by the "finger of God" and that the *basileia* of God "has come upon you," then he has spoken falsely, cannot be trusted, and is not on the side of God. In terms of the literary motif, the request for a sign following on claims like those made in the Beelzebul pericope is thoroughly unremarkable. In effect, "others" in the crowd step forward and say, "Well, you say you are of God, but prove it."

This Evil or Sorry Generation

Whether Jesus proves it or not is another matter. With Q 11:29, the polemical heat seems to turn up: "And he said, 'This generation is an evil generation. It seeks a sign, and a sign will not be given to it except the sign of Jonah.'" This is the second reference to "this generation" in Q. Whether the Q text is best represented in Luke's version ("This generation is an *evil* generation. It seeks a sign") or Matthew's ("An *evil* generation requests a sign"), one thing is clear: this is strong talk. Either this generation is evil because it requests a sign, or all generations that request signs are evil. Does Q's Jesus refuse to give a verifiable sign to this generation or does he concede to the request?[40] Is the "sign of Jonah" a successful sign that proves the truth of Jesus' previous claims or a sort of anti-sign that implicitly critiques the demand that Jesus prove that he is of God? Interpreters often decide this question based on the assumption that Q 11:29 is punitive and thus an implicit critique of those who

---

[40]The exasperation of those giving signs appears in Isa 7:13; Mark 8:12; and *b. Sanh.* 98a. In *b. B. Mes.* 59b, R. Eliezer's endless and successful performance of signs (a word plus a recognizably corresponding event) is rejected by R. Joshua as unconvincing in matters of scholarly halakhah debate.

request a sign.[41] This view is directly linked to one's interpretation of "this generation" in Q, and thus we need to discuss this issue before exploring whether Q's Jesus does provide a sign to legitimate his claims.

There are three ways in which one's approach to "this generation" in the text determines one's reading of the sign of Jonah unit. First, the identification of this text as part of a "controversy discourse" in Q leads to an assumption of distance between Jesus and his opponents. Polemical language (such as "this evil generation"), conjoined with the themes of judgment confirms the identification by Q scholars of the Beelzebul and Sign of Jonah units as parallel texts in a larger context (Q 11:14–52 or Q 10:23–11:52 and 13:34–35[42]) in which the theme of polemic and controversy dominates.[43] On the basis of this polemical language, Q scholars often conclude that whatever the "sign of Jonah" means, it is not an acquiescence to the request for a sign:

> Indeed the opponents request a legitimation sign rather than some other type of miracle. . . . But as 11:29 makes clear, the request for a sign comes from an "evil" and unbelieving group. Under the circumstances, it is hardly likely that Q would comply by granting a legitimation sign.[44]

While the text does identify "this generation" as "evil," it does not identify them as "unbelieving." A survey of the texts with the legitimation sign motif shows that none of them suggests that a request for a sign springs from unbelief in either God or the speaker. When a text indicates the motivation for a request, it is usually a lack of confidence in a prophecy that is too far off in the future to verify or in a teaching that is so hard to swallow that people need some guarantee that it is from God. Thus, the sign request functions in the texts noted above to authorize the words and actions of God among the people through a *verifiable* sign. A successful

[41]Kloppenborg, *Formation*, 131–32; Jacobson, *First Gospel*, 164; Tuckett, *Q*, 265; and Edwards, *Sign of Jonah*, 83.

[42]I agree with Kirk (*Composition*, 309–34) that beginning the larger rhetorical unit at Q 10: 23–24, and including Q 13:34–35 in its Matthean location after the woes against the Pharisees, makes more sense than the traditional division beginning at 11:14.

[43]Lührmann, *Redaktion*, 43; Jacobson, *First Gospel*, 182; Kloppenborg, *Formation*, 147; Rudolf Laufen, *Die Doppelüberlieferungen der Logienquelle und des Markusevangeliums* (Bonn: Hanstein, 1980) 147; Tuckett, *Q*, 289; and Kirk, *Composition*, 309–34.

[44]Kloppenborg, *Formation*, 131–32; see also Kirk, *Composition*, 197. Kirk identifies the programmatic thesis as stating that "this generation's" demand is so deviant as to justify refusal; and yet he confirms that the sign of Jonah is a sign.

sign (word plus corresponding event) can *produce* either belief or unbelief insofar as it can convince, but it is not generated by unbelief.

The parallel texts that do register some critique of signs focus on issues other than unbelief.[45] For example, Deut 13:1–5, Josephus,[46] Mark 13:22, and 2 Thess 2:10–11 criticize those who *believe* the successful signs of false prophets and Satan. Rabbi Joshua (*b. B. Mes.* 59b) rejects the view that successful signs should have any epistemic authority in Torah debate.[47] Ahaz (Isa 7:12) is wary of testing God. Isaiah (7:13), Jesus (Mark 8:12), and Rabbi Joshua b. Levi (*b. Sanh.* 98a) sound a note of exasperation at their audience's need for concrete verification of claims. Paul criticizes the epistemic habits of both Greeks (wisdom) and Jews (signs) in 1 Cor 1:22. And in 1 Cor 1:24, Paul confirms that some Jews and Greeks do believe that Christ himself *is* the necessary proof, that is, the power (δύναμις) of God[48] and the wisdom (σοφία) of God.

If we assume that those who request a sign are being polemically characterized as "evil" for their unbelief, then it is inevitable that we will read the text as preemptively judging them and rejecting their request. Because the accusers are identified by interpreters as "unbelievers," they are also understood as outsiders to the Q community and thus representing Jews who have rejected the message of the Q preachers.

A second way that one's approach determines one's interpretation is by how much weight one gives to the adjective πονηρά for determining whether "this generation" represents those "outside" the Q community. Obviously, πονηρά is a negative term. But a review of its usage in Q reveals the following: (1) it is most often used substantively or generically of persons to describe

[45]Q itself may be able to weigh in on this issue. Q 12:54–56 presents a saying about the crowd's *ability* to interpret the appearance of the sky and thus predict the weather, but their *inability* to interpret the present time (Matthew: signs of the times). This may imply a critique of the request for signs from leaders when the people can look around and make accurate (and therefore trustworthy) predictions about what is going to happen for themselves. Q 17:23 warns the audience not to follow those who say, "Look, he is in the wilderness" or "Look, he is indoors." Mark 13:21–22 attributes similar claims to false prophets who can produce signs. Thus Q may attest an implicit critique of signs, but neither of these sayings criticizes the unbelief of those who request signs. Rather, they may critique the over-dependence on (or susceptibility to) leaders who produce signs.

[46]*J.W.* 2.258–259.

[47]R. Joshua even rejects a voice from heaven on the grounds that Torah no longer resides in heaven but was given to the people on Mt. Sinai (*b. B. Mes.* 59b).

[48]Paul identifies his own efforts to convince the Corinthians as "a demonstration of the Spirit and the power" in 1 Cor 2:4.

the moral opposite of something good (6:35 [IQP: "bad"]; 6:45 [3 times; IQP: "evil"]; 11:34 [IQP: "jaundiced"]; and 19:22 [IQP: "wicked"]); (2) it is used once in Q 6:22 to describe either the speech of those who persecute Jesus' followers (Matt 5:11) or the evaluation that those persecutors give to Jesus' followers (Luke 6:22); (3) it is used once in Q 11:26 to describe the eight spirits that re-inhabit the previously exorcised person; and (4) it is used once in Q 11:13 in the concluding conditional saying about the certainty of answer to prayer:

> Q 11:9–13: I tell you, ask and it will be given to you, search and you will find, knock and it will be opened to you. For everyone who asks receives, and the one who searches finds, and to the one who knocks it will be opened. What person of you, whose child asks for bread, will give him a stone? Or again when he asks for a fish, will give him a snake? So if you [pl.], though evil [πονηροὶ ὄντες], know how to give good gifts to your children, by how much more will the Father from heaven give good things to those who ask him.

This last case is striking. The same adjective used for "this generation" in 11:30 and the spirits in 11:26 is applied directly, in the immediately preceding context, to Q's "insiders," those who should have confidence in their prayer. In addition, seven out of ten uses of πονηρά occur in general exhortations to the Q community (6:35; 6:45 [3 times]; 11:13; 11:34; 19:22). Thus the "insider" audience, when faced with two options (good and evil), is pressed to choose to do (or be) the good and not the evil. So, although we cannot fully discount the negative connotations of πονηρά, it is not obvious that it marks "this generation" as hostile "outsiders." As discussed in chapter 2, it is equally plausible to interpret "this generation" as a collective "we" that is marked temporally, such that Jesus says, "The people of our time are evil. We seek a sign."

The third way that our approach shapes our interpretation is in the translation of πονηρά. BAG lists "evil" (along with "wicked"; "bad"; "base"; and "worthless") as the translation of πονηρά "in the ethical sense." The first translation given by BAG, which refers to the use of the adjective in the physical sense, is "in poor condition, sick."[49] This is the meaning of the adjective in the sayings that follow the Sign of Jonah unit in Q 11:33–35. Given the play

---

[49]BAG, s.v. "πονηρός, ά, όν." LSJ similarly gives the physical meanings first ("in a bad case, in a sorry plight") and then the moral meaning ("worthless, knavish"). LSJ does not give "evil" as a translation for πονηρά, except for the substantive "evil one" in Matt 13:19.

on the physical and ethical meanings of πονηρά in the immediately following unit, is it possible to translate πονηρά in 11:29 with a similar nuance, that is, with "sorry" (meaning, "in a sorry plight") or "in bad condition"?

> This generation is a sorry generation. It seeks a sign, but a sign will not be given to it—except the sign of Jonah. (Q 11:29)

This simple shift creates empathy between Jesus and his interlocutors. It resembles Jesus' sighing reaction to the request in Mark 8:11–13. Where translating the term "evil" connects "this generation" with the demonic evil of the "evil spirits,"[50] the translation "in a bad condition" or "sorry" connects "this generation" with the victim of demon possession, whose condition is "worse" (χείρονα) after the gathering of the seven spirits, and with the "jaundiced eye" in 11:34. This generation is factional (7:31–35) and resists coalition (11:14–26). It requires verifiable proof (11:16, 29) that the *basileia* of God has come upon them. Ultimately, the sorry state of "this generation" reaches a tragic climax in Q when it fulfills Sophia's prophecy that it will kill the prophets and sages whom she has sent to it (Q 11:49–51). For that, says Q, they will pay. If we interpret Q in the context of the cataclysmic destruction of the Jewish fight for freedom from the Roman Empire, then striking a tragic note for a generation that paid with its life is much more appropriate than blaming the victim for blaming itself.[51]

---

[50]Even the translation "evil" here may be misleading and overly influenced by the Christian understanding of all demons as evil. For example, using the LSJ proposal "knavish" significantly alters the depiction of the spirits in 11:24–26.

[51]It often goes unsaid that deuteronomistic theology is a theological process of self-blame and community exhortation, whereby the community made sense of national tragedies such as the exile by claiming that God was punishing Israel for its disobedience. I propose that Q scholars re-evaluate the interpretation of Q's use of deuteronomistic theology as insider/outsider polemic. It may make more sense of the passages in which "this generation" appears to interpret this rhetoric in light of a colonized victim's internalizing of the blame for oppression. From this view, Q's critique of "this generation" would represent the community's theological reflections on their own times rather than a polemical condemnation of Israel and/or its leaders for rejecting Jesus and the Q community. I have proposed this interpretation of Q 11:49–51 in Melanie Johnson-DeBaufre, "The Blood Required of This Generation: Interpreting Communal Blame in a Colonial Context," in *Violence in the New Testament* (ed. Shelly Matthews and Leigh Gibson; New York: T&T Clark, 2005) 22–34. Evald Lövestam has argued that the use of the expression "this generation" in the Christian Testament resembles other Jewish literature that draws attention to "special 'generations' in the history of the world and of Israel." From this view, Q would be interpreting its own time by imagining Jesus offering ultimatums to a

By not overestimating the polemic of Jesus' critique of those who request a sign, the interpretive possibility is allowed that Q's Jesus does indeed provide the sign demanded of him. If Q resembles the other uses of this literary motif, it seems unlikely that it would deploy the motif only to show that Jesus did not prove the trustworthiness of his words when asked to do so. Certainly, Q's Jesus displays the same frustration that Isaiah, Paul, and Rabbi Joshua b. Levi express over the people's epistemic need for verification. But Q 11:29 may also portray Jesus as responding to the crowd's desire for trustworthy answers to their situation: "You will receive no sign *except the sign of Jonah*."

Seeking a Verifiable Sign

From the perspective of the Gospel of Matthew, Q's presentation of Jesus' answer to the request for a sign was too ambiguous. Matthew changes the analogy in Q 11:30 ("For as Jonah became a sign to the Ninevites, so also will the son of humanity be to this generation") to the following:

Matt 12:40: ὥσπερ γὰρ ἦν Ἰωνᾶς ἐν τῇ κοιλίᾳ τοῦ κήτους τρεῖς ἡμέρας καὶ τρεῖς νύκτας, οὕτως ἔσται ὁ υἱὸς τοῦ ἀνθρώπου ἐν τῇ καρδίᾳ τῆς γῆς τρεῖς ἡμέρας καὶ τρεῖς νύκτας.	For just as Jonah was in the belly of the sea monster for three days and three nights, so will the son of humanity be three days and three nights in the heart of the earth.

This revision is quite ingenious, insofar as it guarantees that Jesus clearly provides the sign that is requested and thus guarantees the trustworthiness of Jesus' other teachings and prophecies. Matthew's version completes the fourth and fifth steps of the literary motif. Jesus makes a specific prophecy ("so will the son of humanity be three days and three nights in the heart of the earth") that can soon be verified by those present in the scene, when Jesus himself is buried in a tomb in Matt 27:59–60.[52] Matthew 16:1–4

---

generation like the "wilderness generation" or the "flood generation" (Evald Lövestam, "The ἡ γενεὰ αὕτη Eschatology in Mark 13,30 parr.," in *L'Apocalypse johannique et l'Apocalyptique dans le Nouveau Testament* [ed. Jan Lambrecht; Louvain: Leuven University Press, 1980] 410).

[52]There is some irony in Matthew's decision to explicate the sign of Jonah in this way. According to every gospel account (including Matthew!) Jesus did not spend three nights and three days in the tomb but rather two nights and one day. Thus, by the rules of a legitimation sign, Jesus is a false prophet in Matt 12:40! The confusion arises from Matthew's awareness

also corrects Mark's depiction of Jesus refusing a sign (Mark 8:11–13) by removing the Markan "sighing in his spirit" and adding "except for the sign of Jonah" to Jesus' refusal. Luke seems to make no attempt to rescue Jesus' trustworthiness here.[53] In the Gospel of John, Jesus readily complies with requests for a sign after the incident in the temple (2:19: "Destroy this temple, and in three days I will raise it up") and after Jesus claims that he is sent from God (6:33: "The bread of God is that which comes down from heaven and gives life to the world"[54]). Indeed, apart from Mark 8:11–13, all of those who seek signs in the New Testament receive the signs that they request.[55]

If one begins with the request for a sign as a request for *proof that can be verified by the audience*, and leaves open the possibility that Q's Jesus *does* provide the sign that is requested of him, then certain aspects of the Sign of Jonah unit and the larger Q context stand out which may suggest that Q intends to present Jesus as providing the requested sign. First, the language of visual perception reappears in the double saying in Q 11:31–32: "Look, something more than Jonah/Solomon is here!" Thus, the request for an observable sign (11:16, 29) and the refrain (11:31, 32), which directs the audience to observe the "something more than Jonah/Solomon" that is "here" among them, create rhetorical bookends around the unit. Second, the themes of seeing, seeking,

---

and adoption of the passion predictions of Mark (8:31; 9:31; and 10:33–34), all of which show Jesus predicting that he will rise again "after three days." Left with the elusive "sign of Jonah" in the Q source, Matthew engaged in some creative exegesis of the LXX of Jonah using the number three from the Markan passion predictions as his hermeneutical key. Indeed Matthew's scribalism produces the error insofar as he quotes the LXX here verbatim.

[53]This may be because Luke thinks that the "sign of Jonah" and its interpretation in 11:30 is sufficient to fulfill the request. Luke omits Jesus' refusal to produce a sign in Mark 8:11–13 and includes Jesus' compliance with the disciples' request for a sign from Mark 13:1–13. In Acts, the apostles regularly perform signs as a way to legitimate their message (Acts 4:13–16, 22; 8:12–13; 14:3).

[54]This may not seem like a proper prediction, but Jesus fulfills it by his very presence among them: "Jesus said to them, 'I am the bread of life. Whoever comes to me will never be hungry, and whoever believes in me will never be thirsty'" (John 6:35). Notably, both "the Jews" (6:41–59) and the disciples (6:60–71) complain about and refuse to accept this sign.

[55]Gibson ("Jesus' Refusal," 37–66) argues convincingly that Mark, although not using the word σημεῖον, depicts Jesus providing a legitimation sign in the healing of the paralytic (Mark 2:1–12). Mark 13:1–13 also shows Jesus responding to the disciples' request for a sign. Gibson attributes Jesus' refusal to produce a sign in 8:11–13 to the author's awareness that nationalistic false prophets and messiahs have been producing "signs from heaven" (signs of national liberation akin to God's rescue of the Israelites from Egypt) that mislead the people (Mark 13:22).

and visibility appear in the larger context of the Sign of Jonah unit at Q 10: 23–24; 11:9–10; and 11:33–35:

> Blessed are the eyes which see what you see! For I tell you that many prophets and kings desired to see what you are seeing, and did not see it, and to hear what you are hearing, and did not hear it. (Q 10:23–24)

> And I tell you, Ask, and it will be given you; seek, and you will find; knock, and it will be opened to you. For everyone who asks receives, and whoever seeks finds, and whoever knocks is admitted. (Q 11:9–10)

> No one having lit a lamp puts it in a cellar or under a grain basket, but on a lampstand, that those who enter may see the light. Your eye is the lamp of your body; when your eye is "healthy," your whole body is also full of light; but when it is "unhealthy," your body is full of darkness. Therefore, watch lest the light in you be darkness. (Q 11:33–35)

Thus the audience is affirmed as people who see things that kings and prophets have desired to see (10:23–24), is assured that they will find that which they seek (11:9–10), and is exhorted to recognize (and in some sense internalize[56]) the light that shines visibly among them (11:33–35). All of these allusions to the audience's ability to perceive things around them occur in the immediate context of the Sign of Jonah pericope.

In vv. 32 and 31, Q's Jesus compares "this generation" to the Ninevites and the Queen of the South and thus continues the criticism of "this generation":

> The men of Nineveh will rise up at the judgment with this generation and condemn it, for they repented at the proclamation of Jonah, and look, something more than Jonah is here. (Q 11:32)

> The Queen of the South will be raised up at the judgment with this generation and condemn it, for she came from the ends of the earth to hear the wisdom of Solomon, and look, something more than Solomon is here.[57] (Q 11:31)

---

[56]Kirk suggests that 11:34–35 serves as a concretizing example of the general maxim in 11:33. Thus, the "light shining in the room of 11:33 becomes in 11:34 the inner space of the human illuminated by the lamp of the eye" (*Composition*, 200).

[57]Some interpreters suggest that the Queen of the South version of the double saying

Through these examples from Israel's history, Jesus dares the audience to measure themselves against two different parties, which responded to the preaching of Jonah and the wisdom of Solomon, respectively. Both parties will be witnesses against "this generation" at the judgment[58] because they responded to the preaching and the wisdom.

Most interpreters see a contrast between the positive response of the Ninevites and the Queen and the negative response of "this generation" to Jesus or the Q preachers. However, "this generation" is not criticized in Q for its *negative* response but rather its need for a sign, its desire for visible proof. In the context of a request for a sign, it may be significant that neither the preaching of Jonah nor the wisdom of Solomon is actually a sign. Insofar as signs are *visible* confirmations that someone is of God or that God is acting, neither wisdom nor preaching qualifies. Technically speaking, the one prediction that Jonah provides to the Ninevites ("In forty days, Nineveh shall be overthrown!"; Jonah 3:4) does *not* come to visible fruition.[59] The contrast, therefore, may be between those who trust the message without a visible sign of verification (the men of Nineveh and the Queen of the South) and those who do not trust the message (they request a sign) despite the presence of

---

is tangential (off the subject of Jonah) and related only formally to 11:31 (Jacobson, *First Gospel*, 167; and Tuckett, *Q*, 258). This view overlooks the predominance of sayings that present gendered pairs as part of the argumentation of Q. See the initial work of Alicia Batten, "More Queries for Q," *BTB* 24 (1994) 44–51; and Arnal, "Gendered Couplets," 75–94. These gendered couplets appear at Q 11:31–32; 13:18–21; 15:4–10; 17:27; 17:34–35; and possibly 12:51–53; 7:29; 7:34; and 14:26–27. Arnal points out that "in Q 11:31–32 we have an instance of a gendered couplet in a forensic context in which the male and female elements are positive figures. . . . [T]hey are argumentative supports for the Q contention that both the men and women of 'this generation' are subject to judgment" (ibid., 85–86). The presentation of double examples—regardless of gendered imagery—is also a common feature of Q's argumentation. For example, double examples also appear in Q 9:57–60; 10:13–15; 11:11–12; and 13:18–21.

[58]The judgment imagery in Q 11:31–32 serves a paraenetic function. Kirk concludes that "it is thus incorrect to read into 11:31–32 a rejection of Israel as Lührmann and Schürmann suppose. The examples pointedly refer Jesus' skeptical interlocutors to other ancient auditors— Sheba and the Ninevites—who responded quite differently to wise, authoritative words. The positive response of the queen and the Ninevites, combined with the threat of judgment, serve as inducements to Jesus' auditors, intractable though they may be, to act likewise" (Kirk, *Composition*, 198). See also Migaku Sato, *Q und Prophetie* (WUNT 2.29; Tübingen: Mohr/ Siebeck, 1988) 283.

[59]Indeed, Jonah is aware of this when he gets angry in Jonah 4. The *Lives of the Prophets* is also aware of this when it says that Jonah lived in Gentile territory after returning from Nineveh. "So shall I remove my reproach, for I spoke falsely in prophesying against the great city of Nineveh" (*OTP* 2:392).

visible proof among them. Thus, the men of Nineveh and the Queen of the South may out-perform "this generation" by "hearing" without needing also to "see," that is, without needing visible proof. The rhetorical climax of the unit, therefore, is an exhortation to look around and perceive what is apparent among them and respond positively as the Ninevites and the Queen did.

Both the men of Nineveh and the Queen of the South will give witness against "this generation" at the judgment because both of them responded without needing signs. But "this generation" cannot even see what is apparent all around them. "Look!" Jesus says, "Something more than Jonah is here!" "Look!" he says, "Something more than Solomon is here." Thus, in Q 11: 16, 29–32 "this generation" is characterized primarily as a blind genera- tion—one that cannot see what it should be able to see. The text constructs the encounter between Jesus and the crowds (11:15) as a crucial moment, an epistemic crisis of sorts, the response to which will determine their fate at the judgment.

But what does Jesus want them to see? What sign is verifiable among them? Read in conjunction with Q 11:14–26, πλεῖον ("something more") could point to the events of the *basileia* of God that have come upon the audience (11:20). These include the exorcisms of both Jesus and the "sons" of the accusers (11:19). They may also include the healings by those sent out to the villages (10:9) and by Jesus (7:10), practicing the values of the inaugural sermon, and heeding the teachings of John. In Q 11:29–32 Jesus rebuts the attempt to locate him on the side of false prophets and teachers by pointing to the visible signs of the *basileia* among the people. They must not be blind to their common cause.

There's Something about the "Son of Humanity"

In his discussion of Q 11:16, 29–32, Kloppenborg argues similarly that "the original referents of the 'something greater than Jonah/Solomon' were the eschatological occurrences which signaled the presence of the kingdom."[60] In order to make this conclusion, he separates Q 11:30 from 11:31–32, arguing that the double saying "can easily stand on its own. . . . Once separated from the 'Son of Man' in 11:30, there is no reason to construe 11:31–32 in a christological way. The neuter πλεῖον does not invite such an interpretation."[61] Thus Q 11:31–32 points to the visible presence of the

[60]Kloppenborg, *Formation*, 128.
[61]Ibid.

basileia of God among the people. But does 11:30 mitigate this interpretation? Is the son of humanity Christology incompatible with an emphasis on the importance of recognizing the *basileia* of God?

It is difficult to answer this question. Q 11:29 says that the sign of Jonah is the only sign that will be provided to this generation. Q 11:30 provides an analogical explanation of the "sign of Jonah"[62] "For as Jonah became a sign to the Ninevites, so also the son of humanity will be to this generation."[63] This creates an analogy between two sets of pairs: Jonah/Ninevites and son of humanity/this generation. In Q 11:29, there are only three characters: Jesus (the speaker), this generation (the audience), and Jonah (the sign). If a "sign" is a word or action that can be verified by observation, then it is unclear how Jonah can produce a sign for this generation. The analogy in 11:30 clears this up by introducing a fourth character (the Ninevites) and by referring to Jesus in the third person as the son of humanity. This aligns Jesus (the speaker and the son of humanity) with Jonah and "this generation" with the Ninevites. The analogy also identifies specific persons (Jonah/son of humanity) as the "signs" available to their respective generations.

The shift in verbs in 11:29 and 30 is also significant. In 11:29, no sign "will be given" (δοθήσεται) except the sign of Jonah. This verb corresponds well with other literary treatments of signs: they are requested, and later given. Q 11:30, however, draws on a different verbal field: Jonah "became" (ἐγένετο) a sign, and the son of humanity "will be" (ἔσται) a sign. This verbal shift identifies Jonah and the son of humanity *as the signs* given (presumably by God) to their respective audiences. Many interpreters puzzle over the *tertium comparationis* between Jonah and the son of humanity in 11:30. Three options are debated: (1) the miracles of Jonah's and Jesus' delivery from

---

[62]Even the grammatical meaning of the phrase the "sign of Jonah" presents several problems. One must decide how the genitive ('Ιωνᾶ) functions in the phrase. Possibilities are (1) the appositive genitive ("the sign which was given in the prophet Jonah"); (2) the subjective genitive ("the sign which Jonah gave"); or (3) the objective genitive ("the sign which Jonah experienced"). See Joachim Jeremias, "'Ιωνᾶ," *TDNT* 4:408. Q 11:30 interprets the phrase as an appositive genitive, since it claims that Jonah *became* a sign to the Ninevites. Q 11:32, however, suggests that Jonah's preaching of repentance is the sign given to the Ninevites, which would require the subjective genitive.

[63]The form is a prophetic correlative common in the LXX and Qumran. It also appears in Q 17:24, 26, 30. While Edwards (*Sign of Jonah*, 86) proposes that this form was an "eschatological correlative," Schmidt shows that this is unnecessary since the form works throughout LXX and Qumran literature to explain the present on analogy with the past (Daryl Schmidt, "The LXX *Gattung* 'Prophetic Correlative,'" *JBL* 96 [1977] 517–22).

death;[64] (2) the arrival of Jonah and Jesus as "signs" of the coming judgment and destruction;[65] and (3) Jonah's and Jesus' preaching of repentance.[66] There are problems with all three from the view of Jonah/son of humanity themselves *being* the observable signs. First, the Ninevites did not witness Jonah's rescue from the whale, nor does Q suggest that the audience will witness Jesus' resurrection. Second, Jonah's arrival in Nineveh was not a sign of its destruction and judgment. That outcome was avoided by Jonah's arrival. Third, it is unclear how preaching can be a sign, since a sign's success does not depend on hearing but on seeing.

One possibility emerges if we focus on parallels to the claim that an individual person *is* a sign, rather than attempting to lock down the specific terms of comparison between Jonah and the son of humanity. In his discussion of the Sign of Jonah, Rengstorf notes that "the implied idea that a person can be God's sign is linked with prophetic figures"[67] in the Hebrew Bible. For example, in Isa 20:1–5 and Ezek 12:1–11, the prophets perform actions that are named as a "sign" or a "wonder or omen." In each case, a correlative interpretation[68] is provided and eyewitnesses are present.

> In the year that the commander-in-chief, who was sent by King Sargon
> of Assyria, came to Ashdod and fought against it and took it—at

[64]Schürmann ("QLk 11:14–36," 576–78); Vögtle ("Jonaszeichen," 132–33); Simon Chow ("The Sign of Jonah Reconsidered," *Theology and Life* 15–16 [1993] 53–60). This interpretation focuses on the parallel to either the whale story (and Matthew) or the raising of Jonah by Elijah in the *Lives of the Prophets*.

[65]Bultmann, *History*, 118; Tödt, *Son of Man*, 270–71; Lührmann, *Redaktion*, 41–42; Hoffmann, *Studien*, 157. Jonathan Reed ("The Sign of Jonah [Q 11:29–32] and Other Epic Traditions in Q," in *Re-Imagining Christian Origins* [ed. Elizabeth A. Castelli and Hal Taussig; Valley Forge, Pa.: Trinity, 1996] 130–43) proposes that Jonah was an important figure in the region of the Galilee. He raises the interesting possibility that the common ground between Jonah and the son of humanity is their announcement of judgment on Jerusalem. The tradition that Jonah gave a "portent" of the destruction of Jerusalem is from the *Lives of the Prophets*.

[66]Kloppenborg, *Formation*, 132–33; Tuckett, *Q*, 265; Jacobson, *First Gospel*, 166; Vielhauer, "Jesus und Menschensohn," 151–52; George M. Landes, "Jonah in Luke: The Hebrew Bible Background to the Interpretation of the 'Sign of Jonah' Pericope in Luke 11.29–32," in *A Gift of God in Due Season* (ed. Richard D. Weis and David Carr; JSOTSup 225; Sheffield: Sheffield Academic Press, 1996) 133–63.

[67]Rengstorf, "σημεῖον," 234.

[68]Both of these texts are mentioned by Daryl Schmidt ("LXX *Gattung*") as examples of prophetic correlatives comparable to the correlatives in Q 11:30 and Q 17:24, 26, 30. Schmidt refutes the position of Edwards (*Sign of Jonah*, 47–58) that the "eschatological correlative" is a form created by the Q community.

that time the LORD had spoken by Isaiah son of Amoz, saying, "Go, and loose the sackcloth from your loins and take off your sandals off your feet," and he had done so, walking naked and barefoot. Then the LORD said, "Just as *my servant Isaiah has walked naked and barefoot for three years as a sign [LXX: σημεῖα] and a portent against Egypt and Ethiopia, so shall the king of Assyria lead away the Egyptians as captives and the Ethiopians as exiles*, both young and old, naked and barefoot, with buttocks uncovered, to the shame of Egypt. And they shall be dismayed and confounded because of Ethiopia their hope and of Egypt their boast. In that day *the inhabitants of this coastland will say, 'See, this is what has happened to those in whom we hoped* and to whom we fled for help and deliverance from the king of Assyria! And we, how shall we escape?'" (Isa 20: 1–5; NRSV; my emphasis)

The word of the LORD came to me: Mortal [or, son of humanity], you are living in the midst of a rebellious house, who have eyes to see, but see not, who have ears to hear, but do not hear; for they are a rebellious house. Therefore, mortal [or son of humanity], prepare for yourself an exile's baggage, and go into exile by day *in their sight*. . . . You shall bring out your baggage by day *in their sight*, as baggage for exile. . . . Dig through the wall *in their sight*, and carry the baggage through it . . . for I have made you a sign [LXX: τέρας] for the house of Israel. And I did just as I was commanded. . . . . In the morning the word of the LORD came to me: Mortal [or, son of humanity], has not the house of Israel, the rebellious house, said to you, "What are you doing?" Say to them, "Thus says the LORD God: This oracle concerns the prince in Jerusalem and all the house of Israel in it." Say, *"I am a sign [LXX: τέρατα] for you: as I have done, so shall it be done to them*; they shall go into exile, into captivity." (Ezek 12:1–11; NRSV; my emphasis)

Interpreted in the context of these parallels, the analogy between Jonah and the son of humanity provides the sign, that is, the verifiable word. As Jonah is a sign, so the son of humanity is a sign. While this interpretation leaves open the specific way in which either is a sign to their generations, it draws on the Isaiah and Ezekiel models and suggests that Jonah's and Jesus' own public actions serve as verifiable signs.

The direct analogy between "this generation" and the Ninevites recurs in Q 11:32. Jonah also reappears in an analogical relationship in v. 32, but now the comparison is between Jonah and "something more" (πλεῖον) than Jonah. In the logical structure of the unit, this "something more" could be the son of humanity. But the neuter πλεῖον breaks the symmetry of 11:30 in which the "sign" is a person (Jonah/son of humanity), and denies symmetry to the concluding refrain of v. 32 in which Jonah is compared to "something" and not "someone" more. The referent of the neuter πλεῖον seems to be more general than the "son of humanity" in 11:30. In addition, the neuter πλεῖον removes Jesus from the named cast of characters and returns him to being primarily the speaker (as in 11:29). As Yarbro Collins notes: "Even though vv. 31–32 are placed in the mouth of Jesus, the use of the neuter allows a broader reference than one to the person of the earthly Jesus alone."[69]

Much of the meaning of the passage rests on whether πλεῖον points to the events of the *basileia* or the work of the son of humanity among the people. While Q 11:29 leans toward the recognition of the son of humanity as the *sole* sign provided to this generation, Q 11:31–32 suggests that this generation should imitate the Ninevites and the Queen of the South and trust in what they see around them. In this context, the sign of the son of humanity is the sign of the movement of which he is a part. As with the "coming one" in Q 3:16–17, Q 12, and Q 17, the son of humanity features prominently in the present and future of the Q community, but not necessarily in a way that places sole allegiance to the son of humanity at the heart of the community's values.

A. K. M. Adam says of the Sign of Jonah unit that ultimately we are left with a variety of readings that make sense in the context of the interests and interpretive trends that produced them. He concludes that "correct interpretation" can be invoked only according to "commonly-held assumptions, if we use our terms and ideas in a common sense way, we will have mutually agreed-upon standards for correct interpretation, and on their basis we will be able to judge some interpretations of the Sign of Jonah correct and others incorrect."[70] Of course, common sense is a produced knowledge as well. If we begin with the "common sense" notion that Q 11:16, 29–32 is primarily interested in asserting the superlative value of Jesus over and against his opponents, then we might miss the possibility that the son of humanity texts also press the audience to see Jesus' work as part of something that is greater than the preaching of Jonah and the wisdom of Solomon. At the crucial moment of judgment, the community will be condemned if they have failed to see the proof that the *basileia* of God is all around them.

---

[69]Collins, "Son of Man," 378.
[70]Adam, "Sign of Jonah," 187.

CONCLUSION

Scholarly discourses about eschatology, Jesus, and Q participate in larger contemporary debates about Christian identity in a diverse and pluralistic world. Just as Johannes Weiss countered the prevailing theological understanding of the *basileia* of God with an argument for the "otherness" of the historical Jesus, so recent interpretations of Q challenge the dominant conception of contemporary Christian identity with a Jesus that differs significantly from the Jesus of the Gospels or Paul. The commitment to reconstruct early Christianity as diverse reflects an important contribution to the contemporary public discourse about multiculturalism and pluralism. However, the theological and methodological emphases on origins—particularly in terms of the historical Jesus—limit the potential of these reconstructions to re-envision Christian identity in a pluralistic context, since they ultimately identify one understanding of "Christianity" with the "earliest" understanding. In addition, the equation of Christian identity and Jesus' identity erases the participation of wo/men and diverse communities in the production of Christian self-understanding.

Contemporary scholars offer important critiques of the ideological character of the quest for the pure origins of Christianity and claims to Christian uniqueness. However, biblical scholars prefer to avoid articulating the ethical, political, and theological stakes of their own contributions. This results in a back-and-forth struggle between those who claim authority for their interpretations on dogmatic-theological grounds and those who anchor the authority of their reconstructions in methodology that is allegedly "scientifically" rigorous and value-neutral.[1] My own approach begins from the authority of wo/men's ongoing struggle for equality and well-being for all people. One of the areas that receives particular attention in my analyses of both contemporary discourses and the texts of Q is the way in which our

[1]Schüssler Fiorenza, *Politics*, 5.

interpretations create and negotiate boundary lines between Christians and Jews. In light of the contemporary climate of religious intolerance and the reinforcing of boundary lines between religious groups, my re-readings of Q attempt to give voice to aspects of the tradition that may have fostered solidarity around common ancient visions and thus may serve similar contemporary purposes.

The equation in the scholarly discourse of Christian identity with the identity of Jesus plays a significant role in the interpretation of Q. In the exegetical chapters of this study (chapters 2–3 and 5–6), I illustrate how an interest in the identity of Jesus shapes interpreters' approaches to the text. Taking a different approach—one that re-centers the Q community—makes alternative interpretations possible. For example, in both the children in the marketplace pericope (Q 7:31–35) and the Beelzebul controversy (Q 11: 14–26), the assumption of distance between Jesus and John, between Jesus and "this generation," or between Jesus and his accusers requires that these texts make special claims for Jesus over and against the other characters in the scene. In the case of the Beelzebul pericope, this results in the incompatibility between the claims of Q 11:19 and Q 11:20. Despite the fact that neither Matthew nor Luke appears to have been uncomfortable with the juxtaposition, theories of redactional development, alternative meanings, and polemical critiques are deployed to make sense of the perceived tension between the two claims: that Jesus and the "sons" of the accusers share common cause (11:19), and that Jesus' exorcisms alone represent the *basileia* of God (11:20). The entire unit (11:14–26), I have argued, is better understood as a sustained critique of divisiveness and a plea for solidarity in the face of a common enemy.

Similarly, with the children in the marketplace pericope, we have explored a solution to the long-standing puzzle of the relationship between the simile about children piping a tune and singing a dirge (7:30–31) and its application to the differences between John and Jesus (7:33–34). If we presume a common identity horizon among Jesus, John, and "this generation," then the application provides a structurally parallel and chiastic repetition of the simile that attempts to persuade the audience ("this generation") to dispense with their divisiveness. The criticism of "this generation," therefore, is not for their lack of response to the special messages of John and Jesus but for their judgmental postures toward each other, which do not properly recognize that "*Sophia* is vindicated by all her children."

In an effort to interpret the Q materials with an interest in the values and visions of the movement around Jesus, this study suggests that the John material in Q does not function primarily to work out the identity of the two men John and Jesus in relationship to each other. Rather, the units in Q 7:18–26 and Q 3:7–9, 16–17 can be interpreted as showing a consistent interest in asserting the vision of the *basileia* of God as an alternative to the prevailing systems of the day. Thus, the actions of the community that center the lives of the weak, the least, the sick, and the marginalized are lauded as visible proof of the *basileia* of God. John's opening speech lends urgency to the work of the *baslieia* not to condemn outsiders but to exhort insiders to recognize the crucial moment in which they live and to come to terms with the divine authorization of the values of the *basileia*. Similarly, what the audience can see all around them in the Sign of Jonah pericope should provide the verifiable evidence that the *basileia* of God is upon them.

Centering the communal values of Q does not mean that Jesus is not an important figure in Q. Indeed, Jesus is the authoritative speaker throughout most of Q. In Q 3:16, Jesus is introduced as the "coming one" who stands at the judgment in the future of the text and the audience. This theme is repeated throughout Q, culminating in the warnings to be prepared for the return of the master in Q 12 and the exhortation not to be surprised by the day of the son of humanity. In Q 11:29–32, πλεῖον ("something more") can include the events of the *basileia* and the work of the son of humanity. The question is not whether the Q community valued Jesus; it is whether the text of Q functioned primarily to explicate Jesus' identity and assert his superlative value, or whether Q is interested primarily in the *basileia* of God.

We have examined four texts which suggest that negotiating the identity of Jesus may be of more interest to contemporary interpreters of Q than to Q itself. Reading Q with a focus on Jesus' identity has ethical implications for our reconstruction of Christian origins. Insofar as focusing on the superlative value of Jesus participates in debates about Christian uniqueness, the centering of Jesus can work to erase the presence of others in the movement, create sharp divides between Jesus and his Jewish contemporaries, and constitute Christian identity in relationship to the person of Jesus rather than the vision of God's *basileia*.

There are several directions in which this study could be applied and extended. This book has shown that the process of analyzing our contemporary discourses alongside and toward informing our exegetical work may open up new possibilities for thinking about the texts and materials of early Christianity. A concrete example of this is in the interpretation of "this generation." Q scholars should re-evaluate the common approach to this terminology as insider/outsider polemic. When "this generation" reflects deuteronomistic theology in Q, it is as part of a rhetoric of self-blame and community exhortation. From this view, Q's critique of "this generation" would represent the community's theological reflections on their own times and their own experience in the context of the Roman Empire rather than a polemical condemnation of Israel and/or its leaders for rejecting Jesus and the Q community.[2] This may suggest that a crisis such as the Jewish war (66–73/74 C.E.) presents the most viable context for locating the rhetorical-historical situation of Q.[3]

An additional area in which this study might be applied is in discussions about the redaction of Q. The interpretations of Q presented here do not in themselves represent a refutation of Kloppenborg's stratigraphical proposal. Describing the literary development of Q has not been a primary goal of this investigation. There are two ways, however, in which this study might contribute to the ongoing evaluation of stratigraphic proposals. First, the texts discussed here all come from the Q² stratum. Although Kloppenborg's analysis proceeds on literary analysis, the presence of a common outsider audience and the thematic continuity of Q² are presented as secondary arguments for the viability of this redactional stratum.[4] The theme of the announcement of judgment against this generation and the polemical condemnation of outsiders have been foregrounded as central to Q². However, the theme of the *basileia* of God being present among the people—a theme commonly associated with Q¹—is strong in these units. This calls into question not only the thematic unity criterion of stratigraphic differentiation but also the criterion of an outsider audience.

Second, to some extent the references to Jesus as the son of humanity in Q are grafted[5] onto units that can make sense without such insertions. This

---

[2]See Melanie Johnson-DeBaufre, "The Blood Required of This Generation: Interpreting Communal Blame in a Colonial Context," in *Violence in the New Testament* (ed. Shelly Matthews and Leigh Gibson; New York: T. & T. Clark, 2005) 22–34.

[3]See Matti Myllykoski, "The Social History of Q and the Jewish War," in *Symbols and Strata: Essays on the Sayings Gospel Q* (ed. Risto Uro; Göttingen: Vandenhoeck & Ruprecht, 1996) 143–99. See also, Paul Hoffmann, "The Redaction of Q and the Son of Man: A Preliminary Sketch," in *The Gospel Behind the Gospels* (ed. Ronald A. Piper; Leiden: Brill, 1995) 159–98.

[4]Kloppenborg, *Formation*, 167–70.

[5]See Heinz Schürmann, "Beobachtungen zum Menschensohn-Titel in der Redequelle,"

can be seen primarily in the use of the appellation for Jesus in Q 7:34. Q 7: 31–35 makes claims for the parity of John and Jesus among the people. Jesus' self-reference as the son of humanity may tip the balance in favor of Jesus for the audience but only in association with other uses of the expression for Jesus in Q and in light of the presentation of Jesus as the authoritative speaker in Q. Thus, identifying Jesus as the son of humanity may participate in a larger ideological centering of Jesus in the present and future of the audience. Evidence of this move may be seen in Jesus' association with the "coming one" in 3:16 and the alignment of the sign of Jonah with the sign of the son of humanity in 11:30. However, none of these references to Jesus as the son of humanity require reading the text as making a case for the unique identity of Jesus. If the idea of Jesus as the son of humanity was indeed added to pre-existing units, then the redactional growth of Q may have occurred by a much more piecemeal and unit-by-unit process than the current proposals allow.

The interpretations in this book cohere generally with the proposals that the son of humanity sayings enter the Q tradition somewhat as latecomers. However, we should not conclude that the vision of the *basileia* of God was the *first* ideological orientation of the community only to be *eclipsed* by the centering of Jesus as the son of humanity. That would depend upon notions of pure origins for describing Christian history. It is unlikely that before Q no one thought of anything but the *basileia* and after Q no one bothered to think of it again. As Elisabeth Schüssler Fiorenza points out:

> To read Christian history in terms of the reconstructive model of rapid decline from the heights of radical equality to the valleys of patriarchal institution is to overlook the continuing struggles that have been going on throughout Christian history between those who understand Christian identity as radically inclusive and egalitarian and those who advocate kyriarchal domination and submission.[6]

As we have seen in Q, not all claims to the distinctive value of Jesus automatically remove the focus from the vision of the *basileia*. Rather,

---

Jesus und der Menschensohn: Für Anton Vögtle (Freiburg: Herder & Herder, 1975) 124–47. See, however, the critique by Adela Yarbro Collins ("The Son of Man Sayings in the Sayings Source," in *To Touch the Text: Biblical and Related Studies in Honor of Joseph A. Fitzmyer, S.J.* [ed. Maurya P. Horgan and Paul Kobelski; New York: Crossroad, 1989] 369–89).

[6]Elisabeth Schüssler Fiorenza, "Re-Visioning Christian Origins: In Memory of Her Revisited," unpublished manuscript, 16.

each rhetorical use of that vision and of Jesus as the son of humanity should be evaluated in its context according to its effect on the vision of the liberation and dignity of all people.

There is one final observation about the possibilities for applying and extending this study. Several of these interpretations circle around issues of how we tell the story of the Q community's relationship to their fellow Jews. Using a feminist model of inquiry, we have begun with the contemporary context of religious intolerance and approached the text in light of the ethical imperative to articulate aspects of the tradition that envision solidarity across lines of difference around common visions and values. Neither the children in the marketplace nor the Beelzebul pericope depends upon or seeks to negotiate the Q community's identity over and against Jewish outsiders. This emphasis on issues of religious identity difference, however, is not sufficient to articulate fully the vision of the *basileia*. For example, the androcentric nature of the text still masks the presence of Jewish wo/men in the work of the *basileia*. In the Beelzebul pericope, the common ground that is the primary rhetorical interest of the text is claimed between Jesus (the son [ὁ υἱός] of humanity in 11:30) and the sons (οἱ υἱοὶ ὑμῶν) of the accusers. This linguistically hides the presence of Jewish wo/men as healers among the people. Thus, further re-imagination and historical reconstruction is required to gain a full picture of the Jesus movement.[7] So also, while the double sayings in Q 11:31–32 affirm the availability of the wisdom and *kerygma* to foreigners, represented by the Queen of the South and the men of Nineveh, that availability is mediated in the text by Solomon and Jonah, two native men.[8] In addition, the very language of the *basileia* linguistically frames the vision of an alternative to Roman imperial power in terms of a monarchical and androcentric system and thus uses hierarchical language even as it imagines an alternative.[9] These observations do not undermine my re-readings of the Q material. They rather suggest that the work of envisioning the *basileia* cannot end with the biblical texts and authoritative interpretations of them but must continue to participate in the ongoing public discourse that seeks to shape Christian identity in a diverse world.

---

[7] Tal Ilan, "In the Footsteps of Jesus: Jewish Women in a Jewish Movement," in *Transformative Encounters: Jesus and Women Re-viewed* (ed. Ingrid Rosa Kitzberger; Leiden: Brill, 2000) 115–36.

[8] Kerry M. Craig and Margaret A. Kristjansson, "Women Reading as Men/Women Reading as Women: A Structural Analysis for the Historical Project," *Semeia* 51 (1990) 119–36.

[9] Schüssler Fiorenza, *Politics*, 168–70.

While some interpreters attempt to sort out the exegetical problems created by using the nineteenth-century doctrinal category "eschatology" to organize and classify the concepts and motifs about the future in early Christianity, little attention has been paid to what we are debating and why. Analyzing the contours of the contemporary discourse should be part of the ongoing work of biblical scholars as they participate in larger spheres of meaning-making beyond the academy. I offer this study, therefore, as a contribution to what Elisabeth Schüssler Fiorenza has termed an "ethics of interpretation":

> To propose the ethics of interpretation as a new interdisciplinary area in biblical studies means to overcome the assumed dichotomy between engaged scholarship (such as feminist, postcolonial, African American, queer, and other subdisciplines) and scientific (malestream) interpretation. Whereas the former is allegedly utilizing ethical criteria, the latter is said to live up to a scientific ethos that gives precedence to cognitive criteria. Instead, I would argue that a scientific ethos demands *both* ethical and cognitive criteria that must be reasoned out in terms of standard knowledge and at the same time intersubjectively understandable and communicable.[10]

In this light, my re-readings of the John the Baptist material in Q 3 and 7 and the two interrelated controversy pericopes in Q 11 attempt to disrupt the persistent focus on the identity of Jesus that is apparent in contemporary discourses on eschatology and Q. An approach that attempts to read Jesus in community—as among the children of *Sophia*—creates the possibility that the rhetorical interests of Q are not primarily focused on asserting and negotiating Jesus' singular identity but rather on shaping communal values and promoting solidarity across differences around the vision of the *basileia* of God.

---

[10]Schüssler Fiorenza, *Rhetoric and Ethic*, 195–96.

Bibliography

Adam, A. K. M. "The Sign of Jonah: A Fish-Eye View." *Semeia* 51 (1990) 177–91.

Aitken, W. E. M. "Beelzebul." *JBL* 31 (1912) 34–53.

Allison, Dale C., Jr. *The Jesus Tradition in Q.* Harrisburg, Pa.: Trinity, 1997.

Arnal, William E. "Gendered Couplets in Q and Legal Formulations: From Rhetoric to Social History." *JBL* 116 (1997) 75–94.

———. *Jesus and the Village Scribes.* Minneapolis: Fortress, 2001.

———. "Making and Re-Making the Jesus Sign: Contemporary Markings on the Body of Christ." Pages 308–19 in *Whose Historical Jesus?* Edited by idem and Michel Desjardins. Waterloo, Ontario: Wilfrid Laurier University Press, 1997.

———. "Redactional Fabrication and Group Legitimation: The Baptist's Preaching in Q 3:7–9, 16–17." Pages 165–80 in *Conflict and Invention: Literary, Rhetorical, and Social Studies on the Sayings Gospel Q.* Edited by John S. Kloppenborg. Valley Forge, Pa.: Trinity, 1995.

Aune, D. E. "Eschatology (Early Christian)." Pages 594–609 in vol. 2 of *ABD.* Edited by David Noel Freedman. 6 vols. New York: Doubleday, 1992.

Batten, Alicia. "More Queries for Q." *BTB* 24 (1994) 44–51.

Beker, J. Christiaan. "Biblical Theology Today." Pages 7–34 in no. 6 of *New Theology.* Edited by Martin E. Marty and Dean G. Peerman. London: Collier-Macmillan, 1969.

Berkey, Robert F. "ΕΓΓΙΖΕΙΝ, ΦΘΑΝΕΙΝ, and Realized Eschatology." *JBL* 82 (1963) 177–87.

Betz, Hans Dieter. *Essays on the Sermon on the Mount.* Philadelphia: Fortress, 1985.

Black, Matthew. "The Kingdom Has Come." *ExpTim* 63 (1951–1952) 289–90.

Borg, Marcus J. *Jesus in Contemporary Scholarship.* Valley Forge, Pa.: Trinity, 1994.

Borg, Marcus J. "Portraits of Jesus in Contemporary North American Scholarship," *HTR* 84 (1991) 1–22.

———. "Reflections on a Discipline: A North American Perspective." Pages 9–23 in *Studying the Historical Jesus: Evaluations of the Current State of Research*. Edited by Bruce Chilton and Craig Evans. Leiden: Brill, 1994.

Borsch, Frederick. *The Son of Man in Myth and History*. Philadelphia: Westminster, 1967.

Bretscher, Paul G. " 'Whose Sandals'? (Matt 3.11)." *JBL* 86 (1967) 81–87.

Bultmann, Rudolf. *The History of the Synoptic Tradition*. Translated by John Marsh. New York and Evanston: Harper & Row, 1963. Translation of *Die Geschichte der synoptischen tradition*. Göttingen: Vandenhoeck & Ruprecht, 1921.

———. *Jesus and the Word*. Translated by Louise P. Smith and Erminie Huntress. New York and London: Scribner, 1934. Translation of *Jesus*. Berlin: Deutsche Bibliothek, 1926.

———. *The Presence of Eternity: History and Eschatology*. New York: Harper & Brothers, 1957.

———. *Theology of the New Testament*. 2 vols. New York: Scribner, 1951–1955.

Büschel, Friedrich. "γενεά." Pages 662–65 in vol. 1 of *TDNT*. Edited by G. Kittel and G. Friedrich. Translated by G. W. Bromiley. 10 vols. Grand Rapids: Eerdmans, 1964–1976.

Butts, James R. "Probing the Polling." *Foundations & Facets Forum* 3 (1987) 97–128.

Caird, G. B. *The Language and Imagery of the Bible*. Philadelphia: Westminster, 1980.

Cameron, Ron. "The Anatomy of a Discourse: On 'Eschatology' as a Category for Explaining Christian Origins." *Method and Theory in the Study of Religion* 8 (1996) 231–45.

———. " 'What Have You Come Out To See?' Characterizations of John and Jesus in the Gospels." *Semeia* 49 (1990) 35–69.

Campbell, J. Y. "The Kingdom of God Has Come." *ExpTim* 48 (1936–1937) 91–94.

Caragounis, Chrys C. *The Son of Man: Vision and Interpretation*. Tübingen: Mohr/Siebeck, 1986.

Carmignac, Jean. *Le mirage de l'eschatologie*. Paris: Letouzey et Ané, 1979.

Catchpole, David. "The Beginning of Q: A Proposal." *NTS* 38 (1992) 205–21.

Charlesworth, James H., ed. *The Old Testament Pseudepigrapha*. 2 vols. New York: Doubleday, 1983.

Chow, Simon. "The Sign of Jonah Reconsidered." *Theology and Life* 15–16 (1993) 53–60.

Cicero, Marcus Tullius. *Orationes. English and Latin. Selections. Pro Q. Ligario*. Cambridge, Mass.; Harvard University Press, 1979.

Clark, Kenneth W. "Realized Eschatology." *JBL* 59 (1940) 367–83.

Collins, Adela Yarbro. "The Apocalyptic Son of Man Sayings." Pages 220–28 in *The Future of Early Christianity: Essays in Honor of Helmut Koester*. Edited by Birger A. Pearson et al. Minneapolis: Fortress, 1991.

————. "The Origins of the Designation of Jesus as 'Son of Man.'" *HTR* 80 (1987) 391–407.

————. "The Son of Man Sayings in the Sayings Source." Pages 369–89 in *To Touch the Text: Biblical and Related Studies in Honor of Joseph A. Fitzmyer, S.J.* Edited by Maurya P. Horgan and Paul Kobelski. New York: Crossroad, 1989.

Collins, John J. "The Son of Man in First-Century Judaism." *NTS* 38 (1992) 448–66.

————. "Wisdom, Apocalypticism, and Generic Compatibility." Pages 165–86 in *In Search of Wisdom*. Edited by Leo G. Perdue et al. Louisville, Ky.: Westminster/John Knox, 1993.

Cotter, Wendy, C.S.J. "The Parable of the Children in the Market-Place, Q (Lk) 7:31–35: An Examination of the Parable's Image and Significance." *NovT* 29 (1987) 289–304.

————. "Prestige, Protection and Promise: A Proposal for the Apologetics of Q^2." Pages 117–38 in *The Gospel Behind the Gospels: Current Studies on Q*. Edited by Ronald A. Piper. NovTSup 74. Leiden: Brill, 1995.

————. "Yes, I Tell You, and More than a Prophet: The Function of John in Q." Pages 135–50 in *Conflict and Invention: Literary, Rhetorical, and Social Studies on the Sayings Gospel Q*. Edited by John S. Kloppenborg. Valley Forge, Pa.: Trinity Press, 1995.

Craig, Clarence T. "Realized Eschatology." *JBL* 56 (1937) 17–26.

Craig, Kerry M., and Margaret A. Kristjansson. "Women Reading as Men/ Women Reading as Women: A Structural Analysis for the Historical Project." *Semeia* 51 (1990) 119–36.

Crossan, John Dominic. *The Birth of Christianity*. San Francisco: HarperSan Francisco, 1998.

Crossan, John Dominic. *The Historical Jesus: The Life of a Mediterranean Jewish Peasant*. San Francisco: HarperSanFrancisco, 1991.

———. *Jesus: A Revolutionary Biography*. San Francisco: HarperSanFrancisco, 1995.

Dodd, C. H. *The Parables of the Kingdom*. Rev. ed. New York: Scribner, 1961.

Doty, William G. "Identifying Eschatological Language." *Continuum* 7 (1970) 546–61.

Downing, F. Gerald. *Christ and the Cynics: Jesus and Other Radical Preachers in the First-Century Tradition*. JSOT Manuals 4. Sheffield: JSOT Press, 1988.

Draper, Jonathan A. "The Development of 'The Sign of the Son of Man' in the Jesus Tradition." *NTS* 39 (1993) 1–21.

Dunn, James D. G. "Spirit-and-Fire Baptism." *NovT* 14 (1972) 81–92.

Easton, B. S. "The Beelzebul Sections." *JBL* 32 (1913) 57–73.

Edwards, Richard A. *The Sign of Jonah: In the Theology of the Evangelists and Q*. Naperville, Ill.: Allenson; London: SCM, 1971.

Ehrhardt, Arnold. "Greek Proverbs in the Gospel." Pages 44–63 in *The Framework of the New Testament Stories*. Cambridge, Mass.: Harvard University Press, 1964.

Ehrman, Bart. *Jesus: Apocalyptic Prophet of the New Millennium*. Oxford and New York: Oxford University Press, 1999.

Farmer, William. *The Synoptic Problem: A Critical Analysis*. New York: Macmillan, 1964.

Fleddermann, Harry. "The Beginning of Q." *SBLSP* 24 (1985) 153–59.

———. "John and the Coming One (Matt 3:11–12//Luke 3:16–17)." *SBLSP* 23 (1984) 377–84.

Franzmann, Majella. "Of Food, Bodies, and the Boundless Reign of God in the Synoptic Gospels." *Pacifica* 5 (1992) 17–31.

Freyne, Séan. "Jesus the Wine-Drinker: A Friend of Women." Pages 162–80 in *Transformative Encounters: Jesus and Women Re-viewed*. Edited by Ingrid Rosa Kitzberger. Leiden: Brill, 2000.

Fridrichsen, Anton. "Wer nicht mit mir ist, ist wider mich." *ZWT* 13 (1912) 273–80.

Funk, Robert W. "Apocalyptic as an Historical and Theological Problem in Current New Testament Scholarship." *Journal for Theology and the Church* 6 (1969) 175–91.

———. *Honest to Jesus: Jesus for a New Millennium*. San Francisco: HarperSanFrancisco, 1996.

Funk, Robert W., Roy W. Hoover, and the Jesus Seminar. *The Five Gospels: The Search for the Authentic Words of Jesus*. New York: Macmillan, 1993.

Gager, John G. *Kingdom and Community*. Englewood Cliffs, N.J.: Prentice-Hall, 1975.

Gaston, Lloyd. "Beelzebul." *TZ* 18 (1962) 247–55.

George, A. "Note sur quelques traits lucaniens de l'expression « Par le doigt de Dieu » (Luc XI.20)." *Sciences Ecclésiastiques* 18 (1966) 461–66.

Georgi, Dieter. "The Interest in Life of Jesus Theology as a Paradigm for the Social History of Biblical Criticism." *HTR* 85 (1992) 51–83.

———. "Rudolf Bultmann's *Theology of the New Testament* Revisited." Pages 75–87 in *Bultmann, Retrospect and Prospect*. Edited by Edward C. Hobbs. HTS 35. Philadelphia: Fortress, 1985.

———. "Who is the True Prophet?" Pages 100–126 in *Christians Among Jews and Gentiles: Essays in Honor of Krister Stendahl*. Edited by George McRae et al. Philadelphia: Fortress, 1986.

Gibson, Jeffrey. "Jesus' Refusal to Produce a 'Sign' (Mk 8.11–13)." *JSNT* 38 (1990) 37–66.

Güttgemanns, Ehrhart. *Candid Questions Concerning Gospel Form Criticism*. Translated by W. D. Doty. Pittsburgh: Pickwick, 1979.

Hamerton-Kelly, Robert G. "A Note on Matthew XII.28 Par. Luke XI.20." *NTS* 11 (1964–1965) 167–69.

Hare, Douglas R. A. *The Son of Man Tradition*. Minneapolis: Fortress, 1990.

Harnack, Adolf von. *The Sayings of Jesus: The Second Source of St. Matthew and St. Luke*. Translated by J. R. Wilkinson. New York: Putnam, 1908. Translation of *Sprüche und Reden Jesu. Die Zweite Quelle des Matthäus und Lukas*. Leipzig: J.C. Hinrichs, 1907.

Hartin, Patrick J. " 'Yet Wisdom Is Justified by Her Children' (Q 7:35): A Rhetorical and Compositional Analysis of Divine Sophia in Q." Pages 151–64 in *Conflict and Invention: Literary, Rhetorical, and Social Studies on the Sayings Gospel Q*. Edited by John S. Kloppenborg. Valley Forge, Pa.: Trinity, 1995.

Hick, John, and Paul F. Knitter, eds. *The Myth of Christian Uniqueness: Toward a Pluralistic Theology of Religions*. Maryknoll, N.Y.: Orbis, 1987.

Hoffmann, Paul. "The Redaction of Q and the Son of Man: A Preliminary Sketch." Pages 159–98 in *The Gospel Behind the Gospels: Current Studies on Q*. Edited by Ronald A. Piper. NovTSup 75. Leiden: Brill, 1995.

Hoffmann, Paul. *Studien zur Theologie der Logienquelle*. Münster: Aschendorff, 1972.

Hollenbach, Paul W. "Jesus, Demoniacs, and Public Authorities: A Socio-Historical Study." *JAAR* 49 (1981) 567–88.

Horsley, Richard A. "Logoi Propheton? Reflections on the Genre of Q." Pages 195–209 in *The Future of Early Christianity: Essays in Honor of Helmut Koester*. Edited by Birger A. Pearson et al. Minneapolis: Fortress, 1991.

———. "Q and Jesus: Assumptions, Approaches and Analysis." *Semeia* 55 (1991) 175–209.

———. "Questions about Redactional Strata and the Social Relations Reflected in Q." *SBLSP* 28 (1989) 186–203.

———. "Social Conflict in the Synoptic Sayings Source Q." Pages 37–52 in *Conflict and Invention: Literary, Rhetorical, and Social Studies on the Sayings Gospel Q*. Edited by John S. Kloppenborg. Valley Forge, Pa.: Trinity, 1995.

Horsley, Richard A., and Jonathan A. Draper. *Whoever Hears You Hears Me*. Harrisburg, Pa.: Trinity, 1999.

Humphries, Michael L. *Christian Origins and the Language of the Kingdom of God*. Carbondale and Edwardsville: Southern Illinois University Press, 1999.

Ilan, Tal. "In the Footsteps of Jesus: Jewish Women in a Jewish Movement." Pages 115–36 in *Transformative Encounters: Jesus and Women Reviewed*. Edited by Ingrid Rosa Kitzberger. Leiden: Brill, 2000.

Jacobson, Arland. "Apocalyptic and the Synoptic Sayings Source Q." Pages 403–19 in vol. 1 of *The Four Gospels, 1992: Festschrift for Frans Neirynck*. Edited by Frans Van Segbroeck et al. BETL 100. Leuven: Leuven University Press, 1992.

———. *The First Gospel: An Introduction to Q*. Sonoma, Calif.: Polebridge, 1992.

Järvinen, Arto. "The Son of Man and His Followers: A Q Portrait of Jesus." Pages 180–222 in *Characterization in the Gospels: Reconceiving Narrative Criticism*. Edited by David Rhoads and Kari Syreeni. JSNTSup 184. Sheffield: Sheffield Academic Press, 1999.

Jeremias, Joachim. " ᾽Ιωνᾶς." Pages 406–10 in vol. 4 of *TDNT*. Edited by G. Kittel and G. Friedrich. Translated by G. W. Bromiley. 10 vols. Grand Rapids: Eerdmans, 1964–1976.

Johnson, Luke Timothy. *The Real Jesus: The Misguided Quest for the Historical Jesus and the Truth of the Traditional Gospels.* San Francisco: HarperSanFrancisco, 1996.

Käsemann, Ernst. "Lukas 11:14–28." Pages 242–48 in *Exegetische Versuche und Besinnungen.* Göttingen: Vandenhoeck & Ruprecht, 1960.

Kazmierski, Carl R. "The Stones of Abraham: John the Baptist and the End of the Torah (Matt 3,7–10 par. Luke 3,7–9)." *Bib* 68 (1987) 22–40.

Kee, Howard Clark. "Jesus: A Glutton and a Drunkard." *NTS* 42 (1996) 374–93.

Killagen, John. "The Return of the Unclean Spirit (Luke 11,24–26)." *Bib* 74 (1993) 45–59.

Kirk, Alan. "Breaching the Frontier: Going Public with the Hidden Transcript in Q 11." Paper presented at the annual meeting of the Society of Biblical Literature. Denver, Colo., 2001.

―――. *The Composition of the Sayings Source: Genre, Synchrony, and Wisdom Redaction in Q.* NovTSup 91. Leiden: Brill, 1998.

―――. "Liminality and Transformative Wisdom in Q." *NTS* 45 (1999) 1–18.

―――. "Upbraiding Wisdom: John's Speech and the Beginning of Q (Q 3: 7–9, 16–17)." *NovT* 40 (1998) 1–16.

Kloppenborg, John S. "City and Wasteland: Narrative World and the Beginning of the Sayings Gospel (Q)." *Semeia* 52 (1990) 145–60.

―――. *The Formation of Q: Trajectories in Ancient Wisdom Collections.* Philadelphia: Fortress, 1987.

―――. "Jesus and the Parables of Jesus in Q." Pages 275–319 in *The Gospel Behind the Gospels: Current Studies on Q.* Edited by Ronald A. Piper. NovTSup 75. Leiden: Brill, 1995.

―――. "Q 11:14–20: Work Sheets for Reconstruction." *SBLSP* 24 (1985) 133–51.

―――. *Q Parallels.* Sonoma, Calif.: Polebridge Press, 1988.

―――. "The Sayings Gospel Q: Recent Opinion on the People Behind the Document." *Currents in Research: Biblical Studies* 1 (1993) 9–34.

―――, ed. *The Shape of Q: Signal Essays on the Sayings Gospel.* Minneapolis: Fortress, 1994.

―――. "Symbolic Eschatology and the Apocalypticism of Q." *HTR* 80 (1987) 287–306.

―――. "A Synopsis for Q [11:14–26]." *SBLSP* 24 (1985) 127–32.

Kloppenborg, John S. "The Theological Stakes in the Synoptic Problem." Pages 93–120 in vol. 1 of *The Four Gospels, 1992: Festschrift for Frans Neirynck*. Edited by Frans Van Segbroeck et al. BETL 100. Leuven: Leuven University Press, 1992.

Kloppenborg Verbin, John S. *Excavating Q*. Minneapolis: Fortress, 2000.

Koester, Helmut. *Ancient Christian Gospels*. Philadelphia: Trinity, 1990.

———. "Early Christianity for the Perspective of the History of Religions: Rudolf Bultmann's Contribution." Pages 59–74 in *Bultmann, Retrospect and Prospect*. Edited by Edward C. Hobbs. HTS 35. Philadelphia: Fortress, 1985.

———. "The Historical Jesus and the Cult of the *Kyrios Christos*." *Harvard Divinity Bulletin* 24 (1995) 13–18.

———. "Jesus the Victim." *JBL* 111 (1992) 3–15.

———. "Jesus' Presence in the Early Church." *Cr St* 15 (1994) 541–57.

———. "Q and Its Relatives." Pages 49–63 in *Gospel Origins & Christian Beginnings*. Edited by James E. Goehring. Sonoma, Calif.: Polebridge, 1990.

Koester, Helmut, and James M. Robinson. *Trajectories through Early Christianity*. Philadelphia: Fortress, 1971.

Landes, George M. "Jonah in Luke: The Hebrew Bible Background to the Interpretation of the 'Sign of Jonah' Pericope in Luke 11.29–32." Pages 133–63 in *A Gift of God in Due Season*. Edited by Richard D. Weis and David Carr. JSOTSup 225. Sheffield: Sheffield Academic Press, 1996.

Laufen, Rudolf. *Die Doppelüberlieferungen der Logienquelle und des Markusevangeliums*. Bonn: Hanstein, 1980.

Leivestad, Ragnar. "Exit the Apocalyptic Son of Man." *NTS* 18 (1972) 243–67.

Levine, Amy-Jill. "Who's Catering the Q Affair? Feminist Observations on Q Paraenesis." *Semeia* 50 (1990) 145–61.

———. "Women in the Q Communit(ies) and Traditions." Pages 150–70 in *Women & Christian Origins*. Edited by Ross Shepard Kraemer and Mary Rose D'Angelo. Oxford and New York: Oxford University Press, 1999.

Lindars, Barnabas. "Re-enter the Apocalyptic Son of Man." *NTS* 22 (1975) 52–72.

Linton, Olof. "The Demand for a Sign from Heaven." *Studia Theologica* 19 (1965) 112–29.

———. "The Parable of the Children's Game." *NTS* 22 (1975–1976) 159–79.

Lövestam, Evald. "The ἡ γενεὰ αὕτη Eschatology in Mk 13,30 parr." Pages 403–13 in *L'Apocalypse johannique et l'Apocalyptique dans le Nouveau Testament*. Edited by Jan Lambrecht. Louvain: Leuven University Press, 1980.

Lührmann, Dieter. *Die Redaktion der Logienquelle*. Neukirchen-Vluyn: Neukirchener Verlag, 1969.

Mack, Burton L. "The Kingdom Sayings in Mark." *Foundations & Facets Forum* 3 (1987) 1–47.

———. *The Lost Gospel: The Book of Q and Christian Origins*. San Francisco: HarperSanFrancisco, 1993.

———. *A Myth of Innocence: Mark and Christian Origins*. Philadelphia: Fortress, 1988.

———. "Social Formation." Pages 283–96 in *Guide to the Study of Religion*. Edited by Willi Braun and Russell T. McCutcheon. London and New York: Cassell, 2000.

Malina, Bruce J. "Christ and Time: Swiss or Mediterranean?" *CBQ* 51 (1989) 1–31.

Marcus, Joel. "The Beelzebul Controversy and the Eschatologies of Jesus." *New Testament Tools and Studies* 28 (1999) 247–77.

Marshall, I. Howard. "Slippery Words: I. Eschatology." *ExpTim* 81 (1978) 264–69.

Mason, Steve. "Fire, Water and Spirit: John the Baptist and the Tyranny of Canon." *Studies in Religion* 21 (1992) 163–80.

McCowan, C. C. "The Scene of John's Ministry and its Relation to the Purpose and Outcome of His Mission." *JBL* 59 (1940) 113–31.

Meadors, Edward P. *Jesus the Messianic Herald of Salvation*. Tübingen: Mohr/Siebeck, 1995.

Mearns, Chris. "Realized Eschatology in Q? A Consideration of the Sayings in Luke 7.22, 11.20 and 16.16." *Scottish Journal of Theology* 40 (1987) 189–210.

———. "The Son of Man Trajectory and Eschatological Development." *ExpTim* 97 (1985) 8–12.

Meynet, Roland. "Qui donc est «Le plus fort»?" *Revue biblique* 90 (1983) 334–50.

Miller, Robert J. *The Complete Gospels*. San Francisco: HarperSanFrancisco, 1994.

———. "Elijah, John, and Jesus in the Gospel of Luke." *NTS* 34 (1988) 611–22.

Moule, C. F. D. "The Influence of Circumstance on the Use of Eschatological Terms." *JTS* 15 (1964) 1–15.

Myllykoski, Matti. "The Social History of Q and the Jewish War." Pages 143–99 in *Symbols and Symbols: Essays on the Sayings Gospel Q*. Edited by Risto Uro. Göttingen: Vandenhoeck & Ruprecht, 1996.

Neirynck, Franz. "Recent Developments in the Study of Q." Pages 29–75 in *Logia. Les paroles de Jésus*. Edited by Joël Delobel. Leuven: Leuven University Press, 1982.

Nickelsburg, George. "Eschatology (Early Jewish)." Pages 579–94 in vol. 2 of *ABD*. Edited by David Noel Freedman. 6 vols. New York: Doubleday, 1992.

Oakman, Douglas E. "Rulers' Houses, Thieves, and Usurpers: The Beelzebul Pericope." *Forum* 4 (1988) 109–23.

Perrin, Norman. *Jesus and the Language of the Kingdom*. Philadelphia: Fortress, 1976.

———. *Rediscovering the Teaching of Jesus*. London: SCM, 1967.

Piper, Ronald A. *Wisdom in the Q-Tradition*. Cambridge: Cambridge University Press, 1989.

Plaskow, Judith. "Feminist Anti-Judaism and the Christian God." *JFSR* 7 (1991) 99–108.

Polag, Athanasius. *Die Christologie der Logienquelle*. WMANT 45. Neukirchen-Vluyn: Neukirchener Verlag, 1977.

Räisänen, Heikki. "Exorcisms and the Kingdom: Is Q 11:20 a Saying of the Historical Jesus?" Pages 119–42 in *Symbols and Strata: Essays on the Sayings Gospel Q*. Edited by Risto Uro. Helsinki: Finnish Exegetical Society; Göttingen: Vandenhoeck & Ruprecht, 1996.

Reed, Jonathan. "The Sign of Jonah [Q 11:29–32] and Other Epic Traditions in Q." Pages 130–43 in *Re-Imagining Christian Origins*. Edited by Elizabeth A. Castelli and Hal Taussig. Valley Forge, Pa.: Trinity, 1996.

Reimarus, Hermann Samuel. *Fragments*. Edited by Charles H. Talbert. Translated by Ralph S. Fraser. Philadelphia: Fortress, 1970.

Reiser, Marius. *Jesus and Judgment: The Eschatological Proclamation in Its Jewish Context*. Translated by Linda M. Maloney. Minneapolis: Fortress, 1997.

Rengstorf, K. H. "σημεῖον." Pages 200–261 in vol. 7 of *TDNT*. Edited by G. Kittel and G. Friedrich. Translated by G. W. Bromiley. 10 vols. Grand Rapids: Eerdmans, 1964–1976.

Rivkin, Ellis. "Locating John the Baptizer in Palestinian Judaism: The Political Dimension." *SBLSP* 22 (1983) 79–85.

Robbins, Vernon K. "Rhetorical Composition & the Beelzebul Controversy." Pages 161–93 in *Patterns of Persuasion in the Gospels*. Edited by Burton L. Mack and Vernon K. Robbins. Sonoma, Calif.: Polebridge, 1989.

Robinson, J. A. T. "Elijah, John, and Jesus: An Essay in Detection." *NTS* 4 (1957–1958) 263–81.

Robinson, James M. "The Jesus of Q as Liberation Theologian." Pages 259–74 in *The Gospel Behind the Gospels: Current Studies on Q*. Edited by Ronald A. Piper. NovTSup 75. Leiden: Brill, 1995.

———. "The Q Trajectory: Between John and Matthew via Jesus." Pages 173–94 in *The Future of Early Christianity: Essays in Honor of Helmut Koester*. Edited by Birger A. Pearson et al. Minneapolis: Fortress, 1991.

———. "The Sayings Gospel Q." Pages 361–88 in vol. 1 of *The Four Gospels, 1992: Festschrift for Frans Neirynck*. Edited by Frans Van Segbroeck et al. BETL 100. Leuven: Leuven University Press, 1992.

Robinson, James M., Paul Hoffmann, and John S. Kloppenborg. *The Critical Edition of Q*. Hermeneia. Minneapolis: Fortress, 2000.

Rodd, C. S. "Spirit or Finger." *ExpTim* 72 (1960–1961) 157–58.

Sato, Migaku. *Q und Prophetie*. WUNT 2.29. Tübingen: Mohr/Siebeck, 1988.

———. "Wisdom Statements in the Sphere of Prophecy." Pages 139–58 in *The Gospel Behind the Gospels: Current Studies on Q*. Edited by Ronald A. Piper. NovTSup 75. Leiden: Brill, 1995.

Sauter, Gerhard. "The Concept and Task of Eschatology—Theological and Philosophical Reflections." *Scottish Journal of Theology* 41 (1988) 499–515.

Schmidt, Daryl. "The LXX *Gattung* 'Prophetic Correlative.'" *JBL* 96 (1977) 517–22.

Schmidt, Karl L. "βασιλεία." Pages 579–93 in vol. 1 of *TDNT*. Edited by G. Kittel and G. Friedrich. Translated by G. W. Bromiley. 10 vols. Grand Rapids: Eerdmans, 1964–1976.

Schotroff, Luise. "Itinerant Prophetesses: A Feminist Analysis of the Sayings Source Q." Pages 347–60 in *The Gospel Behind the Gospels: Current Studies on Q*. Edited by Ronald A. Piper. NovTSup 75. Leiden: Brill, 1995.

Schotroff, Luise. "The Sayings Source Q." Pages 510–34 in *Searching the Scriptures: A Feminist Commentary*. Edited by Elisabeth Schüssler Fiorenza. Vol. 2 of *Searching the Scriptures*. Edited by Elisabeth Schüssler Fiorenza. New York: Crossroad, 1994.

Schulz, Siegfried. *Q: Die Spruchquelle der Evangelisten*. Zürich: Theologischer Verlag, 1972.

Schürmann, Heinz. "Beobachtungen zum Menschensohn-Titel in der Redequelle." Pages 124–47 in *Jesus und der Menschensohn: Für Anton Vögtle*. Freiburg: Herder & Herder, 1975.

———. "QLk 11:14–36." Pages 576–78 in vol. 1 of *The Four Gospels 1992: Festschrift for Frans Neirynck*. Edited by Frans Van Segbroeck et al. BETL 100. Leuven: Leuven University Press, 1992.

———. "Der Zeugnis der Redequelle für die Basileia-Verkündigung Jesu." Pages 121–200 in *Logia. Les paroles de Jésus*. Edited by Joël Delobel. Leuven: Leuven University Press, 1982.

Schüssler Fiorenza, Elisabeth. "Eschatology of the NT." *IDBSup* (1976) 271–77.

———. *Jesus and the Politics of Interpretation*. New York: Continuum, 2000.

———. *Jesus: Miriam's Child, Sophia's Prophet*. New York: Continuum, 1994.

———. "The Phenomenon of Early Christian Apocalyptic: Some Reflections on Method." Pages 295–316 in *Apocalypticism in the Mediterranean World and the Near East*. Edited by David Hellholm. Tübingen: Mohr/Siebeck, 1983.

———. "Re-Visioning Christian Origins: In Memory of Her Revisited." Unpublished manuscript.

———. *Rhetoric and Ethic: The Politics of Biblical Interpretation*. Minneapolis: Fortress, 1999.

———. *Wisdom Ways: Introducing Feminist Biblical Interpretation*. Maryknoll, N.Y.: Orbis, 2001.

Schweitzer, Albert. *The Quest of the Historical Jesus*. First English translation, 1910. Translation by W. Montgomery. New York: MacMillan, 1968. German original, 1906.

Seeley, David. "Futuristic Eschatology and Social Formation in Q." Pages 144–53 in *Reimagining Christian Origins: A Colloquium Honoring Burton L. Mack*. Edited by Elizabeth A. Castelli and Hal Taussig. Valley Forge, Pa.: Trinity, 1996.

Segovia, Fernando F. "'And They Began to Speak in Other Tongues': Competing Modes of Discourse in Contemporary Biblical Criticism." Pages 1–34 in *Reading from This Place: Social Location and Biblical Interpretation in the United States*. Edited by idem and Mary Ann Tolbert. Minneapolis: Fortress, 1995.

Sevenich-Bax, Elisabeth. *Israels Konfrontation mit den letzten Boten der Weisheit*. MthA 21. Altenberge: Oros Verlag, 1993.

Shirock, Robert. "Whose Exorcists Are They?" *JSNT* 46 (1992) 41–51.

Shrenk, Gottlob. "δικαίοω." Pages 177–255 in vol. 2 of *TDNT*. Edited by G. Kittel and G. Friedrich. Translated by G. W. Bromiley. 10 vols. Grand Rapids: Eerdmans, 1964–1976.

Smith, Jonathan Z. *Drudgery Divine: On the Comparison of Early Christianities and the Religions of Late Antiquity*. Chicago: University of Chicago Press, 1990.

Steck, Odil Hannes. *Israel und das gewaltsame Geschick der Propheten*. WMANT 23. Neukirchen-Vluyn: Neukirchener Verlag, 1967.

Sugirtharajah, Rasiah. "'What Do Men Say Remains of Me?' Current Jesus Research and Third World Christologies." *Asian Journal of Theology* 5 (1991) 336–37.

Sullivan, Clayton. *Rethinking Realized Eschatology*. Macon, Ga.: Mercer University Press, 1988.

Swetnam, James, S.J. "No Sign of Jonah." *Bib* 66 (1985) 126–30.

———. "Some Signs of Jonah." *Bib* 68 (1987) 74–79.

Taylor, Joan E. *The Immerser: John the Baptist Within Second Temple Judaism*. Grand Rapids, Mich.: Eerdmans, 1997.

Tödt, Heinz Eduard. *The Son of Man in the Synoptic Tradition*. Translated by Dorothea Barton. Philadelphia: Westminster, 1965.

Trumbower, Jeffrey A. "The Role of Malachi in the Career of John the Baptist." *JSNTSup* 104 (1994) 28–41.

Tuckett, Christopher M. *Q and the History of Early Christianity*. Edinburgh: T&T Clark, 1996.

Uro, Risto. "John the Baptist and the Jesus Movement: What Does Q Tell Us?" Pages 231–55 in *The Gospel Behind the Gospels: Current Studies on Q*. Edited by Ronald A. Piper. NovTSup 75. Leiden: Brill, 1995.

Vaage, Leif E. *Galilean Upstarts: Jesus' First Followers According to Q*. Valley Forge, Pa.: Trinity Press, 1994.

Vaage, Leif E. "More Than a Prophet, and Demon-Possessed: Q and the 'Historical John.'" Pages 181–202 in *Conflict and Invention: Literary, Rhetorical, and Social Studies on the Sayings Gospel Q*. Edited by John S. Kloppenborg. Valley Forge, Pa.: Trinity Press, 1995.

———. "The Son of Man Sayings in Q: Stratigraphical Location and Significance." *Semeia* 55 (1991) 103–29.

Vaage, Leif E., and John S. Kloppenborg. "Early Christianity, Q and Jesus: The Sayings Gospel and Method in the Study of Christian Origins." *Semeia* 55 (1991) 1–14.

Van Cangh, J. M. "'Par l'esprit de Dieu—par le doigt de Dieu' Mt 12,28 par. Lc 11,20." Pages 337–42 in *Logia. Les paroles de Jésus*. Edited by Joël Delobel. Leuven: Leuven University Press, 1982.

Vassiliadis, Petros. "The Function of John the Baptist in Q and Mark." *Theologia* 46 (1975) 405–13.

———. "The Original Order of Q: Some Residual Cases." Pages 379–87 in *Logia. Les paroles de Jésus*. Edited by Joël Delobel. Leuven: Leuven University Press, 1982.

Vielhauer, Philipp. "Gottesreich und Menschensohn in der Verkündigung Jesu." Pages 55–91 in *Aufsätze zum Neuen Testament*. TB 31. Munich: Kaiser Verlag, 1965.

Vögtle, Anton. "Der Spruch vom Jonaszeichen." Pages 103–36 in *Das Evangelium und die Evangelien*. Düsseldorf: Patmos, 1971.

Walker, William O., Jr. "The Son of Man: Some Recent Developments." *CBQ* 45 (1983) 584–607.

Webb, Robert L. "The Activity of John the Baptist's Expected Figure as the Threshing Floor (Matthew 3.12 = Luke 3.17)." *JSNT* 43 (1991) 103–11.

Weiss, Johannes. *Die Idee des Reiches Gottes in der Theologie*. Giessen: Ricker, 1901.

———. *Jesus' Proclamation of the Kingdom of God*. Edited, translated, and introduction by Richard Hyde Hiers and David Larrimore Holland. Forward by Rudolf Bultmann. Philadelphia: Fortress, 1971. Translation of *Die Predigt Jesu vom Reiche Gottes*. Göttingen: Vandenhoeck & Ruprecht, 1892.

Williams, James G. "Neither Here Nor There: Between Wisdom and Apocalyptic in Jesus' Kingdom Sayings." *Forum* 5 (1989) 7–30.

Wink, Walter. *The Human Being: Jesus and the Enigma of the Son of the Man*. Minneapolis: Fortress, 2002.

Woodward, Kenneth L. "The Other Jesus." *Newsweek* (March 27, 2000) 51–60.

Zeller, Dieter. "Die Bildlogik des Glechnisses Mt 11.16f. / Lk 7.31f." *ZNW* 68 (1977) 252–57.

Index of Ancient Sources

Aesop
Fables 27b   48n24

Apocrypha
4 Ezra
4.51   180n36
6.11, 20   180n36
7.26   180n36
8.63–9.2   180n36

3 Maccabees
2:5   96
2:21   70n91

Sirach
4:11   45, 57n47
6:23   57
15:1–2   57n47
18:24   93n39
36:8–10   93n37
39:28   93n39
44:17   93nn38,39
48:1   97
48:1–11   74
48:8   110n89
48:9   98

48:10   98, 111
48:15   157n81

Tobit
13:5   157n81

Wisdom of Solomon
7:22–8:1   1n2
10:6   96, 98, 107
17:3   157n81

Cicero
Pro Q Ligario Orat
33   158

1 Clement
11.1   96, 96n45, 107

Dead Sea Scrolls
1 QS
3.6–9   108n85

1 Q 27
Fr. 1, col. 1, 5 180n35

Didache
9:4   157n81

Gospel of Thomas
35   155
46   75n111
78   74

Hebrew Bible
Genesis
13:10–11   96n45
18:17–19   107
19:17   96n45
19:20   96
19:24   96
19:25   96n45
19:28   96n45
19:29   96n45, 98, 101

Exodus
3:5   83n7, 108n84
3:9–12   179n30
4:1–9   179n30
8:19   153
20:22–23:33 73n102
21:1   73n102
23:20   72–73, 97

Numbers
14:11–12, 22 179n30

Deuteronomy
13:1–5   183
13:1–12   179n30
21:18–21   59n50

Joshua
5:15   83n7, 108n84

Judges
6:14–18   179n30

1 Samuel
2:27–36   179n30
10:1–8   179n30
14:8–10   179n30

2 Samuel
22:17   157

1 Kings
13:1–5   179n30
17   97

2 Kings
2   74, 97
19:28–31   179n30
20:1–11   179n30

2 Chronicles
32:24   179n30

Nehemiah
9:6–10   179n30

Psalms
17:15   157
78:42–43   179n30
105:26–27   179n30
117:26a   110
135:8–9   179n30
143:6   157

Proverbs

2:1	57n47
8:1–36	1n2
8:32	45, 57
9:1–6	1n2
23:20–21	59

Ecclesiastes

3:4	46n14

Isaiah

5:24	98n53
7:10–25	178
7:12	183
7:13	181n40, 183
17:13	101n64
20:1–5	192–93
26:19	64
29:5	101n64
29:18–19	64
33:10–12	98n53, 101n64
35:5–6	64
37:29–32	179n30
38:7–8, 22	179n30
40:3	74n106
41:15	101n64
61	22–23
61:1	64

Jeremiah

13:24	101n64

Ezekiel

12:1–11	192–93
37:1–4	108n85

Daniel

2:35	101n64

Hosea

13:3	101n64

Joel

2:28–29	108n85

Jonah

2:1	171
3:4	189
4	189n59

Micah

4:12	101n64

Zephaniah

2:2	101n64

Zechariah

9:9	110
13:7–9	157n81

Malachi

3	97
3:1	72–73, 73n105, 74, 96n49, 97
3:1–2a	97
3:2b–3	97
3:5	73nn101,105, 97
3:19–20a	98
3:22–23	98, 111
3:24	98
4:5–6	73–74n105, 74

Herodotus
History
1:114   48n24

John Chrysostom
Homily 41 on Matthew 12:25–26
                148

Josephus
Antiquities
8.347   180n38
10.28   180n38
20.97–99   180n38
20.167–168   180n38
20.188   180n38

Jewish War
2.258–259   180n38, 183n46
2.261–263   180n38
6.258, 288   180n38

Life
64–65   70n92

Lucian of Samosata
Herotimus
68   69–70

New Testament (and Q)
Matthew
1:1–6   82
3:5   95
3:7   105n74
3:11   83n7
3:12   83n8
5:11   184
5:40   104n73

7:15   105n74
7:18–19   104
7:19   105n74
9:34   140n26
12:22–30,43–45
               131–32, 173
12:2   105, 140n26, 173
12:28   105n74, 146n48
12:29   134n6, 155
12:31–37   173
12:36–37   173n10
12:38   173
12:32   105
12:34   84, 104
12:38–42   169
12:40   186
12:41–42   171
12:45   135n7
13:19   184n49
16:1–4   169, 173, 186
16:4   170n 4
17:12–13   96
21:28–32   57n46, 59n54, 60
23:33   84, 104, 105n74
24:3   180n37
27:59–60   186

Mark
1:2   72n98, 74n106
1:2–6   82
1:7   83n7, 108n83
2:1–12   187n55
3:21   60n57
3:22   140
3:22–26   131, 174
3:23   141n33, 143n40
3:24–25   143n40

Mark *continued*

3:26	142n39
3:27	134n6, 155
3:28–30	173n9, 174n12
3:30	133
4:3–9, 14–20	51n30
8:11	170n3, 173, 174
8:11–13	169, 185, 187
8:12	170n4,173, 181n 40, 183
8:31	187n52
9:12	96n48
9:13	96
9:31	187n52
9:36–40	150, 161
9:40	66
10:33–34	187n52
13:1–13	187n53, 187n55
13:4	180n37
13:21–22	183n45
13:22	180n36, 183, 187n 55
13:30	79n121
16:17, 20	180n36

Luke

1:17	96n48
1:76	96n48
2:7	180
2:11–12	180
2:16	180
3:1–6	82
3:3	95
3:10–14	60n56, 105–6
3:11	105–6
3:16	83n7
3:17	83n8
6:22	184

7:21	65n73
7:29–30	57, 59, 60
11:14–26	131–32
11:14–32	174
11:15	135n7
11:16	135n7, 174
11:17	142n34
11:21–22	134n6, 155
11:29	172
11:29–32	169
21:7	180n37

John

1:21	97
1:27	83n7
2:18–22	180n37
2:19	187
2:19–25	74n106
6:28–34	180n37
6:33	187
6:35	187n54
6:41–59	187n54
6:60–71	187n54
7:20	60n57
8:48, 52	60n57
10:20, 21	60n57

Acts

3:21	96n48
4:13–16, 22	180n37, 187n53
8:12–13	180n37, 187n53
13:25	83n7
14:3	180n37, 187n53

1 Corinthians

1:22	180n37, 183
1:24	183
2:4	183n48

1 Thessalonians
1:10   93, 100n63
2:14–16   93

2 Thessalonians
2:9   180n37
2:10–11   183

Revelation
13:13–14   180n37

Q
3:3   82
3:7   24, 69n87, 84,
              92, 96, 99–102,
              106, 107n78
3:7–9   60, 67, 74n105,
              82, 99–102,
              105n75, 108–09
3:7–9, 16–17 15, 25, 44,
              74n108, 81–113,
              197
3:7–7:35   43–44, 56n41
3:8   44, 56n41,
              99–102, 106,
              107
3:9   97, 98, 99–104,
              105n74, 109, 111
3:16   43, 44, 62, 83n7,
              96, 97, 101,
              108nn83, 85,
              110, 197, 199
3:16–17   66, 83n7, 97, 98,
              108–112, 194
3:17   96, 101, 108–09,
              111, 157n81
4:1–13   69n87

4:1–7:10   44
4:5–6   167
6:20b   20–21, 65, 77, 167
6:21   103
6:22   184
6:22–23   112
6:27   104
6:29   104, 106
6:30   104
6:35   184
6:36   104
6:37–42   143n40
6:41–42   144n42
6:43–44   101n64, 102–03,
              104, 135n10,
              142n36,143n40,
              144n42, 173
6:45   103n72, 142n36,
              185
6:46   105n76
6:46–49   103–04
7:1–10   64n71, 69n87
7:10   190
7:18   44, 63, 65,
              69n87, 109
7:18–19   63
7:18–23   43, 62–67, 69, 75,
              78, 110, 111n96,
              145n46
7:18–28   60, 78, 110n89,
              197
7:18–35   15, 25, 43–81,
              110
7:22   59n51, 63–66, 67,
              77, 110, 110n89,
              167

Q continued

7:23	62, 63, 66–67
7:24	69–70, 75, 82n3
7:24–26	69, 70–71n93, 71n94, 74
7:24–28	43, 68–77, 78, 96, 145n46
7:26	69, 71nn93, 94, 73, 74
7:27	69, 71, 72–75, 96n49, 97, 110
7:28	69, 71, 75–76, 167
7:29	189n57
7:30–31	196
7:31	47–48, 50
7:31–35	15–16, 43–63, 75, 77, 78, 80, 145n46, 184, 196, 199
7:32	49–55, 142n36
7:33	135n8
7:33–34	47–55, 59nn51, 53, 60, 70n93, 75n110, 196
7:34	189n57, 199
7:35	1, 1n2, 24, 44, 47, 55–60, 67
9:57–60	173n11, 189n57
9:58	142n36
10:2	135n10,157n81
10:2–10	101n64
10:9	64n71, 65, 66, 150, 167, 190
10:12	96
10:13–15	65n72, 85, 88, 189n57
10:16	112
10:21	77
10:23	167
10:23–24	66,182n42, 188
10:23–11:52	182
11:2–4, 9–13	135,142n36, 43n40
11:3	103
11:4	104
11:5–8	144n42
11:9–10	188
11:9–13	184
11:11–12	144n42, 189n57
11:13	184
11:14	64n71, 132, 135–36, 140, 181, 182n42
11:14–15	160, 172
11:14–17	166
11:14–18	136
11:14–20	16, 65, 135, 139, 154, 161
11:14–23	135n7, 137n20
11:14–26	15, 25, 66n80, 131–168, 185, 190, 196
11:14–32	135n7, 150–52
11:14–52	182
11:15	133, 135–36, 140– 45, 147, 150, 156, 170n2, 172, 173, 178, 190
11:15–18	140–44
11:16	132–33, 170–74, 178, 181, 185, 187
11:16, 29–32	15, 25, 80, 169–94
11:17	133, 135–37, 141–44, 160

Q continued

11:17–18	135, 145, 155, 156n74,160, 164, 165
11:17–19	159
11:17–20	135
11:18	133, 135n9, 136, 137n20, 140, 142, 143n40, 144, 153, 160
11:19	16, 132–33, 135–36, 137n20, 138, 139, 143, 154, 160, 162, 163n97, 165, 190, 196
11:19–20	144–54, 160, 163n98, 164, 181
11:20	16, 132–33, 134n6, 135–39, 154, 155, 160, 162, 165, 190, 196
11:20–26	159
11:21–22	134–35, 137n20, 142, 154–58, 160, 161, 163n99, 165
11:21–26	154–65
11:22	134, 135
11:23	66n80, 134, 135, 137n20, 147, 150, 151n63, 154, 157– 61, 164, 165
11:24	134–35

11:24–26	132, 135, 137n20, 154, 160, 162–65, 172n7, 185
11:25	134
11:26	134, 172n7, 184
11:29	170–71, 172, 176, 181, 185, 186, 187, 191, 194
11:29–30	170
11:29–32	88, 135, 177, 190, 197
11:29–35	137n20
11:30	169, 171, 172, 174–78, 184, 185, 187n53,190–93, 199, 200
11:31	171, 172
11:31–32	150, 171, 176n20, 187, 189n57, 189n58, 190, 194, 200
11:32	133, 170–71, 172, 191n62, 193–94
11:33–35	176n20, 184, 188
11:34	184, 185
11:39	140n26
11:42–52	167
11:43	140n 26
11:49	1n2
11:49–51	58, 79–80, 110n91, 185
12:2–9	143n40
12:8–9	112, 177
12:10	173

Q continued
12:22–31   143n40
12:24–28   142n36
12:28   111
12:29–31   103
12:30   112
12:33   142n36
12:39   111n95
12:40   101n68, 103,
        111, 177
12:42–46   103, 111n95
12:49   111
12:51–53   189n57
12:53   111
12:54–55   103–4, 173
12:54–56   183n45
13:18–21   189n57, 189n57
13:24   142n36
13:24–29   104
13:26–27   67
13:28   135n10
13:30   77n118
13:34–35   110, 182
13:35   101n68, 109, 110
14:16–26   104
14:26   111
14:26–27   189n57
14:35   111
15:4–10   189n57
16:16   96
17:1–2   77
17:3   104
17:20–21   66
17:22–37b   111
17:23   183n45
17:24   111, 191n63

17:26   191n63
17:24–30   177
17:27   189n57
17:28–30   96, 98
17:30   111, 191n63
17:33   77n118
17:34–35   111–12, 142n36,
        189n57
19:13   111
19:15   111
19:22   184
19:23   111

Oxyrhynchus Papyri
1224   161n93

Polybius
History
208.2   59n52

Pseudepigrapha
Jubilees
16.5   96n45

Lives of the Prophets
10   189n59, 192n64,
        192n65

Psalms of Solomon
2:15   57n45
3:3–8   56–57
4:8   57n45
8:7   57n45
8:2   57n45
8:26   57n45
9:2   57n45

Sibylline Oracles
4.165   108n85

Pseudo-Crates
Epistle
29   70n93

Pseudo-Diogenes
Epistle
12   70n93
28   70n93

Quintilian
Institutio Oratoria
6.3.63   141n32

Rabbinic Literature
b. Sanh. 98a   179n31, 181n40,
                   183
b. B. Mes. 59b
                   179n32, 181n40,
                   183

Septuagint
3 Kingdoms
14:15   70n91

Tertullian
Adversus Marcionem
4.26.10   152–53

Index of Subjects and Select Secondary Literature

Abraham, 100; children of, 44, 56n41, 96, 102, 106–8

Adam, A. K. M., 169, 194

Allison, Dale, 6, 31–32, 76n114, 88n21, 147, 150

anti-Judaism and interpretation, 90–91, 116–18, 121–22, 129–30

apocalyptic, interpretation of, 85–86, 87–91, 175, 177. *See also* judgment

apologetics, Christian, 116–17, 124, 127

Arnal, William, 37, 89–90, 92n34, 111nn94, 96, 125n39, 126nn40, 41, 127–28, 171n6

audience of Q. *See* identity: of Q community in relationship to outsiders/other Jews

baptism, 108–09

basileia of God: and "coming one," 65–67, 69; and John, 67n83, 68–77; as a moral/ethical program, 4–5; as future event, 4, 131–32; existential interpretation of, 119; in Q, 20–24, 36, 65–67, 112–13, 131–68, 190–91, 197, 199, 200; translation of, 20n60

basileia of Satan, 154–62

Berger, Klaus, 159, 160

Betz, Hans Dieter, 21–22

Bretscher, Paul, 83n7, 108n84

Bultmann, Rudolf, 64n69, 118–19, 123n29, 136, 146n47, 175

Cameron, Ron, 47, 70n93, 71n96, 76n116

Christology, 122–23, 129–30, 138n22, 139, 146–47, 149, 153–54, 160, 165–66, 175–77, 191. *See also* Son of Humanity

Collins, Adela Yarbro, 175, 194

"coming one," 43, 44, 63, 63n68, 65–67, 73, 75, 77, 95, 97, 108–12, 197, 199

comparison: for genealogy, 22–24, 117, 127–28; for locative purposes, 38, 40, 87, 92, 93–94, 94n40

controversy stories: in Q, 139, 150–52, 182–83

Cotter, Wendy, 48n22, 53, 89, 90n29
Crossan, John Dominic, 3, 6n14, 29, 86, 91
Cynic hypothesis/comparison, 6, 7, 21, 35, 37, 58n49, 60n58, 70–71n93, 71n94, 86, 121, 123–25, 127–28

Deuteronomistic theology, 185n51, 198
diversity, of early Christianity, 27, 28–29, 31, 34n29, 41, 195
Dodd, C. H., 138

Easton, B. S., 146
Edwards, Richard, 176–77, 191n63
Elijah, 74, 95–98, 110n89, 111, 192n64
Elisha, Jesus as, 110n89
eschatology: defining the term, 3, 3n6, 6, 6n18, 7n21, 12, 92n35, 138n24; doctrinal category, 3, 3n6, 91–95, 116, 118–21, 123, 201; of Jesus, 4–5, 123, 137–38, 156n74, *See also* Jesus, apocalyptic, and judgment
ethics of interpretation, 10, 11–17, 29, 94, 201

feminist/liberationist criticism, 8, 14, 23n73, 33n26, 114–15, 117–18, 121, 122, 125, 200
Fleddermann, Harry, 82, 84, 100
Freyne, Séan, 50n27, 59n52, 61n61, 123n28
Fridrichsen, Anton, 158n87, 160–61

Funk, Robert, 30, 40–41

Georgi, Dieter, 33, 118–20, 123n29, 124
Gaston, Lloyd, 140n28
gendered pairs: in Q, 171n6, 189n57
Gospel of Thomas, 3, 18, 36, 74, 75n111, 155
Güttgemanns, Ehrhart, 120

Harnack, Adolf von, 5
Hartin, Patrick, 56n43, 60n59
Herod Antipas, 70
historical Jesus: as foreign to modern world, 4–5, 118, 195; quest of, 4–5, 17, 20, 30, 32, 33, 36–37, 88–89, 90–91, 123n28, 126, 137–38, 174–75
Hollenbach, Paul, 166n105
Horsley, Richard, 13n39, 18, 35n32, 54n36, 66n76, 76n114, 79–80, 82n3, 88n21, 90n28, 108n85, 137n17
Humphries, Michael, 131, 137, 140n27, 141, 142n33, 144, 152, 156, 159–61, 164, 165, 166

identity: of Q community in relationship to outsiders/other Jews, 15–16, 52n31, 78–80, 90, 102, 106–8, 112–113, 139, 144, 148, 150–52, 165–67, 177, 183–84, 185n51, 198, 200. *See also* Jesus: relation to Christian identity interpretation: effects of, 90, 94; objective/value-free/scientific, 9, 10, 24, 32, 40, 116, 124–25, 129–30, 195. *See also* apologetics, Christian; ethics of interpretation

Jacobson, Arland, 43, 47, 67n82, 69n85, 79, 107n78, 108n85, 142n33, 144, 154, 158, 166

Jesus: contemporary discourses about, 28, 85–86, 88, 94, 115, 122–23; eschatological vs. non-eschatological, 4, 6, 7, 20, 22–23, 37, 64n69, 86, 94, 123, 125, 146, 165–66; relation to Christian identity, 8, 28–29, 31, 33, 36, 41, 71n93, 78, 88, 94, 114, 122, 126, 129, 177, 195–96; uniqueness of, 28, 112, 114–30, 131–32, 139, 145–47, 150, 153–54, 166, 197, 199. *See also* historical Jesus

Jesus Seminar, 3, 6, 7, 18, 36

Jewish responses to Jesus/Q. *See* identity: in relation to outsiders/other Jews

John: as Elijah, 74–75, 96–98, 110n89; baptism of, 59–60, 69n87, 108n85, 109; eschatology of, 85, 89, 91–95, 107n81; Q's affirmation of, 60–61, 67n83, 75, 77–78

Johnson, Luke Timothy, 7, 31, 126

Jonah, 186, 189, 191–92

judgment: in Q, 85, 88–91, 112–113, 169–70, 177; interpretation of,

85–91; rhetorical function of, 92–95, 99–106, 109, 112–13

Käsemann, Ernst, 146

Killagen, John, 163, 164n103

kingdom of God, *see basileia* of God

Kirk, Alan, 44, 65n75, 76n114, 82n3, 88n21, 99n59, 102n71, 109n86, 121n22, 133n3, 137, 141n32, 142, 144n42, 145, 156–57, 159–60, 165–66, 167, 172, 175, 182n42

Kleinlitaratur, 120

Kloppenborg, John, 13, 38–39, 51n30, 58, 65n73, 67n83, 76n14, 82n3, 95–96, 107, 107n78, 120–21, 123, 124, 133n3, 136, 141n33, 142n39, 150–51, 155, 157–58, 190; redactional proposal, 5–7, 19, 79, 87–88, 88n21, 121n22, 198

Koester, Helmut, 27n1, 66n77, 119–20

kyriarchy, 14n42

Lot, story of, 82n3, 95–96, 98, 107, 111. *See also* Sodom

Lövestam, Evald, 79n121, 85n51

Lührmann, Dieter, 78–79, 136n13, 176

Mack, Burton, 6, 30–31, 33, 34, 36, 71n93, 89–90n26, 116–17, 118, 125, 177

Marcus, Joel, 156n74

Meadors, Edward, 36–37, 138n22

Meinertz, Max, 79, 79n121
myth, mythmaking, mythologizing, 31–32, 33, 35, 71n93, 177

Nave, Guy, 102n70
Noah, 111

origins, quest for pure, 116–18, 125, 127–28, 132, 138, 195, 199
Overbeck, Franz, 120

Patte, Daniel, 10–11, 13
Perrin, Norman, 175
Piper, Ronald, 143n40, 153–54
Plaskow, Judith, 122, 129
postmodern biblical criticism/postmodern situation, 8–11, 37, 125

Q: as alternative view of Jesus, 5, 27, 32, 34, 125n33; as orally derived text, 18–19, 35n32, 54n36, 88n21; date and location, 19n57, 198; dichotomies in interpretation of, 35–36, 37, 38, 41, 71n93, 78, 88; genre of, 35, 38–40, 87–88, 120–21; hypothesis, 1n1, 17, 18; IQP reconstruction of, 18, 46, 46nn14,15, 52n31, 57n46, 62–63, 68, 82–83, 84, 110n92, 132–34, 135nn8,10, 155, 170–71, 184; Luke's redaction of, 54, 57, 65n73, 104–06, 147; Matthew's redaction of, 84, 96, 104–06, 147; popular discourse about, 17, 18, 30; redactional proposals, 19, 70n93, 78–79, 87–91, 198–99.

See also identity: of Q community; controversy stories in Q

Räisänen, Heikki, 147, 158
reconstruction of Q. See Q:IQP reconstruction of
redaction of Q. See Kloppenborg, John; Q:redactional proposals
Reed, Jonathan, 192n65
Reiser, Marius, 85–86, 91
Robbins, Vernon, 141n32
Robinson, James, 6, 60, 89n25, 120

Sato, Migaku, 88n21, 99n58
Schulz, Siegfried, 87, 136n13, 141n33
Schürmann, Heinz, 175–76
Schüssler Fiorenza, Elisabeth, 8, 8n23, 11–12, 14, 14n42, 20n59, 30n11, 32, 41n54, 117–18, 121, 124n31, 126, 129–30, 201. See also ethics of interpretation
Schweitzer, Albert, 3n6, 4–5, 6, 121
Shirock, Robert, 149–50
Sign: request for, 178–81
Smith, Jonathan Z., 40n51, 116–17, 118, 120, 121, 124–25, 127–28, 141
Sodom, story of, 82n3, 95–96, 98, 112. See also Lot
Son of humanity (or Son of Man), 20n60, 43, 46, 49n25, 61–62, 75n110, 103, 111–12, 169, 174–75, 176, 177, 186, 190–94, 199. See also Christology

Sophia: children of, 44–45, 56–62; messengers of, 58, 185; translation of, 1n2

Sugirtharajah, Rasiah, 23n73

Steck, O. H., 79

Taylor, Joan, 100n61

"this generation," 43, 45, 47, 50–51, 53, 55, 57n46, 61–62, 78–80, 106, 172, 176, 181–86, 188–90, 196, 198; judgment on, 15, 48, 52, 78–79, 87

Tödt, Heinz Eduard, 174–75

Tuckett, Christopher, 6, 22–23, 34n28, 44–45, 48n22, 58n48, 65n74, 79–80, 82n3, 88n21, 90n28, 99n57, 108n85

two-source hypothesis, 1n1, 17–18, 19

uniqueness of Jesus. *See* Jesus: uniqueness of

Uro, Risto, 89n26, 108n85

Vaage, Leif, 21–24, 58n49, 59nn51, 53, 67n81, 70n93, 76n115, 175–76, 177

Vielhauer, Philipp, 175

Weiss, Johannes, 4–5, 121, 175, 195

wilderness in Q, 69, 70, 71n93, 82n3

wisdom of God, *see Sophia*

wo/men, 14, 33n26, 118, 129, 200

wrath of God, 82, 84, 92–93, 98, 99–101, 107, 109

Harvard Theological Studies

55. Johnson-DeBaufre, Melanie. *Jesus Among Her Children: Q, Eschatology, and the Construction of Christian Origins*, 2005.

54. Hall, David D. *The Faithful Shepherd: A History of the New England Ministry in the Seventeenth Century*, 2006.

53. Schowalter, Daniel N., and Steven J. Friesen, eds. *Urban Religion in Roman Corinth: Interdisciplinary Approaches*, 2004.

52. Nasrallah, Laura. *"An Ecstasy of Folly": Prophecy and Authority in Early Christianity*, 2003.

51. Brock, Ann Graham. *Mary Magdalene, The First Apostle: The Struggle for Authority*, 2003.

50. Trost, Theodore Louis. *Douglas Horton and the Ecumenical Impulse in American Religion*, 2002.

49. Huang, Yong. *Religious Goodness and Political Rightness: Beyond the Liberal-Communitarian Debate*, 2001.

48. Rossing, Barbara R. *The Choice between Two Cities: Whore, Bride, and Empire in the Apocalypse*, 1999.

47. Skedros, James Constantine. *Saint Demetrios of Thessaloniki: Civic Patron and Divine Protector, 4th–7th Centuries c.e.*, 1999.

46. Koester, Helmut, ed. *Pergamon, Citadel of the Gods: Archaeological Record, Literary Description, and Religious Development*, 1998.

45. Kittredge, Cynthia Briggs. *Community and Authority: The Rhetoric of Obedience in the Pauline Tradition*, 1998.

44. Lesses, Rebecca Macy. *Ritual Practices to Gain Power: Angels, Incantations, and Revelation in Early Jewish Mysticism*, 1998.

43. Guenther-Gleason, Patricia E. *On Schleiermacher and Gender Politics*, 1997.

42. White, L. Michael. *The Social Origins of Christian Architecture* (2 vols.), 1997.

41. Koester, Helmut, ed. *Ephesos, Metropolis of Asia: An Interdisciplinary Approach to its Archaeology, Religion, and Culture*, 1995.

40. Guider, Margaret Eletta. *Daughters of Rahab: Prostitution and the Church of Liberation in Brazil*, 1995.

39. Schenkel, Albert F. *The Rich Man and the Kingdom: John D. Rockefeller, Jr., and the Protestant Establishment*, 1995.

38. Hutchison, William R. and Hartmut Lehmann, eds. *Many Are Chosen: Divine Election and Western Nationalism*, 1994.

37. Lubieniecki, Stanislas. *History of the Polish Reformation and Nine Related Documents*. Translated and interpreted by George Huntston Williams, 1995.

– Davidovich, Adina. *Religion as a Province of Meaning: The Kantian Foundations of Modern Theology*, 1993.

36. Thiemann, Ronald F., ed. *The Legacy of H. Richard Niebuhr*, 1991.

35. Hobbs, Edward C., ed. *Bultmann, Retrospect and Prospect: The Centenary Symposium at Wellesley*, 1985.

34. Cameron, Ron. *Sayings Traditions in the Apocryphon of James*, 1984. Reprinted, 2004,

33. Blackwell, Albert L. *Schleiermacher's Early Philosophy of Life: Determinism, Freedom, and Phantasy*, 1982.

32. Gibson, Elsa. *The "Christians for Christians" Inscriptions of Phrygia: Greek Texts, Translation and Commentary*, 1978.

31. Bynum, Caroline Walker. Docere Verbo et Exemplo: *An Aspect of Twelfth-Century Spirituality*, 1979.

30. Williams, George Huntston, ed. *The Polish Brethren: Documentation of the History and Thought of Unitarianism in the Polish-Lithuanian Commonwealth and in the Diaspora 1601–1685*, 1980.

29. Attridge, Harold W. *First-Century Cynicism in the Epistles of Heraclitus*, 1976.

28. Williams, George Huntston, Norman Pettit, Winfried Herget, and Sargent Bush, Jr., eds. *Thomas Hooker: Writings in England and Holland, 1626–1633*, 1975.

27. Preus, James Samuel. *Carlstadt's* Ordinaciones *and Luther's Liberty: A Study of the Wittenberg Movement, 1521–22*, 1974.

26. Nickelsburg, George W. E. *Resurrection, Immortality, and Eternal Life in Inter-testamental Judaism*, 1972.

25. Worthley, Harold Field. *An Inventory of the Records of the Particular (Congregational) Churches of Massachusetts Gathered 1620–1805*, 1970.

24. Yamauchi, Edwin M. *Gnostic Ethics and Mandaean Origins*, 1970.

23. Yizhar, Michael. *Bibliography of Hebrew Publications on the Dead Sea Scrolls 1948–1964*, 1967.

22. Albright, William Foxwell. *The Proto-Sinaitic Inscriptions and Their Decipherment*, 1966.

21. Dow, Sterling, and Robert F. Healey. *A Sacred Calendar of Eleusis*, 1965.

20. Sundberg, Jr., Albert C. *The Old Testament of the Early Church*, 1964.

19. Cranz, Ferdinand Edward. *An Essay on the Development of Luther's Thought on Justice, Law, and Society*, 1959.

18. Williams, George Huntston, ed. *The Norman Anonymous of 1100 A.D.: Towards the Identification and Evaluation of the So-Called Anonymous of York*, 1951.

17. Lake, Kirsopp, and Silva New, eds. *Six Collations of New Testament Manuscripts*, 1932.

16. Wilbur, Earl Morse, trans. *The Two Treatises of Servetus on the Trinity: On the Errors of the Trinity, 7 Books, A.D. 1531. Dialogues on the Trinity, 2 Books. On the Righteousness of Christ's Kingdom, 4 Chapters, A.D. 1532*, 1932.

15. Casey, Robert Pierce, ed. Serapion of Thmuis's *Against the Manichees*, 1931.

14. Ropes, James Hardy. *The Singular Problem of the Epistles to the Galatians*, 1929.

13. Smith, Preserved. *A Key to the Colloquies of Erasmus*, 1927.

12. Spyridon of the Laura and Sophronios Eustratiades. *Catalogue of the Greek Manuscripts in the Library of the Laura on Mount Athos*, 1925.

11. Sophronios Eustratiades and Arcadios of Vatspedi. *Catalogue of the Greek Manuscripts in the Library of the Monastery of Vatopedi on Mt. Athos*, 1924.

10. Conybeare, Frederick C. *Russian Dissenters*, 1921.

9. Burrage, Champlin, ed. *An Answer to John Robinson of Leyden by a Puritan Friend: Now First Published from a Manuscript of A.D. 1609*, 1920.

8. Emerton, Ephraim. *The* Defensor pacis *of Marsiglio of Padua: A Critical Study*, 1920,

7. Bacon, Benjamin W. *Is Mark a Roman Gospel?* 1919.

6. Cadbury, Henry Joel. 2 vols. *The Style and Literary Method of Luke*, 1920.

5. Marriott, G. L., ed. Macarii Anecdota: *Seven Unpublished Homilies of Macarius*, 1918.

4. Edmunds, Charles Carroll and William Henry Paine Hatch. *The Gospel Manuscripts of the General Theological Seminary*, 1918.

3. Arnold, William Rosenzweig. *Ephod and Ark: A Study in the Records and Religion of the Ancient Hebrews*, 1917.

2. Hatch, William Henry Paine. *The Pauline Idea of Faith in its Relation to Jewish and Hellenistic Religion*, 1917.

1. Torrey, Charles Cutler. *The Composition and Date of Acts*, 1916.

Harvard Dissertations in Religion

In 1993, Harvard Theological Studies absorbed
the Harvard Dissertations in Religion series.

31. Baker-Fletcher, Garth. *Somebodyness: Martin Luther King, Jr. and the Theory of Dignity*, 1993.

30. Soneson, Jerome Paul. *Pragmatism and Pluralism: John Dewey's Significance for Theology*, 1993.

29. Crabtree, Harriet. *The Christian Life: The Traditional Metaphors and Contemporary Theologies*, 1991.

28. Schowalter, Daniel N. *The Emperor and the Gods: Images from the Time of Trajan*, 1993.

27. Valantasis, Richard. *Spiritual Guides of the Third Century: A Semiotic Study of the Guide-Disciple Relationship in Christianity, Neoplatonism, Hermetism, and Gnosticism*, 1991.

26. Wills, Lawrence Mitchell. *The Jews in the Court of the Foreign King: Ancient Jewish Court Legends*, 1990.

25. Massa, Mark Stephen. *Charles Augustus Briggs and the Crisis of Historical Criticism*, 1990.

24. Hills, Julian Victor. *Tradition and Composition in the* Epistula apostolorum, 1990.

23. Bowe, Barbara Ellen. *A Church in Crisis: Ecclesiology and Paraenesis in Clement of Rome*, 1988.

22. Bisbee, Gary A. *Pre-Decian Acts of Martyrs and* Commentarii, 1988.

21. Ray, Stephen Alan. *The Modern Soul: Michel Foucault and the Theological Discourse of Gordon Kaufman and David Tracy*, 1987.

20. MacDonald, Dennis Ronald. *There Is No Male and Female: The Fate of a Dominical Saying in Paul and Gnosticism*, 1987.

19. Davaney, Sheila Greeve. *Divine Power: A Study of Karl Barth and Charles Hartshorne*, 1986.

18. LaFargue, J. Michael. *Language and Gnosis: The Opening Scenes of the Acts of Thomas*, 1985.

12. Layton, Bentley, ed. *The Gnostic Treatise on Resurrection from Nag Hammadi*, 1979.

11. Ryan, Patrick J. *Imale: Yoruba Participation in the Muslim Tradition: A Study of Clerical Piety*, 1977.

10. Neevel, Jr., Walter G. *Yāmuna's Vedānta and Pāñcarātra: Integrating the Classical and the Popular*, 1977.

9. Yarbro Collins, Adela. *The Combat Myth in the Book of Revelation*, 1976.

8. Veatch, Robert M. *Value-Freedom in Science and Technology: A Study of the Importance of the Religious, Ethical, and Other Socio-Cultural Factors in Selected Medical Decisions Regarding Birth Control*, 1976.

7. Attridge, Harold W. *The Interpretation of Biblical History in the* Antiquitates judaicae *of Flavius Josephus*, 1976.

6. Trakatellis, Demetrios C. *The Pre-Existence of Christ in the Writings of Justin Martyr*, 1976.

5. Green, Ronald Michael. *Population Growth and Justice: An Examination of Moral Issues Raised by Rapid Population Growth*, 1975.

4. Schrader, Robert W. *The Nature of Theological Argument: A Study of Paul Tillich*, 1976.

3. Christensen, Duane L. *Transformations of the War Oracle in Old Testament Prophecy: Studies in the Oracles Against the Nations*, 1975.

2. Williams, Sam K. *Jesus' Death as Saving Event: The Background and Origin of a Concept*, 1972.

1. Smith, Jane I. *An Historical and Semantic Study of the Term "Islām" as Seen in a Sequence of Qur'an Commentaries*, 1970.

This book was produced at the offices of Harvard Theological Studies, located at the Harvard Divinity School, Cambridge, Massachusetts:

Managing Editor:	Margaret Studier
Copy editor:	Glenn Snyder
Typesetters:	Cory Crawford Randall Short Richard Jude Thompson
Proofreaders:	Randall Short Richard Jude Thompson

The indexes were prepared by Melanie Johnson-DeBaufre. The Greek font, SymbolGreekII, used in this book is available from Linguist's Software, Inc. PO Box 580, Edmonds, WA 98020-0580, USA, tel (425) 775-1130 www.linguistsoftware.com.